FOURTH EDITION

AMERICAN Government

& TEXAS POLITICS

Stacey Jurhree, Ph.D.

Kendall Hunt
publishing company

Kendall Hunt
publishing company

www.kendallhunt.com
Send all inquiries to:
4050 Westmark Drive
Dubuque, IA 52004-1840

Contents

The objective of *American Government & Texas Politics* is to give the reader a simple but more concrete knowledge of how American Government and Texas Politics operate. Too many traditional political science and government textbooks spend excessive time on concepts, phrases, and paradigms that are really not relevant to the average American citizen's life. In fact, several of these texts appear to be written to impress professors and their peers more than to help the American Citizenry understand governmental actions and events. Also, traditional textbooks have a tendency only to focus on the institutions of government, thus leaving out the other aspects of government that affect one's life. *The Revelation of American Government and Texas Politics: The Illumination* seeks to ratify these situations.

This small piece is designed to do the following:

1. Give the readers a more comprehensive analysis of American Government and Texas Politics,
2. Give the readers theories and analyses that have not only applied in the past, but also apply today,
3. Teach the readers not just about the institutions of government, but how politics applies to their day-to-day lives,
4. Teach the readers the art of intellectualism.

The Revelation of American Government and Texas Politics: The Illumination's purpose is not to embrace any particular ideological perspective; nor does it attempt to make the readers liberals or conservatives, or Democrats or Republicans. The fundamental purpose of this book is to attempt to tell the truth about the operation of American Government and Texas Politics with very minimal romanticism.

American Government & Texas Politics, is simple without being ordinary, the chapters are short without being shallow, brief without being dwarfed, positive without being stilted, and comprehensive without being complicated. It does not embrace any particular ideological perspective; nor does it attempt to make the readers liberals or conservatives, or Democrats or Republicans. The fundamental purpose of this text is to attempt to tell the truth about the systematic operation of American Government and Texas Politics with very minimal romanticism.

Each chapter begins with a poem in the form of a political message. For example, Chapter 11 is titled "Political Parties." In American Government and Texas Politics

To many Americans, the Democrats and the Republicans are the same,
all both parties do is play the political game.

The Republicans claim to fight for the man at the top.
Whereas the Democrats claim to fight for the man down below.
Nonetheless, the objective of both parties is to maintain the status quo.

When political problems arise, each party blames one another,
neither party is truly concerned about the middle-class brother.

Both parties make promises that they cannot keep.
It is enough even to make a grown man weep.

The political parties must represent U.S. citizens as a whole.
Anything less than this would be downright wicked and cold.

—The Bowtie Professor

American Government: Poli-ology

At one time, the American political system was government for the people and by the people. However, this no longer appears to be the case. Both political parties in Washington are in the back pockets of powerful multinational corporations. The Democratic party is full of poverty pimps and race hustlers. Whereas the Republican party are strictly for the rich and are constantly quoting bibilical scriptures, and a God which many of them deny by their actions.

Rome was a Republican form of government. The U.S. also is a Republican form of governenment, and just as the Roman Empire fail down the slippery slope of immorality, the United States of America is currently going down that same path of destruction. Many of us have heard the saying "history repeats itself". History only repeats itself because men seem to never learn from their mistkes. Any nation that does what is right in its own eyes is doomed to fail. The only way that the U.S. can save itself is to turn back to the true Christian principles that she once claimed to believe in and cherished.

—The Bowtie Professor

Name _____ **Date** _____

Explain:

_____

_____

_____

_____

_____

_____

_____

_____

_____

_____

_____

_____

_____

_____

_____

_____

_____

_____

_____

The study of government, politics and political institutions is known as Political Science. Political Science and the role of government in our daily activities has impacted the American citizenry in every aspect of our lives. Unfortunately, most of the American population knows very little about government and politics and several of them really don't care to know. One reason for this is due to the fact that too many U.S. citizens cannot relate government and politics to their dominant social paradigm or world view. Another reason is because so many of the American citizenry have become very distrustful of government and the politicians who run it. So many Americans have become fed up with big government spending and elected officials who work to help the rich get richer at the expense of the poor and working class. The American governmental system appears to no longer reward its citizens for positive behavior. Those who work hard to enjoy the fruits of their labor are undermined by political officials who pass legislation to take from a man who is working and give to a man who can work but won't. Whatever happened to an American political culture in which the work ethic was valued and individuals took responsibility for their actions? Whatever happened to an American political culture when individuals would stand for something and not go for anything? We have a nation of individuals and

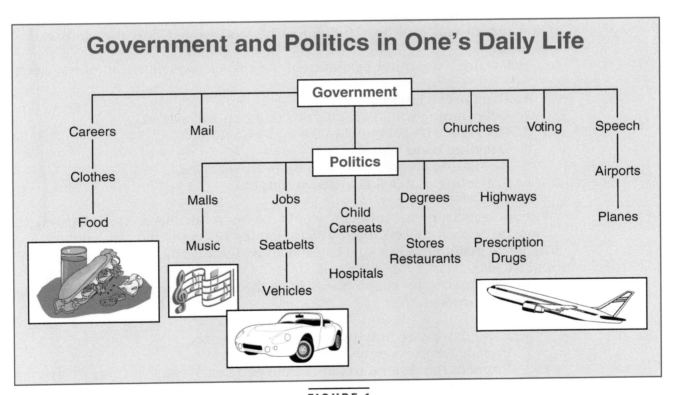

FIGURE 1
No one can escape the hand of visible and invisible Government.

groups who think that the world owes them something simply because they are white, black, Hispanic, Asian, gay, lesbian or happen to be a woman. American society is filled with individuals who see themselves as victims, and it is the government through the mass media who has helped to perpetuate such nonsense. Government is very much needed and without it individuals could not function adequately within a society. However, in the Republic of the United States, the government has violated its limitations which is the rule of law which is sometimes known as Constitutionalism. The governmental system of the U.S. along with its elected officials have overstepped its boundaries by taking power from the local entities in the areas of education, social welfare, health care, and religious freedom. Therefore, the question that must be raised is "what role should government play in our lives?" **Government** is the rule or authority of a state or country that legitimately controls the actions and affairs of the people. Many Americans do not realize how powerful governmental bodies are, and the impact that these institutions have on their daily lives. All government is politics, and all politics is intertwined within government. **Politics** is the science or art of government, or the allocation of political, economic, and social resources within a social unit. Government and politics touches every aspect of human activity. Whether it is seatbelt requirement laws or requiring a child to be in a car seat, the visible and invisible hand of government is present practically everywhere.

Figure 1 shows how government and politics become a reality in our lives. Government can and does influence the food we eat and the clothes that we wear.

Below are a few other examples of the role of government in our society:

1. Drug prescriptions,
2. Determining which schools our children will attend,
3. Deciding who gets tax breaks and who doesn't,
4. Deciding bond issues,
5. Regulating corporations and other businesses,
6. Protecting our civil liberties and rights.

Without government, societies would be in total chaos as expressed by Thomas Hobbes in *Leviathan 1651*. Hobbes believed that government was needed to maintain peace, and law and order, because men were selfish, brutal, and wicked.

In fact, successful governments have the tendency to possess or serve the following purposes:

1. Establish peace and justice within its society,
2. Provide for the common defense,
3. Promote the general welfare of the people,
4. Regulate society,
5. Secure the blessing of liberty,
6. Transfer income.

These elements in one way or other fit the description of the U.S. government, as well as many European nations. Many have referred to this as a **Constitutional Democracy,** a government that regularly enforces recognized limits on those who govern, and allows the voice of people to be regularly heard through free and fair elections. The American political system is one that allows:

1. Majority rule expressed in fair and free elections,
2. The protection of minority rights against the majority,
3. The protection of individual's rights, known as Civil Liberties,
4. Equality of the law for all citizens, which are usually known as Civil Rights.

The rule of law in U.S. politics controls every aspect of government bodies and, thus, places limitations upon both elected and unelected officials. This is sometimes referred to as **Constitutionalism,** which means how power is granted, dispersed, and limited. Without constitutionalism, governmental officials would have ultimate power, and the U.S. would not be a **Representative Democracy** in which those who have power gain and retain it by winning fair and free elections, whereby all adult citizens are allowed to participate. Too many American citizens, however, do not appear to be concerned at all about the government and politics within and outside their communities. In fact, the average U.S. citizen probably could not identify the following:

1. The mayor of one's city,
2. The chairperson of one's school board,
3. The city councilperson of one's district,
4. The state representative of one's district,
5. The state senator of one's district,
6. The U.S. Representative of one's district,
7. The U.S. Senators of one's state.

The major reason for the apathy and unawareness of government and politics among the American citizenry is probably due to the fact they have not and cannot relate government to their daily lives. Figure 2 shows the three basic steps in how government becomes a reality, both in our individual and collective lives. The **Revelation of Government** reveals its values and beliefs to its citizenry. The **Inspiration of Government** means government writes down its beliefs and values in a document such as a constitution. Finally, the **Illumination of Government** is how government applies to its citizens on a daily basis. Once citizens can see the impact of government and politics in their daily lives, maybe then they will take more of an active role in the political process through various forms of political participation.

Government and politics are so essential within any society because they:

1. Help one become aware of his or her political environment,
2. Help individuals to become familiar with politicians who make laws that affect their lives on a daily basis,

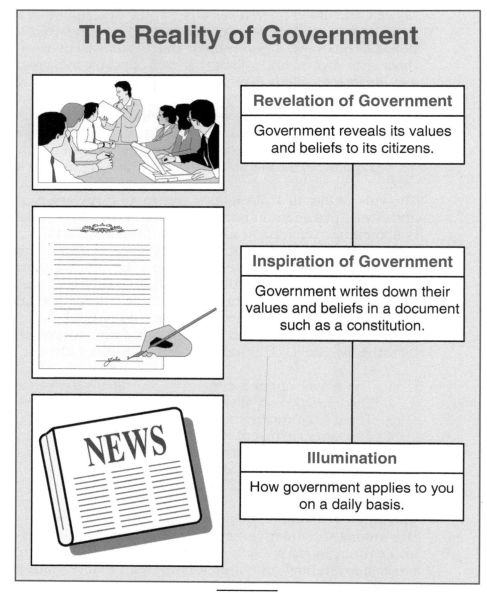

The Reality of Government

Revelation of Government

Government reveals its values and beliefs to its citizens.

Inspiration of Government

Government writes down their values and beliefs in a document such as a constitution.

Illumination

How government applies to you on a daily basis.

FIGURE 2

3. Give individuals a sense of political efficacy,
4. Help individuals to become rational voters,
5. Enable one to discuss government and politics intellectually,
6. Enable one to understand terminology used by both politicians and the mass media,
7. Enable one to know how government and politics operate in one's society as a whole.

All Americans in one way or another are directly affected by the policies and choices of government. Liberals in the U.S. believe that government should take strong, positive action to solve the nation's economic and social problems; they have a tendency to support programs which are designed to alleviate poverty, redistribute income from wealthier citizens to poorer ones, and to regulate the activities of multinational corporations. Conservatives, on the other hand, believe the individual is primarily responsible for his or her own plight. They are less supportive of big government, especially in the areas of social welfare programs and business regulations. Nevertheless, both liberals and conservatives do believe that working within the American political process is still the most positive way to bring about change in our society.

Box 1-1 raises the question of the absence of government.

When reading the list in Box 1-1, one can clearly see that without government we would not have the following elements, which are in the preamble of the U.S. Constitution:

1. Establishment of justice and ensuring domestic tranquility,
2. Providing for the common defense,
3. Promoting the general welfare of the people,
4. Regulating society,
5. Securing the blessings of liberty,
6. Transferring income.

BOX 1-1

WHAT IF THERE WAS NO GOVERNMENT?

1. The weak would be overtaken by the strong.
2. There would be no protection for one's Civil Liberties.
3. There would be no protection for one's Civil Rights.
4. There would not be any collective or public goods.
5. Life would be in a state of confusion and short-lived.
6. There would be the proliferation of Demagogues.
7. How would crime be regulated?
8. How would one receive his or her mail?
9. Who would regulate businesses and multinational corporations?
10. What would be the basis of laws?
11. If someone were to walk up and kill you, how would that person be dealt with?
12. There would be no social welfare programs for both the poor and wealthy.
13. There would be no protections for minorities and women.
14. The poor would be at the mercy of the rich.
15. There would be no protection from external aggression outside the U.S.

The point that is being made here is that without government, there would be no peace. Without government, there would be no providing for the common defense or promoting the general welfare of the people. One would have to forget about the regulating of society or of securing the blessings of liberty, and there would be no transferring of income. Barbarism would be the way for any society that tried to exist without some formal type of government. Niccolo Machiavelli expressed this view in *The Prince;* he depicted the origin of government as standing between weak individuals who were not able to protect themselves from the aggressions of the strong and mighty and, thus, needed the state in order to survive. Government and law are needed to curb human greed and ambition.

■ CONCLUSION

Government is the only social organization which extends to society as a whole and which can legitimately use force when necessary. Some political scientists believe that the American political system is controlled by a group of individuals known as elites. Others believe the Pluralist view in which competing interest groups struggle for political power, and that no one group really controls American politics. Nevertheless, the American governmental system is characterized by the classical liberalist philosophy which consists of liberty, equality, and property.

Suggested Readings

Bouza, Anthony V. *The Decline and Fall of the American Empire: Corruption, Decadence, and the American Dream.* New York: Plenum Press, 1996.

Easton, David. *The Political System.* New York: Knopf, 1953.

Glendon, Mary Ann. *Rights Talk: The Impoverishment of Political Discourse.* New York: Free Press, 1991.

Greenberg, Edward S. and Benjamin I. Page. *The Struggle for Democracy.* New York: Addison-Wesley, 2001.

Lasswell, Harold. *Politics: Who Gets What, When and How.* New York: McGraw-Hill, 1936.

Tolchin, Susan J. *The Angry American: How Voter Rage is Changing the Nation.* Boulder, CO: Westview Press, 1996.

Weisberg, Jacob. *In Defense of Government: The Fall and Rise of Public Trust.* New York: Scribner, 1996.

CHAPTER 1
<u>STUDY GUIDE</u>

After reading and studying this chapter, one should be able to either explain, define, or identify the following:

1. What were Bowtie Professor's views concerning American government?

2. Identify or define the following concepts:
    a. Government
    b. Politics
    c. Constitutional democracy
    d. Constitutionalism
    e. Representative democracy
    f. Niccolo Machiavelli
    g. Thomas Hobbes

3. Explain or identify the following:
    a. Figure 1
    b. Figure 2
    c. Box 1-1
    d. The Prince
    e. Leviathan

4. Give a few examples of the role of government in our society.

5. Identify the four major principles that are allowed in the American political system.

6. Explain the six major purposes that successful governments have a tendency to possess.

7. List at least seven politicians or elected officials the average American citizen probably could *not* identify.

8. List the seven reasons why government and politics are so essential within any society.

9. List the six elements in the preamble of the U.S. Constitution.

10. What was the conclusion of this chapter?

TRUE/FALSE MULTIPLE CHOICE SAMPLE TEST

1. No one can escape the hand of visible and invisible government.
   a. True
   b. False

2. Niccolo Machiavelli wrote the book, *The Prince.*
   a. True
   b. False

3. The Reality of Government consists of 3 major elements.
   a. True
   b. False

4. How power is granted, dispersed, and limited is known as politics.
   a. True
   b. False

5. Government is *not* the only social organization that can extend to a society as a whole.
   a. True
   b. False

6. The book, *Leviathan,* was written by Herbert Spencer.
   a. True
   b. False

7. The Revelation of Government reveals its values and beliefs to its citizenry.
   a. True
   b. False

8. The transfer of income is a major purpose of government.
   a. True
   b. False

9. According to Bowtie Professor, the god of America is materialism.
   a. True
   b. False

Name _____ Date _____

10. Government and politics are so essential because they do *not* give one a sense of political efficacy.
  a. True
  b. False

11. Politics is the rule or authority of a state or country that legitimately controls the actions and affairs of the people.
  a. True
  b. False

12. The Pluralists believe that competing interest groups struggle for political power.
  a. True
  b. False

13. Some political scientists believe that the American political system is controlled by a group of individuals known as the elites.
  a. True
  b. False

14. The American governmental system is characterized by the classical socialist philosophy.
  a. True
  b. False

15. Government and laws are needed to curb human greed and ambition.
  a. True
  b. False

16. _____ is the science or art of government.
  a. Constitutional democracy
  b. Government
  c. Constitutionalism
  d. Politics
  e. Leviathan

17. The _____ of government means that the government writes down its beliefs and values in a document such as a constitution.
  a. Revelation
  b. Inspiration

    c. Illumination

    d. Admiration

    e. Representation

18. There are _____ reasons why government and politics are so essential within any society.

    a. 3

    b. 4

    c. 5

    d. 6

    e. 7

19. _____ believe that the individual is primarily responsible for his or her own plight.

    a. Conservatives

    b. Liberals

    c. Elitists

    d. Pluralists

    e. Socialists

20. believe that the government should take a strong and active role in order to solve the nation's problems.

    a. Pluralists

    b. Bureaucrats

    c. Liberals

    d. Conservatives

    e. Elitists

21. All American citizens in one way or another are directly affected by the:

    a. Elitists

    b. Pluralists

    c. Liberals

    d. Government

    e. All of the above

22. Thomas Hobbes wrote the book:

    a. *The Prince*

    b. *Leviathan*

    c. *Politics in America*

    d. *Government and Power*

    e. *Systems Theory*

23. Political Science is the study of government, politics and:

    a. Status

    b. Political Institutions

    c. Money

    d. Voters

    e. Bureaucrats

24. Which of the following wrote the book, *The Prince?*

    a. Thomas Hobbes

    b. Herbert Spencer

    c. Niccolo Machiavelli

    d. John Locke

    e. Karl Marx

25. means how power is granted, dispersed, and limited.

    a. Constitutionalism

    b. Constitutional democracy

    c. Government

    d. Power

    e. All of the above

26. According to this chapter, Americans know very little about government and:

    a. Foreign policy

    b. Politics

    c. Crime

    d. Social Welfare

    e. Gun control

27. The U.S. citizenry have become very _____ of government and politicians.

    a. Pleased

    b. Aware

    c. Distrustful

    d. Angry

    e. All of the above

28. Both Rome and the U.S. has _____ forms of government.
- **a.** Democratic
- **b.** Federal
- **c.** Republican
- **d.** Unitary
- **e.** Confederate

29. Those who work hard in the U.S. to experience the "American Dream," are undermined by:
- **a.** Republicans
- **b.** Democrats
- **c.** Progressives
- **d.** Political Officials
- **e.** Liberals

30. The Bowtie Professor compared the U.S. with:
- **a.** Germany
- **b.** France
- **c.** Spain
- **d.** Greece
- **e.** Rome

Texas Government: The Republic

There is an individual in Texas political history who was marginalized in his efforts to bring about a change to the state. He is looked upon by traditional Texas historians as a tyrant. However, to some of us he was a hero.

Edmund Jackson Davis was the governor of Texas during the Radical Reconstruction period, and he implemented changes which were beneficial to the newly freed slaves and this did not go well with the Anglo citizens of the state.

E. J. Davis favored such legislation as the Reconstruction Act of 1857, the Wade-Davis Bill, the Civil War Amendments, and other measures which ensured a better quality of life for the former slaves.

E. J. Davis was not a tyrant as projected by the good old boy system. He was a man who wanted change for those who had been dented the rights and privileges that other groups enjoyed. After was this not the reason we had the American Revolutionary War.

—The Bowtie Professor

Name _____ **Date** _____

Explain:

_____

_____

_____

_____

_____

_____

_____

_____

_____

_____

_____

_____

_____

_____

_____

_____

_____

_____

_____

The political history of Texas is usually described from a historical romanticized perspective. Most of the traditional historians have painted a near perfect picture of the state. Texas political history has not always been the positive image projected by those of the past. Instead, it has been a state of terror and hostility against people of color who came into its territory. While some were forced to enter the state others came voluntarily. Nevertheless, the political history of Tejas, has been the combination of the good, the bad, and the ugly. The framework that most Texas government and politic books use explain the politics and history of the state along with the political and economic changes within its territory. The early politics of the state began to revolve around both the pro-union and secessionist crowd. However, before Texas could even get to this point, there had to be a relationship between the state and Mexico. Moses Austin, a native of Connecticut, abandoned his unsuccessful business activities in Missouri and turned his attention to Texas. He was not successful in getting a land grant from the Mexican government to settle a group of European families, but his son Stephen F, Austin was able to make such an accomplishment. Austin was able to settle about 300 families in Tejas. He was a highly educated man who spent five years in the Missouri legislature, a district judge in Arkansas, a federal judge in Arkansas, and also operated a large farm. His actions would lead Texas to the beginning of a new era. Texas is a very unique state within itself. It is the second largest state both populationally and geographically. Only California has more people and Alaska has more land mass. The Greek philosopher Aristotle once stated that "politics is the highest science." To the Texas citizenry, no matter who you are or where you go within the state, you cannot escape from the direct or indirect influence of Texas government and politics. Whether it is car insurance, the kind of water you drink, the safety or nonsafety of the streets you walk or the highways you drive on, or emission sticker requirements on our vehicles, or the college tuition we pay, among countless other examples, the Texas political arena is present everywhere within and in some cases outside the state.

As conventional wisdom has it, the name Texas means **Tejas,** meaning friends or allies. This name was applied by the Spanish explorers and missionaries who came upon a Native American Confederacy whom they discovered in the territory. The Native Americans quite naturally were the first people in Tejas; however, later on came the Spanish, French, Mexicans, and the Americans.

Each group ruled within the following time periods:

1. Spanish Flag (1519)
2. French Flag (1685)
3. Mexican Flag (1825)
4. Republic Flag (1845)
5. Confederate Flag (1861)
6. United States Flag (1845, 1865)

As the story goes on, we all probably have heard about the two major battles which took place in which Texas would gain its independence from Mexico around 1836. Both the battles of the Alamo and San Jacinto would result in the Mexican government giving up Texas, plus all the territories west of Texas and south of Oregon for $15 million. This was known as the **Treaty of Guadalupe.** Texas would later become a state on December 29, 1845. It was the 28th state to be admitted into the Union, only after pro-annexation Democratic James K. Polk was elected president. The annexation articles allowed Texas the privilege of dividing itself into five states.

Box 2-1 shows some of the key players and events in the development of Texas government and history.

The early statehood and secession movement in Texas started around 1846 to 1864, revolved around the pro-Union crowd and the secessionist forces. Texas wanted to secede from the Union, first of all, because the general government of the Union would play favoritism to some states and give them rights and privileges, which did not include Texas; second, the general government of the Union would exclude Texas from the major decision-making process; third, Northern people were considered to be race traitors by Southerners because they wanted to abolish slavery and preached racial equality for all men; fourth, there was a great deal of animosity and chaos among the slave states; fifth and

BOX 2-1

1. **Moses Austin**—the father of Stephen F. Austin. He was a native of Connecticut who abandoned his unsuccessful business activities in Missouri and turned his attention to Texas.
2. **Stephen F. Austin**—was given a land grant by the Mexican government to settle 300 families in Texas. Austin was a highly educated man who spent five years in the Missouri legislature, was a district judge in Arkansas, served as a federal judge in Arkansas, and also operated a farm.
3. **Antonio Lopez de Santa Anna**—president of Mexico and general of the Mexican army.
4. **Sam Houston**—general of the Texas military forces who defeated Santa Anna at San Jacinto.
5. **Emily Morgan**—slave, mulatto girl who was very instrumental in helping to defeat Santa Anna at the battle of San Jacinto. She has been known as the "Yellow Rose of Texas."
6. **The Battle of the Alamo**—took place in San Antonio, Texas, in which about 187 white men and Texas Mexicans fought against larger Mexican forces for 11 days before being annihilated. According to research, there were only two or three survivors.
7. **The Battle of San Jacinto**—a battle which lasted only 18 minutes in which Sam Houston and his forces defeated General Santa Anna and his Mexican forces. Santa Anna was forced to sign a treaty or be executed.
8. **Texas**—was able to gain its independence from Mexico around 1836.
9. **Treaty of Guadalupe**—Mexicans gave up Texas plus all territories west of Texas and south of Oregon for $15 million dollars.
10. **Texas Statehood**—Texas became a part of the Union on December 29, 1845. It was the 28th state to be admitted into the Union.

finally, the election of Abraham Lincoln as president meant one thing to Texans and that was the loss of white rights. As a result of these factors, Texas seceded from the Union and joined the Confederate States of America in March of 1861. During this time both black and white abolitionists were hanged all through the state, which included cities like Austin, Dallas, Denton, and other major areas. White Southerners feared equality for blacks, dissolution of the Union, and the loss of their rights. As a result, Ku Klux Klan activities began taking place throughout the South in the late 1860's to intimidate the following groups:

1. freed African American slaves
2. foreigners
3. Mexicans
4. Jews
5. Catholics

The KKK activities of intimidation included violent beatings which usually resorted in death, torture—tar and feathers, branding, hangings, or threats of castration on the above groups if any of them were perceived to have gotten out of line. Nevertheless, the Confederacy still collapsed and Texas was occupied by Union troops on June 19, 1865. This day has been known as "June-teenth," or Emancipation Day, long celebrated by African Americans in Texas. "June-teenth" became an official state holiday in 1979.

Box 2-2 elaborates on the myth of "June-teenth."

The point I am making here is that African American slaves in Texas were not walking around unaware of their freedom for a period of approximately two

BOX 2-2

Conventional wisdom in Texas believes in the mythical notion that African American slaves were free in Texas for two years and did not know it. The systematic research on slavery has caused me to believe that this is a major misconception for the following reasons:

1. There were free African American populations both in Texas and surrounding Southern states. These free blacks informed the slaves about their freedom.
2. Many abolitionists, though many of them were killed, informed the slaves concerning their freedom.
3. Several black soldiers from Texas, who fought in the Union, were able to get the word of freedom back home to the slaves.
4. How does one explain the fact that rebellious literature on the freedom of slaves and equality for all men was able to infiltrate through Texas, and the information or voice of freedom came into the ears of the slave community?
5. When Abraham Lincoln signed the "Emancipation Proclamation," January 1, 1863, the news traveled all across the Union, both North and South; but remember, Texas joined the Confederate States of America in March of 1861. Therefore, Texas as well as the other Southern states did not honor the Emancipation Proclamation.

years. Many of them knew they were free immediately after the Emancipation Proclamation was signed. The white power structure in Texas did not allow the slaves to have freedom because, as stated earlier, Texas—as well as other southern states—did not honor the Emancipation Proclamation; and the sad thing about this is that if you were to ask the average Texan, black or white, what is the true meaning behind "June-teenth," nine out of ten would give the misconception concerning "June-teenth" as his or her response.

Texas during the post Civil War era had to go through a serious Reconstruction period. During this particular time, Edmund Jackson Davis was the governor; he was pretty much hand picked by the Radical Republican party. The post Civil War period excluded Confederate soldiers and officials from voting, experienced the rise of the Ku Klux Klan as a result of black activity, and allowed the blacks codes and the ex-slaves to vote Republican. Nevertheless, the Great Compromise of 1877 was truly the overthrow of both the Radical Republicans and the Reconstruction era, not only in Texas but in the other southern states as well.

■ THE TEXAS POLITICAL CULTURE

The political culture of Texas has been that of **Individualism,** a belief reinforced by the frontier tradition, that citizens are capable of taking care of themselves with very little governmental assistance. In fact, most Texans believe in **Social Darwinism,** which is that the level of success or failure a person reaches is, for the most part, entirely up to him or her. In Texas, however, as well as in most state governments, political power is concentrated in the hands of a few elite citizens known as the "Establishment." Some have referred to this as the **Traditional Political Culture.** This does not mean that individuals or groups outside the Establishment or the Traditional Culture cannot prosper within the state, but it does mean major public policy issues are in the interest of established families and influential social groups.

The diversity of Texas is evident in its varied and often distinct cultural regions; and those of the less privileged classes hold the view that government's primary responsibility is to promote the general welfare of the people and should use its authority and power to improve the social and economic well-being of all its citizens.

Box 2-3 lists the distinct economic regions of Texas.

BOX 2-3

1. High Plains Region
2. Northwest Texas Region
3. Metroplex Region
4. Upper East Texas Region
5. Southeast Texas Region

6. Gulf Coast Region
7. Central Texas Region
8. South Texas Region
9. West Texas Region
10. Upper Rio Grande Region

■ CONCLUSION

Texas is no longer the backwards frontier state as most outsiders visualize it to be; and the state itself has reached the high levels of both urbanization and physical mobility. The state itself has experienced significant demographic, social, and economic changes over the four decades that have transformed state politics, governmental institutions, race and class relations, and public policies.

Suggested Readings

Bouvier, Leon F. and Dudley L. Poston, Jr. *Thirty Million Texans?* Washington, D.C.: Center for Immigration Studies, 1993.

Buener, Walter L. and Robert A. Calvert, eds. *Texas Through Time: Evolving Interpretations.* College Station: Texas A & M University Press, 1991.

Calvert, Robert A. and Arnoldo Deleon. *The History of Texas.* Arlington Heights, Illinois: Harlan Davidson, 1990.

Fehrenbach, T.R. *Lone Star: A History of Texas and the Texans.* New York: MacMillan, 1968.

McComb, David G. *Texas: A Modern History.* Austin: University of Texas Press, 1989.

O'Connor, Robert F., ed. *Texas Myths.* College Station: Texas A & M University Press, 1986.

Zamora, Emilio. *The World of the Mexican Worker in Texas.* College Station: Texas A & M University Press, 1993.

CHAPTER 2
STUDY GUIDE

After reading and studying this chapter, one should be able to either explain, define, or identify the following:

1. What were Bowtie Professor's views concerning Texas Government: The Republic?

   _____

   _____

2. Who stated that "politics" is the highest science?

   _____

3. List the six flags that have waved over Texas.

   _____

   _____

   _____

   _____

   _____

   _____

4. Identify the following:
   a. Treaty of Guadalupe

   _____

   _____

   b. The Battle of San Jacinto

   _____

   _____

    c. Emily Morgan

_____

_____

    d. The Battle of the Alamo

_____

_____

    e. Sam Houston

_____

_____

    f. Antonio Lopez de Santa Anna

_____

_____

    g. Stephen F. Austin

_____

_____

    h. Moses Austin

_____

_____

5. When did Texas become a state?

_____

6. When did Texas gain its independence from Mexico?

_____

7. What does the name mean?

_____

8. Who was the U.S. president when Texas became a state?

_____

9. In which period did the secession movement in Texas begin?

_____

10. List the five reasons why Texas wanted to secede from the Union.

_____

_____

_____

_____

_____

11. When did Texas join the Confederate States of America?

_____

12. Which groups did the Ku Klux Klan intimidate throughout the South in the late 1860s?

_____

13. Explain the myth concerning June-teenth in Box 2-2.

_____

_____

14. When did June-teenth become an official state holiday?

_____

15. Identify the following:

    a. Individualism

_____

_____

    b. Social Darwinism

_____

_____

    c. Traditional political culture

_____

_____

    d. The 10 distinct cultural regions of Texas

_____

_____

15. What was the conclusion of the chapter?

_____

_____

TRUE/FALSE MULTIPLE CHOICE SAMPLE TEST

1. Throughout the South in the late 1860s, the Ku Klux Klan intimidated Native Americans.

    a. True

    b. False

Name _____   Date _____

2. Texas became a state on December 28, 1845.
   a. True
   b. False

3. "June-teenth" became a state holiday in 1979.
   a. True
   b. False

4. Moses Austin was a native of Connecticut.
   a. True
   b. False

5. Stephen F. Austin was given a land grant to settle 400 families by the Mexican government.
   a. True
   b. False

6. Stephen F. Austin spent 5 years in the Arkansas legislature.
   a. True
   b. False

7. The level of success or failure one reaches is, for the most part, left up to him or her. This is known as social status.
   a. True
   b. False

8. Emily Morgan has been known as the "Yellow Rose of Texas."
   a. True
   b. False

9. Texas gained its independence from Mexico around 1836.
   a. True
   b. False

10. The Battle of the Alamo lasted only 18 minutes.
    a. True
    b. False

11. Texas is no longer the backward frontier state as most outsiders visualize it.
     a. True
     b. False

12. The Great Compromise of 1877 was the overthrow of Radical Reconstruction.
     a. True
     b. False

13. The Great Compromise of 1850 was the overthrow of the Radical Republicans.
     a. True
     b. False

14. The name Texas means which means friends or allies.
     a. True
     b. False

15. Only Alaska is geographically larger than Texas.
     a. True
     b. False

16. Which state is populationally larger than Texas?
     a. Alaska
     b. New York
     c. California
     d. Florida
     e. Pennsylvania

17. The Battle of Alamo lasted about:
     a. 18 minutes
     b. 11 days
     c. 14 hours
     d. 3 weeks
     e. 6 months

18. Which group was intimidated in the late 1860s by the Ku Klux Klan?
     a. Foreigners
     b. Jews
     c. Catholics

    d. Mexicans

    e. Spaniards

19. Texas joined the Confederate States of America in:

    a. March 1861

    b. April 1860

    c. June 1863

    d. September 1864

    e. May 1862

20. _____ was the U.S. president when Texas became a state.

    a. James Monroe

    b. John Q. Adams

    c. Theodore Roosevelt

    d. James K. Polk

    e. Grover Cleveland

21. The Mexicans ruled Texas around:

    a. 1519

    b. 1685

    c. 1825

    d. 1845

    e. 1861

22. The Greek philosopher stated that "politics is the highest science."

    a. Pluto

    b. Aristotle

    c. Socrates

    d. Nietzsche

    e. Nemesis

23. Moses Austin was a native of:

    a. Missouri

    b. San Jacinto

    c. Arkansas

    d. Connecticut

    e. Texas

24. The "Emancipation Proclamation" was signed on:
    a. January 1, 1863
    b. February 3, 1861
    c. March 10, 1870
    d. August 15, 1861
    e. October 9, 1850

25. Several black soldiers from _____ fought in the Union.
    a. Georgia
    b. Alabama
    c. Texas
    d. Connecticut
    e. New Jersey

26. According to the Bowtie Professor, E.J. Davis was a _____.
    a. Tyrant
    b. Hero
    c. Prince
    d. Chief
    e. Nazis

27. E.J. Davis supported the:
    a. Reconstruction Act of 1867
    b. Morrill Grant of 1866
    c. Ex-Confederate Soldiers
    d. Judicial Review
    e. Article V of the Texas Constitution

28. What does E.J. in Davis stand for?
    a. Eddie Jones
    b. Edward Johnson
    c. Eric Jude
    d. Edmund Jackson
    e. Emmit Justin

29. Which of the following is not a distinct economic region of Texas?
    a. West Texas Region
    b. Southeast Texas Region
    c. Gulf Coast Region
    d. Metroplex Region
    e. Low Plains Region

30. The post-Civil War period excluded ex-Confederate soldiers and _____ from voting.
    a. Blacks
    b. Foreigners
    c. Catholics
    d. Mexicans
    e. Officials

Classical Liberalism: America's Political Culture

Chapter 3

The American political culture has become that of entitlement. Many individuals and groups believe that they have a right to things in life, that they did not: earn. Everywhere one turns he or she will notice people whining and complaining about the things they don't have, and are ungrateful for the things that they do have.

Playing the victim role is very common in our culture today. If I do not reach my goals or objectives, I just can blame it on someone else. I want a nice car, but I don't want to work for it. I want to become a doctor, but I am not willing to go to school to become one. Instead, I want things handed to me on a silver platter.

This is the political culture of America today. The attitude of entitlement. We have a generation of individuals who thinks that it is the government's responsibility to take care of them. Narcissism is the way of life for many in our culture, and this started during the social welfare state. The social welfare state (previously known as Modern Reform Liberalism) has destroyed the family, church, education, and American communities as a whole.

The U.S. must return back to the political culture of Classical Liberalism which caused its citizenry to be more responsible for their actions and the daily activities of their lives, and not look for the federal government for handouts, which has caused many to lose both their individual dignity and freedom.

—The Bowtie Professor

Name _____ **Date** _____

Explain:

_____

_____

_____

_____

_____

_____

_____

_____

_____

_____

_____

_____

_____

_____

_____

_____

_____

_____

America's political culture has gone through a serious transformation in the last few decades. By **political culture** I mean a widely shared set of views, values, attitudes, and beliefs about how individuals feel and think their government should be organized and run. Classical Liberalism has been the historical idea of America's political culture. The **Classical Liberal Theory** grew out of the 18th century and stresses the importance of individual dignity and freedom, equality, private property, limited government, and popular consent.

Figure 3 shows the major elements of the Classical Liberalist political philosophy.

One can see that these four major elements have been embedded in America's political culture since the nation began; and as a result of this political philosophy, one will always come across the following key terms when explaining American political culture:

1. *Natural Rights*—rights of all citizens to dignity and worth.
2. *Political Equality*—the belief that the law should apply equally to all and that every person's vote counts equally.
3. *Equality of Opportunity*—the elimination of artificial barriers to success in life, and the opportunity for everyone to strive for success.
4. *Popular Consent*—the idea that a just government must derive its powers from the consent of the people it governs.
5. *Free Market*—an economic system in which prices are controlled by supply and demand and in which regulation by government is minimal.

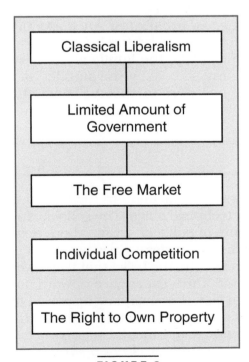

FIGURE 3
The four major elements of Classical Liberalism.

6. *Individual Freedom and Dignity*—the belief that the individual liberty is just as important as the welfare of the community, and that the individual should be allowed to pursue those endeavors which would allow him self-worth and respect.
7. *Ideology*—the values and beliefs of citizens and how they view the proper role of government and political power.
8. *A Republic Form of Government*—a political system whereby elected leaders make public policies.
9. *Theocracy*—a political system whereby religious leaders claim divine guidance.

The primary sources of America's political culture are the family, schools, religion, and the mass media. I will discuss each of these briefly because each one of these primary sources are agents of political socialization, which is the learning of values, beliefs, and opinions concerning government and politics.

■ FAMILY

The family, historically, in the United States was that of the patriarch nuclear family, which consisted of the father, mother, and children. In the patriarch family, the oldest male was usually in charge. Later, the American family was that of the patriarch nuclear extended family which consisted of the husband, wife, children, and other relatives living in, such as either a grandmother or grandfather, or an aunt or uncle. As time went on, the traditional American family became the matriarch family in which the oldest female was in charge.

Unequivocally, the family is the first form of government, and one could measure any society by the stability of its social fabric, which is the family. In fact, if one were to observe some of the social ills of America's society, it could be traced back to the breakdown of the traditional American family.

■ SCHOOLS

The purpose of education in the United States was the transmission of knowledge and technical skills. The schools and educational processes are very powerful agents of political socialization. Acquiring an education is the key to success for most American citizens, which in a sense ushers many of us into the **American Dream,** the belief that if one works hard, he or she will have economic success and, thus, experience upward mobility in a land of opportunity. Education in the U.S., however, has appeared to be dumbed-down in the last twenty-five years or so. Not only this, but also the work ethic does not appear to be as valued in our governmental society as it was several years ago. Traditionally in the U.S., education was not open to the general American citizenry and most of us were grateful just to acquire a high school diploma. A college degree was out of the question because it was too expensive and, therefore, out of reach for

most Americans. In our day and time, however, this is not the case. Practically any individual in our political system can go to some system of higher learning and receive some type of formal training. It is truly up to the individual to determine whether he or she wants to prosper in America's society.

■ RELIGION

Religion, in a nutshell, can be defined as a system of values and beliefs. America is a nation which was built on Judeo Western Christian principles. Figure 4 shows the backbone of America's civilization. One can clearly see

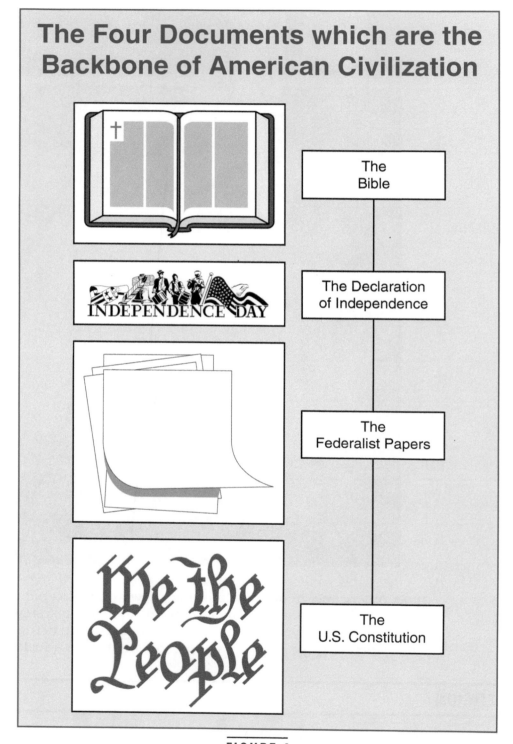

The Four Documents which are the Backbone of American Civilization

The Bible

The Declaration of Independence

The Federalist Papers

The U.S. Constitution

FIGURE 4

that the Bible, the Declaration of Independence, the Federalist Papers, and the U.S. Constitution historically have been the strength of America's political culture. Let it be known, however, that religion is not necessarily synonymous with God or Christianity.

As stated earlier, **Religion** is just a system of values and beliefs. Therefore, if my religion were Marxism or Existentialism then my values and beliefs would be based on these systems. Within our religious beliefs in the U.S. comes an institution known as the **Church,** an organization for public or private worship or religious services. In America there have been four types of churches. They are the emotional, traditional, intellectual, and the spiritual. All of them fall within the realm of Christianity. The emotional church is one in which the congregation is not that educated, and the ministers do not possess any formal training. This type of church bases everything it does purely on emotions and, in many cases, lacks spiritual growth. The traditional church is one in which reality and truth are based on the traditions of their forefathers more than on the Bible itself. In fact, many members of this type of church believe in the traditions of men more than in the power of God. The intellectual church is one in which the vast majority of the congregation are highly educated and the ministers usually hold doctoral degrees in Theology or Divinity. In the intellectual church, there is very limited room for emotions. In fact, some have referred to the intellectual church as God's frozen chosen. The spiritual church is one that does what the Bible says to do. In the spiritual church, the members of the congregation can back up practically everything they do with the Bible. The church as an institution is definitely a powerful agent of political socialization.

■ MASS MEDIA

Finally, the media is a very powerful agent because the mass media engages in both perception and image making. For example, the average American citizen probably will never have the opportunity to walk up and shake the hand of the president of the United States. Through the media, however, the average citizen would get the perception that he is a very powerful person.

The mass media in the United States can give both positive and negative perceptions of any type of noun, meaning any person, place, or thing. For example, how has the media projected the following groups?

1. Small-town people
2. Poor white southerners
3. Hispanics
4. African Americans
5. Uneducated people
6. Fat people
7. Little people
8. Educators

If the mass media projects the above groups or individuals in a positive light, then society as a whole will view them in a positive light.

American political culture has constantly had to deal with the following issues on an ongoing basis:

1. **Race**—a grouping of human beings who have certain inheritable physical peculiarities in common.
2. **Class**—the rank or division of a society who are alike in some way.
3. **Gender**—the grouping of human beings into certain classes, such as masculine, feminine, and neuter.
4. **Ethnicity**—a social division based on national origin, religion, and language, often within the same race, which includes a sense of attachment to that group.
5. **Socioeconomic Status**—a division of the population based on occupation, income, and education.
6. **Ethnocentrism**—is judging another culture or group based on one's own background, attitudes, and biases.
7. **Cultural Relativity**—is judging a particular group or culture on its own standards and not on the standards of another group or culture.
8. **Cultural Pluralism**—is when a group or individual is allowed to keep many of its cultural and social differences while being able to still participate in the dominant culture.
9. **Counterculture**—a group or subculture who challenges the beliefs and practices of mainstream society.

■ CONCLUSION

Political culture exists in the United States within the realm of the classical liberalism. There are a variety of subcultures within the dominant culture because so many Americans hold both similar and different attitudes and beliefs about how government and the political process should work. Perhaps the most notable tension in the American political culture is that we simultaneously believe in a democratic society based on political equality, which involves having an equal voice in shaping our laws and politics.

Suggested Readings

Greenburg, Edward S. *Capitalism and the American Political Ideal.* Armonk, New York: Sharpe Publishers, 1985.

Hunter, James D. *Culture Wars: The Struggle to Define America.* New York: Basic Books, 1991.

Huntington, Samuel. *The Clash of Civilizations and the Remaking of the World Order.* New York: Simon and Schuster, 1996.

Jamieson, Kathleen Hall. *Dirty Politics: Deception, Distraction, and Democracy.* New York: Oxford University Press, 1992.

Kautz, Stevens. *Liberalism and Community.* Ithaca, New York: Cornell University Press, 1996.

Lowi, Theodore J. *The End of Liberalism.* New York: Norton, 1979.

Martin, William. *With God on Our Side: The Rise of the Religious Right in America.* New York: Broadway Publishers, 1996.

CHAPTER 3
STUDY GUIDE

After reading and studying this chapter, one should be able to either explain, define, or identify the following:

1. What were the Bowtie Professor's views concerning Classical Liberalism: America's Political Culture?

_____

_____

2. List the four documents that are the backbone of American civilization?

_____

_____

_____

_____

3. Define the following concepts:
   a. Race

_____

   b. Class

_____

   c. Gender

_____

   d. Ethnicity

_____

   e. Socioeconomic status

_____

   f. Ethnocentrism

_____

   g. Cultural relativity

_____

   h. Cultural pluralism

_____

   i. Counterculture

_____

4. List the four elements of classical liberalism.

_____

_____

_____

_____

5. Name and explain the primary sources of America's political culture.

_____

_____

_____

6. Identify the following:
   a. Political culture

_____

   b. Popular consent

_____

    c. Political equality

_____

    d. Free market

_____

    e. Equality of opportunity

_____

    f. Natural rights

_____

    g. Ideology

_____

    h. Theocracy

_____

    i. Individual freedom and dignity

_____

7. Explain the first form of government

_____

_____

8. What are the four primary sources of political socialization?

_____

_____

_____

_____

9. Explain the four types of churches.

_____

_____

_____

_____

10. Identify the following:
   a. American dream

_____

   b. A republic form of government

_____

   c. Religion

_____

   d. Figure 4

_____

11. What was the conclusion of this chapter?

_____

_____

_____

TRUE/FALSE MULTIPLE CHOICE SAMPLE TEST

1. Four documents are the backbone of American civilization.
   a. True
   b. False

2. Religion is a system of values and beliefs.
   a. True
   b. False

3. Unequivocally, the family is the first form of government.
   a. True
   b. False

4. Historically, the family in the United States was that of the matriarch.
   a. True
   b. False

5. The only purpose of education in America was the transmission of technical skills.
   a. True
   b. False

6. The schools and education are very powerful agents of political socialization.
   a. True
   b. False

7. One primary source of political culture is the mass media.
   a. True
   b. False

8. The intellectual church is known as "God's frozen chosen."
   a. True
   b. False

9. Political culture exists in the United States within the realm of classical socialism.
   a. True
   b. False

10. Class is a division of the population based on occupation, income, and education
    a. True
    b. False

11. Socioeconomic status is the rank or division of a society with members who are alike in some way.
    a. True
    b. False

12. There are four major elements of classical liberalism.
    a. True
    b. False

13. According to Bowtie Professor, victimization seems to be the attitude of many Americans.
    a. True
    b. False

14. The elements of classical liberalism have been embedded in America's political culture.
    a. True
    b. False

15. The classical liberalist theory grew out of the 19th century.
    a. True
    b. False

16. If one works hard and gains educational success, he or she is believed to experience the:
    a. American environment
    b. American dream
    c. Social status
    d. Upward mobility theory
    e. New conservative achievement

17. Education in the United States over the last years appears to have been "dumbed down."
    a. 15
    b. 20
    c. 25
    d. 30
    e. 35

18. _____ allow all citizens to have dignity and worth.
    a. Civil liberties
    b. Civil rights
    c. Human rights
    d. Natural rights
    e. Individual rights

19. Which of the following is *not* an agent of political socialization?

    a. Mass media

    b. Church

    c. Schools/education

    d. Family

    e. Theocracy

20. The _____ church does what the Bible says to.

    a. Spiritual

    b. Emotional

    c. Intellectual

    d. Traditional

    e. Religion

21. The mass media engages in perception and:

    a. Negativism

    b. Emotionalism

    c. Image making

    d. Spiritualism

    e. sensationalism

22. There are _____ documents that are the backbone of American civilization.

    a. 3

    b. 4

    c. 5

    d. 6

    e. 7

23. Each of the four types of churches in America fall within the realm of:

    a. Relativism

    b. Rationalism

    c. Christianity

    d. Subjectivism

    e. Pragmatism

24. _____ is the belief that every person's vote counts.
    a. Equality of opportunity
    b. Equality of results
    c. Political equality
    d. Popular consent
    e. Classical liberalism

25. _____ can be defined as a system of values and beliefs.
    a. Religion
    b. Politics
    c. Theocracy
    d. Ideology
    e. Political culture

26. The U.S. should return back to:
    a. Democracy
    b. Classical Liberalism
    c. Federalism
    d. Socialism
    e. Rationalism

27. _____ seems to be the attitude of many Americans today.
    a. Republicanism
    b. Socialism
    c. Narcissism
    d. Relativism
    e. Pragmatism

28. Most of the American citizenry are born with the _____ mentality.
    a. Welfare
    b. Entitlement
    c. New Age
    d. Socialist
    e. Democratic

29. Classical Liberalism has changed to:
    a. Modern Reform Liberalism
    b. Democratic Socialism
    c. Existentialism
    d. Communism
    e. Relativism

30. The purpose of education in America is the transmission of knowledge and:
    a. Information
    b. Technology
    c. Technical Skills
    d. Democratic Ideas
    e. Higher Learning

The U.S. Constitution: A Masterpiece

Chapter 4

The U.S. Constitution is a document which is supposed to guide the nation. However, many of us can see that several elected officials really do not adhere to it. The U.S. Constitution has become just like the bible, many individuals and groups quote it, but do not live by it. The Articles of Confederation was America's first Constitution. It was a unicameral system, whereby each state had one vote. The objectives of the Articles were to establish a league of friendship, perpetuate unity among the states, provide full faith and credit, and return wanted fugitives. Nevertheless, the Articles of Confederation barely lasted eight years.

Our current U.S. Constitution is a masterpiece, but it is constantly being used and manipulation by the super-rich in the United States who are sometimes referred to as the one percenters. The one percenters practically has the majority of lawmakers in Washington in their back pockets. Therefore, the middle class and the poor in America, do not have a chance. Even though this was not the intent of the frramers, the U.S. is turning into an oligarchy, As a result, the U.S. Constitution will become void. What a shame.

—The Bowtie Professor

Name _____ **Date** _____

Explain:

_____

_____

_____

_____

_____

_____

_____

_____

_____

_____

_____

_____

_____

_____

_____

_____

_____

_____

_____

The political history leading up to the U.S. Constitution is pretty interesting. The background of the original 13 colonies was about sixty percent English. The colonies were either royal or proprietary. Governors of the royal colonies were appointed by the king, and the Penns owned Pennsylvania and Delaware. Connecticut and Rhode Island had charters granted to them in the 17ᵗʰ century, allowing for self government and, thus, they elected their own government.

The original 13 colonies are as follows:

Northern	Middle	Southern
New Hampshire	New York	Virginia
Massachusetts	Delaware	North Carolina
New Jersey	Pennsylvania	South Carolina
Connecticut		Georgia
Rhode Island		Maryland

As time went on, the Americans became sick and tired of being politically oppressed and economically exploited by the British. Therefore, the following events are a few factors that led to the American Revolutionary War:

- **Sugar Act**—taxed sugar, wine, coffee, and other products commonly exported to the colonies.
- **Declaratory Act**—stated that the British government could do anything that was necessary to keep the American colonies in line.
- **Quartering Act**—required the Americans to house and feed the British troops when the troops entered the colonial areas. This act was also called the Mutiny Act.
- **Stamp Act**—required Americans to pay for their own protection and defense out of the revenues from the sale of stamped paper to be used on some 50 items such as pamphlets, newspapers, playing cards, and college diplomas.
- **Townsend Act**—taxed colonial imports of paint, tea, lead, and paper.
- **Taxation Without Representation**—taxed on goods and other products, but did not have an American in the British parliament.
- **The East India Company (1773)**—the British parliament gave exclusive rights to this company to sell tea to American dealers (The Boston Tea Party).
- **The Intolerable Acts**—closed the port of Boston, which was a drastic economic penalty for a city that depended so heavily on trading.

All of the above actions were taken by the British parliament against the Americans, to keep them in line. Yet the American colonies refused to be taxed without representation; and they believed that when a government neglects its responsibilities to a people and oppresses that people, they have a right to overthrow that government. This quite naturally has been known as the Revolutionary Philosophy which would later be found in the Declaration of Independence. The colonies decided to no longer honor British laws; at the First Continental Congress, the colonies boycotted British goods and seven of them sent delegates to Philadelphia. This later was followed by the colonies raising a standard army and commissioning Thomas Jefferson to write the Declaration of Independence.

It is interesting, however, to note how the Americans were able to gain their freedom by using British documents, such as the British Magna Carta (1215), The Colonial Charters (1630-1732), The Mayflower (1620), The Charter Oak Affair (1685-1688), and John Locke, *Second Treatise on Government*.

The call for freedom by the American colonies was ironic in itself. Here we have the colonies calling for freedom and independence from King George III and the British parliament, and yet they themselves had men in bondage. For example, Thomas Paine's "American Crisis" and "Common Sense" basically pointed out that the American Revolution was not only a revolution for Americans to gain their freedom, but it was a revolution for all mankind. This was so far from the truth, considering that slavery as an institution would end far after the American Revolutionary War was won by the colonies. Nonetheless, the colonies gained their freedom and independence from the British empire and then began to set up their own form of government.

The **Articles of Confederation** was America's first constitutional government. It was a unicameral system, whereby each state had one vote. The exercise of most powers required approval of at least nine states, and amendments to the Articles required the consent of all the states. The purposes of the articles are as follows:

1. To establish a league of friendship
2. To perpetuate unity among the states
3. To provide full faith and credit
4. To return wanted fugitives

These objectives were not enough to keep the Articles into existence, and due to Daniel Shay's rebellion, the Articles of Confederation barely lasted eight years. Daniel Shay, along with other farmers, seized the county courthouses and disrupted the trials of the debtors in Springfield, Massachusetts in August of 1786. Later, Shay and his men attacked the federal arsenal at Springfield but were repulsed. Daniel Shay's rebellion brought out the weaknesses of the Articles and the American colonies realized it was time to develop a different governmental system.

The articles were weak because of the following:

1. They lacked a strong central government
2. Could not tax the states
3. Could not print or coin money
4. Did not have a standard army
5. Could not regulate interstate commerce

Even though the Articles of Confederation had many defects, the confederation was able to get the passage of the **Northwest Ordinance of 1787,** which established a basic pattern of government for new territories north of the Ohio River. The Articles were definitely a trial and error for the freely new colonies and now it was time for them to draft a new document. It was time for a constitutional convention.

The constitutional Convention of 1787 totaled 55 delegates, which consisted of 13 affluent individuals, 19 slave owners, 21 were rich, 27 were former officers in the American Revolutionary War, and 33 were lawyers. The two major plans put forth at the convention were the Virginia and New Jersey Plans. The **Virginia Plan** was a bicameral or two-house legislature with the lower house being elected by direct popular vote, and the upper house being elected by the lower house. Whereas the **New Jersey Plan** was a unicameral or one-house legislature with equal state representation, regardless of population. The Federalists, by and large, wanted the Virginia Plan and the Anti-Federalists pushed for the New Jersey Plan. Roger Sherman of Connecticut proposed the **Great Compromise,** or some would call it the **Connecticut Compromise** because of the role that the Connecticut delegates played in proposing it. This plan called for a two-house legislature in which house members would be elected by popular vote based on population, and the upper house would be chosen by state legislatures. The South could also count their slaves as three-fifths of a person. The South wanted to count their slaves as three-fifths of a person to gain more representation in Congress. At first, southerners wanted their slaves to be counted equally as free whites, but northerners objected; therefore, the three-fifths clause was acceptable to both sides.

With this in mind, one would have to ask: "What did the framers intend when it came to the issue of slavery?" A careful examination of the U.S. Constitution and the debates that led to its formation reveals that the framers' intentions were to protect the institution of slavery. Explicit protections of slavery—though the word appears nowhere in the text—are to be found in five places in the U.S. Constitution:

- **Article I, Section 2** said that three-fifths of all slaves would be counted both in setting representation in Congress and in assessing what each state's contribution would be, if a "direct tax" were levied on the states.
- **Article I, Section 9, Paragraph 1** The slave importation clause forbade Congress to ban the African slave trade before 1808, and it did not require Congress to end the trade even after that date.
- **Article I, Section 9, Paragraph 4** declared that any capitation (head) tax imposed had to take into account the three-fifths clause. This clause redundantly reaffirmed that the three-fifths clause would apply to any other type of direct tax imposed.
- **Article IV, Section 2, Paragraph 3** The Fugitive Slave Law clause, which stated that states could not emancipate fugitive slaves and that runaways must be returned to their owners "on demand."

- **Article 5** forbade any amendment of the slave importation or capitation clauses before 1808.

Other clauses gave indirect protection to slavery, such as **Article I, Section 8, Paragraph 15,** which guaranteed federal support to "suppress insurrections." It is no wonder that the great abolitionist Wendell Phillips called the document a "pro-slavery compact," while his ally William Lloyd Garrison called it "a covenant with death," an "agreement with Hell." If one wanted to research further into the criticism of the Founding Fathers' actions regarding slavery, he or she would probably want to read Paul Finkelman's book, *Slavery and the Founders: Race and Liberty in the Age of Jefferson.*

Some of the major players at the Constitutional Convention were: **James Madison,** whose efforts were crucial in assembling the convention and whose voluminous notes provided the most complete records of the daily meeting; **George Mason,** a delegate from Virginia who was very instrumental in later having the Bill of Rights included in the constitution; **Alexander Hamilton,** a delegate from New York whose crucial role came after the convention when he wrote several essays in various New York papers, which later persuaded the state to adopt the new constitution; **George Washington,** who was unanimously appointed as the president of the convention. Some have argued that Washington was appointed because of his heroism in the war. **Benjamin Franklin** was considered to be the delegate who was full of wisdom and knowledge, since he was the oldest at the convention. Franklin was the president of America's first abolitionist organization, the **Pennsylvania Society for the Abolition of Slavery. Governor Morris** of Pennsylvania was the most eloquent spokesman for a strong central government. Morris also worked on the final draft of the constitution and fashioned its literary style. **John Dickenson,** a delegate from Delaware, representing the smallest state in the Union, nonetheless called for a strong central government and he also suggested the Senate be patterned after the British House of Lords. The U.S. Constitution was written in a four-month moment of time, yet it has reflected a century and a half of practical political experience.

A **constitution** is a document that spells out what government can and cannot do, what the rights of individual citizens are, how government officials are to be chosen, and how long they may serve. Yet **Charles Beard,** in his book *American Government,* gives two operational definitions of a constitution:

1. A general system of laws, customs, and institutions pertaining to the government of that country.
2. A formal document or social contract drafted by a representative assembly and ratified by a special procedure for determining public assent.

Definition (1) is more of an international description of any governmental body. Definition (2), however, applies more to the U.S. Constitution because our document is a social contract that was drafted by a representative assembly and ratified by a special procedure for determining public assent.

By far, the U.S. Constitution is a masterpiece. It has been in force since 1789, and except for the period prior to and during the Civil War, has had all but universal acceptance and legitimacy. Political scientist and historian **Herman Pritchett,** in his book *American Constitution,* gives four major purposes of the U.S. Constitution:

1. To provide the structure of the governmental system, its organs, and its institutions of public authority.
2. To authorize the power the government is to have and allocate the power among its different branches.
3. To state the limitations of governmental power so that there will be a balance between individual civil liberties and governmental authority.
4. To provide a means other than a violent revolution by which the constitutional design can adapt to future changes and necessities.

Pritchett's objectives of the U.S. Constitution definitely highlight why the U.S. as a nation has been able to escape the kinds of despotism and governmental chaos that has afflicted so many other peoples. Box 4-1 highlights some of the issues the Founding Fathers were concerned about when perfecting the constitutional document.

The U.S. Constitution is approximately seven thousand words, consisting of seven Articles and 27 Amendments.

The seven Articles are as follows:

Article I   Legislation/Congress
Article II   Executive/Presidency
Article III   Judicial/Federal Courts
Article IV   Interstate Relations
Article V   The Amending Power
Article VI   The Supremacy Act
Article VII   R atification

BOX 4-1

1. Voting
2. Presidential Selection
3. Bill of Rights
4. Commerce
5. National Supremacy
6. Republicanism
7. Separation of Powers
8. Checks and Balances
9. Federalism
10. Judicial Review

In due time, many of the above concerns would be dealt with even after many of the framers had passed on.

According to Professor Yecats, the 27 amendments of the constitution can be broken into four major categories, which are: Civil Liberties, Civil War, Civil Rights, and Government Protection Amendments.

The Civil Liberties Amendments are those amendments from one through ten:

Amendment 1	Speech, press, petition, assembly, religion
Amendment 2	Right to bear arms
Amendment 3	No quartering of troops
Amendment 4	No searches and seizures without a warrant
Amendment 5	Due process of law, no self-incrimination, right to a fair trial
Amendment 6	Right to have a lawyer in criminal cases
Amendment 7	Right to have a jury trial in certain civil cases
Amendment 8	No cruel and unusual punishment, no excessive bails and fines
Amendment 9	Enumerated powers, the protection of liberties not spelled out in the other amendments
Amendment 10	Reserved powers given to the states

Civil Liberties are those rights which protect the citizens from an overbearing government. Civil Liberties are also called the Bill of Rights. Amendments 13, 14, and 15 are known as Civil War Amendments; and quite naturally, it is obvious why they are referred to as the Civil War Amendments, because they were put in the constitution right after the Civil War. These Amendments are:

Amendment 13	Abolished slavery
Amendment 14	Gave Blacks citizenship, due process clause, equal protection of the law
Amendment 15	Gave black males the right to vote

Note: The 13th, 14th, and 15th Amendments are both Civil War and Civil Rights Amendments.

The Civil Rights Amendments are:

Amendment 19	Gave women the right to vote
Amendment 24	Struck down the poll tax
Amendment 26	Gave those 18 years of age and older the right to vote

Civil Rights are those privileges in which a nation guarantees political and social equality for all its citizens, whereby the government sometimes will have to step in and protect its citizenry from each other.

Government Protection Amendments are those in which the government protects itself from its citizenry or they keep the operation of government running smoothly.

Amendment 11	Cannot sue the federal court system; this also includes foreigners
Amendment 12	The electoral college, how the president is selected
Amendment 16	Have to pay a federal income tax
Amendment 17	Senators elected by popular vote
Amendment 18	Prohibition, forbidding the sale of alcoholic drinks and liquors
Amendment 20	The president will take office on January 20 at 12:00 p.m.
Amendment 21	Made it legal for the states to sell alcoholic beverages
Amendment 22	Limits the president to two terms in office
Amendment 23	Washington D.C., three electoral votes
Amendment 25	Presidential disabilities
Amendment 27	Congressional pay raises

Table 4-1 gives examples of how the four major categories of Amendments of the U.S. Constitution are used.

TABLE 4-1

I. Civil Liberties
   A. The right to pray
   B. The right to bear arms
   C. Freedom of speech
   D. Due process of law
   E. No self-incrimination
II. Civil War
   A. Abolished slavery
   B. Black citizenship
   C. Due process clause
   D. Equality of the law
   E. Black males get the right to vote
III. Civil Rights
   A. The right to vote
   B. Cannot be discriminated against based on race, class, gender, religion, color, or age
   C. Allowed to go into public accommodations such as restaurants and hotels
   D. To have equal access to jobs, housing, and recreational activities
IV. Government Protection Amendments
   A. One cannot sue the federal courts
   B. The presidential selection
   C. The federal income tax
   D. Senators elected by the people

■ CONCLUSION

The U.S. Constitution has been hailed as a stroke of political genius. It clearly reflects the basic values of the framers in its emphasis on popular sovereignty, liberty, and a republican form of government. It has generally been conceded to be the most successful and influential document ever written, and the framers established a government to be operated by ordinary people. They did not anticipate Americans would be so virtuous and civic-minded that they could be trusted to operate a government without checks and balances.

Suggested Readings

Beard, Charles. *An Economic Interpretation of the Constitution.* New York: MacMillan, 1913.

Dworkin, Ronald. *Freedom's Law: The Moral Reading of the Constitution.* Cambridge, Massachusetts: Harvard University Press, 1997.

Evans, Sarah M. *Born for Liberty: A History of Women in America.* New York: Free Press, 1997.

Gerber, Scott Douglas. *To Secure These Rights: The Declaration of Independence and Constitutional Interpretation.* New York: New York University Press, 1995.

Hofstadter, Richard. *The American Political Tradition.* New York: Vintage Books, 1948.

Morison, Samuel E. *The Oxford History of the American People.* New York: Oxford University Press, 1965.

Wood, Gordon S. *The Creation of the American Republic.* New York: Norton, 1972.

CHAPTER 4
STUDY GUIDE

After reading and studying this chapter, one should be able to either explain, define, or identify the following:

1. List the 13 colonies according to their geographical locations.

_____

_____

_____

2. Explain the background of the 13 colonies.

_____

_____

_____

3. Identify the following:
    a. Intolerable Acts

    _____

    b. East India Company (1773)

    _____

    c. Taxation without Representation

    _____

    d. Townsend Act

    _____

    e. Stamp Act

    _____

    f. Quartering Act

_____

    g. Declaratory Act

_____

    h. Sugar Act

_____

4. What is the Revolutionary Philosophy?

_____

_____

5. What were the Bowtie Professor's views concerning the U.S. Constitution?

_____

_____

_____

6. Identify the following:
    a. Articles of Confederation

_____

    b. Northwest Ordinance of 1787

_____

    c. Virginia Plan

_____

    d. New Jersey Plan

_____

    e. Connecticut Compromise

_____

7. What are the four purposes of a constitution?

_____

_____

_____

_____

8. Give two operational definitions of a constitution.

_____

_____

9. What are the seven Articles of the U.S. Constitution?

_____

_____

_____

_____

_____

_____

_____

10. What are the four major categories of the U.S. Constitution?

_____

_____

_____

_____

11. Name and explain the 27 Amendments of the U.S. Constitution.

_____

_____

_____

_____

_____

_____

_____

_____

_____

_____

_____

_____

_____

_____

_____

_____

_____

_____

_____

_____

_____

_____

_____

12. Identify the following:
   a. Charles Beard

_____

   b. Herman Pritchett

_____

   c. James Madison

_____

   d. Paul Finkelman

_____

   e. John Dickenson

_____

   f. George Mason

_____

   g. Governor Morris

_____

   h. Alexander Hamilton

_____

   i. George Washington

_____

    j. Wendell Phillips

_____

    k. William Lloyd Garrison

_____

13. List the five reasons why the Articles of Confederation failed.

_____

_____

_____

_____

_____

14. What were the four objectives of the Articles of Confederation?

_____

_____

_____

_____

15. Which articles of the U.S. Constitution protected the institution of slavery?

_____

16. What was the conclusion of this chapter?

_____

_____

_____

TRUE/FALSE MULTIPLE CHOICE SAMPLE TEST

1. There are 27 amendments to the U.S. Constitution.
   a. True
   b. False

2. According to Herman Pritchett, one purpose of a constitution is to provide the structure of the governmental system.
   a. True
   b. False

3. Amendment 3 of the U.S. Constitution is the right to bear arms.
   a. True
   b. False

4. Alabama is one of the original 13 colonies.
   a. True
   b. False

5. The Taxation Act taxed tea, lead, and paper.
   a. True
   b. False

6. The New Jersey Plan was a unicameral system.
   a. True
   b. False

7. The 13 colonies were about 60 percent English.
   a. True
   b. False

8. The Articles of Confederation barely lasted 8 years.
   a. True
   b. False

9. The Virginia Plan was a tricameral system.
   a. True
   b. False

10. New Jersey is one of the original 13 colonies.
    a. True
    b. False

11. Charles Beard wrote the book American Constitution.
    a. True
    b. False

12. Herman Pritchett wrote the book American Government.
    a. True
    b. False

13. There are 17 articles in the U.S. Constitution.
    a. True
    b. False

14. The 13th Amendment to the U.S. Constitution gave women the right to vote.
    a. True
    b. False

15. Amendment 23 to the U.S. Constitution gave Washington, D.C., 3 electoral votes.
    a. True
    b. False

16. Which of the following was *not* an Act?
    a. Stamp
    b. Quartering
    c. Taxation
    d. Sugar
    e. Townsend

17. The National Ordinance of 1787 passed during the:
    a. Articles of Confederation
    b. Virginia Plan
    c. New Jersey Plan
    d. Connecticut Compromise (1789)
    e. East India Company (1773)

18. Which of the following was *not* one of the original 13 colonies?
- **a.** New York
- **b.** Maine
- **c.** Rhode Island
- **d.** Georgia
- **e.** Virginia

19. The 26th Amendment to the U.S. Constitution gave _____ the right to vote.
- **a.** Blacks
- **b.** Women
- **c.** Those 18 or older
- **d.** Hispanics
- **e.** Native Americans

20. No quartering of troops is Amendment of the U.S. Constitution.
- **a.** 3
- **b.** 4
- **c.** 5
- **d.** 6
- **e.** 7

21. An Economic Interpretation of the Constitution was written by:
- **a.** John Locke
- **b.** Herman Pritchett
- **c.** Paul Finkelman
- **d.** Wendell Phillips
- **e.** Charles Beard

22. There were _____ reasons why the Articles of Confederation failed.
- **a.** 2
- **b.** 3
- **c.** 4
- **d.** 5
- **e.** 6

23. Which of the following stated that the U.S. Constitution was a "covenant with death"?
    a. Paul Finkelman
    b. Charles Beard
    c. Herman Pritchett
    d. William Lloyd Garrison
    e. Wendell Phillips

24. Amendment 4 of the U.S. Constitution is:
    a. The right to bare arms
    b. No searches and seizures without a warrant
    c. No quartering of troops
    d. The right to vote
    e. The right to have a lawyer in criminal cases

25. Which of the following was the president of the Pennsylvania Society for the Abolition of Slavery?
    a. Governor Morris
    b. John Dickenson
    c. Wendell Phillips
    d. William Lloyd Garrison
    e. Benjamin Franklin

26. The U.S. is turning into a (an):
    a. Monarchy
    b. Oligarchy
    c. Democracy
    d. Equilibrium
    e. Welfare State

27. The U.S. Constitution was written in a _____ moment of time.
    a. Two
    b. Three
    c. Four
    d. Five
    e. Six

28. John Dickenson was a delegate from _____.
   a. New York
   b. Massachusetts
   c. Connecticut
   d. Delaware
   e. Virginia

29. The Stamp Act stamped about _____ different items.
   a. 50
   b. 40
   c. 30
   d. 20
   e. 10

30. The super-rich are sometimes referred to as the:
   a. Elite
   b. Illuminati
   c. Establishment
   d. Oligarchy
   e. One Percenters

The Texas Constitution: Transformation

The Texas Constitution of 1869 was a very radical document. It conformed to the wishes of the Radical Reconstructionists. It contained many "modern" features such as annual legislative sessions, an appointed judiciary, and generous salaries for state officials.

This constitution was used by the Reconstruction governor E.J. Davis. Governor Davis implemented the Radical Reconstruction measures such as the disfranchisement for ex-Confederate soldiers, unlimited voting for the newly freed slaves, supported the Reconstruction Act of 1867, and demanded the use of the Civil War Amendments.

Many have argued that E.J. was a tyrant while others have claimed that he was a hero. To the Anglos in Texas during the Reconstruction period, Davis was a nightmare, but to the freed slave population, he was a hero. Who is giving the facts and who is giving the interpretation?

—The Bowtie Professor

Name _____ **Date** _____

Explain:

_____

_____

_____

_____

_____

_____

_____

_____

_____

_____

_____

_____

_____

_____

_____

_____

_____

_____

Any system operates according to a set of rules that specify what kinds of inputs and outputs are acceptable and how the conversion structure is to be organized. In a governmental system, this set of rules is commonly called a constitution. The Texas Constitution, unlike the U.S. Constitution, is a long and drawn-out document. The U.S. Constitution has barely 7,000 words, whereas the Texas Constitution has more than 80,000 words. With 364 amendments in 1996, it is the fourth most frequently amended state constitution. The only state constitution which is longer is that of Alabama. Texas has had seven constitutions in its existence, but only five since it became a state on December 29, 1845.

Box 5-1 lists and briefly describes the seven Texas constitutions.

The Texas Constitution, like any other document, has both its general principles and objectives. The three major principles of the Texas Constitution are **Popular Sovereignty, Governmental Limitations,** and **Separation of Powers.** Popular Sovereignty is the idea that a just government gains its power from the consent of the people it governs. Governmental Limitations is the

---

BOX 5-1

1. The Constitution of Coahuila y Tejas was adopted in 1827; it recognized Texas when it was colonized by Anglo settlers under Stephen F. Austin as a Mexican state with Coahuila, its neighbor south of the Rio Grande River.
2. The Constitution of the Republic of Texas of 1836 was drafted during the War of Independence and ratified soon after the war ended. It was modeled after the U.S. Constitution but guaranteed the continuation of slavery.
3. The Statehood Constitution of 1845 was written when Texas was admitted into the Union. This constitution was regarded as the best one produced by the state.
4. The Civil War Constitution of 1861 was adopted by Texans after the state seceded from the Union and joined the Confederacy in 1861.
5. The Constitution of 1866 was a short-lived constitution under which Texas sought to be readmitted to the Union after the Civil War and before the Radical Reconstructionists took control of Congress.
6. The Reconstruction Constitution of 1869 conformed to the wishes of the Radical Reconstructionists. This constitution contained many "modern" features such as annual legislative sessions, an appointed judiciary, and generous salaries for state officials.
7. The Texas Constitution 1876 was adopted at the end of Reconstruction, while Texas was still a rural, frontier state. Amended many times since being adopted, it remains in effect today. It is a highly restrictive and anti-governmental document drafted by Texans reacting to the abuses of the Radical Reconstructionists and the oppressive administration of Governor Edmund Jackson Davis. Tight restrictions were placed on the governorship, the legislature, and other state officials, which today inhibit the ability of the state government to respond to the complex needs of what is now a growing urban state.

constitutional principle that distinguishes between individual civil liberties and governmental authority. Separation of Powers is the same in the Texas Constitution as it is in the U.S. Constitution, which is the division of authority among three distinct branches of government; the legislative, executive, and judicial branches serve as checks and balances on each other's power.

Below are a few examples of the Texas system of checks and balances:

1. Vetoes
2. Judicial review
3. Impeachment
4. Confirmation

The four major purposes or objectives of the Texas Constitution are, first, to give **Legitimacy to the Government.** Government is the only social organization that extends to society as a whole, and it has legitimacy when its citizenry accepts its actions as fair and just. Secondly, to **Organize Government** is another purpose of the Texas Constitution. Government must have structure by establishing offices responsible for basic governmental functions and defining their relationships to each other. Third, to **Provide Power to the State Government.** The Texas Constitution must and does provide power for the state government; however, this power must be subject to the U.S. Constitution's division of powers based on our system of federalism. Fourth and finally, **Limitations on Governmental Authority.** Texans support the belief in limited government, which has produced the Bill of Rights in the Texas Constitution and other constitutional protections against arbitrary governmental action.

Box 5-2 lists the 17 Articles of the Texas Constitution.

BOX 5-2

Article I	Bill of Rights
Article II	The Powers of the Government
Article III	Legislative Department
Article IV	Executive Department
Article V	Judicial Department
Article VI	Suffrage
Article VII	Education and Public Free School
Article VIII	Taxation and Revenue
Article IX	Counties
Article X	Railroads
Article XI	Municipal Corporations
Article XII	Private Corporations
Article XIII	Spanish and Mexican Land Titles
Article XIV	Public Land and Land Office
Article XV	Impeachment
Article XVI	General Provisions
Article XVII	Mode of Amending the Constitution of the State

> **BOX 5-3**
>
> ### A MOMENT OF THOUGHT: E.J. DAVIS AND THE TEXAS RECONSTRUCTION CONSTITUTION OF 1869
>
> For it has been said that history means that he is telling his-story. History has two major components, *facts* and *interpretation.* The interpretation component can be very dangerous and misleading because it can shape the worldview of those who came along later in life. In reference to Edmund Jackson Davis, during the Reconstruction Era in Texas, most of the research projects him as a tyrant. It is the good old boy intellectuals and so-called scholars, however, who project him in such a negative light. Remember, to the Nazis, Hitler was a hero; but to the Jews, he was a nightmare. To the Anglos in Texas during the Reconstruction period, E.J. Davis was a nightmare, but to the newly freed African American slave population he was a hero. In other words, E.J. Davis was an "Abraham Lincoln" for black folks in Texas at the time of his governorship. Why? It is very simple. He implemented Radical Reconstruction measures that benefited the newly freed slaves. Examples are the following:
>
> 1. Davis demanded disfranchisement for ex-Confederate soldiers.
> 2. Davis favored unlimited voting for African Americans.
> 3. Davis included African Americans in key political organizations.
> 4. Davis strongly believed in the Reconstruction Act of 1867.
> 5. He also favored the Wade–Davis Bill.
> 6. He also implemented the Civil War Amendments.
>
> The list could go on, but I will stop here. E.J. Davis was not a tyrant as projected by the good old boy scholars. He was a man who wanted change, for those who had been in bondage for so many years. He was a man of both vision and of political transformation. Any time that there is a change in any political system, there are those who will resist because they are not able to deal with the metamorphosis that is taking place. Remember, history means he is telling his story. It is time for you and me to tell our story.
>
> Professor Yecats

■ CONCLUSION

Texas, like most other states, has functioned under a series of constitutions, each of which has contributed to the state's constitutional legacy. Each is appropriately understood from the perspective of the period in which it was adopted.

Suggested Readings

Bruff, Harold H. "Separation of Powers Under the Texas Constitution." *Texas Law Review.* 68 (June 1990): 1337-67.

Cnudde, Charles F., and Robert E. Crew, Jr. *Constitutional Democracy in Texas.* St. Paul: West Publishers, 1989.

Harrington, James C. "Framing a Texas Bill of Rights Argument." *St. Mary's Law Journal.* 24 (1993): 399-442.

Lutz, Donald S. "The Texas Constitution." *In Perspectives on American and Texas Politics: A Collection of Essays, eds.* Dubuque, Iowa: Kandall/Hunt, 1987, pp.193-211.

May, Janice C. *The Texas Constitution Revision Experience in the 70's.* Austin: Sterling Swift, 1975.

McKay, Seth Shepard. *Seven Decades of the Texas Constitution of 1876.* Lubbock: Texas Technical College, 1943.

Miller, Lawrence. "The Texas Constitution." *Texas Politics: A Reader, eds.* New York: Norton, 1997, pp.16-31.

CHAPTER 5
STUDY GUIDE

After reading and reviewing this chapter, one should be able to either explain, list, define, or identify the following:

1. Identify the 17 articles of the Texas Constitution.

_____

_____

_____

_____

_____

_____

_____

_____

_____

_____

_____

_____

_____

_____

2. What are the four major purposes of the Texas Constitution?

_____

_____

_____

_____

3. Explain Box 5-3 concerning E.J. Davis and the Texas Reconstruction Constitution of 1869.

_____

_____

4. Identify the three major principles of the Texas Constitution.

_____

_____

_____

5. What were the Bowtie Professor's views concerning the Texas Constitution?

_____

_____

_____

6. Name and explain the seven Texas Constitutions.

_____

_____

_____

_____

_____

_____

_____

7. What did this chapter conclude?

_____

_____

_____

TRUE/FALSE MULTIPLE CHOICE SAMPLE TEST

1. The Texas Constitution is the longest constitution in the United States.
   a. True
   b. False

2. Popular sovereignty is a major principle of the Texas Constitution.
   a. True
   b. False

3. The Statehood Constitution of 1836 was the Independence Constitution.
   a. True
   b. False

4. Texas has had seven constitutions in its history.
   a. True
   b. False

5. Article XV of the Texas Constitution is impeachment.
   a. True
   b. False

6. Vetoes would be an example of the Texas system of checks and balances.
   a. True
   b. False

7. E.J. Davis demanded disfranchisement for ex-Confederate soldiers.
   a. True
   b. False

8. History has three major components.
    a. True
    b. False

9. Article VI is the Powers of the Government.
    a. True
    b. False

10. The "good old boy scholars" thought that E.J. Davis was a tyrant.
    a. True
    b. False

11. Article V is the Executive Department.
    a. True
    b. False

12. The Civil War Constitution was that of 1865.
    a. True
    b. False

13. The Texas Constitution has more than 80,000 words.
    a. True
    b. False

14. Texas became a state on December 28, 1845.
    a. True
    b. False

15. The Tejas y Coahuila Constitution was that of 1829.
    a. True
    b. False

16. Which of the following was not a Texas Constitution?
    a. 1827
    b. 1836
    c. 1848
    d. 1861
    e. 1876

17. Texas has had _____ constitutions in its history.

    a. 5
    b. 6
    c. 7
    d. 8
    e. 9

18. The Judicial Department is Article _____ of the Texas Constitution.

    a. III
    b. IV
    c. V
    d. VI
    e. VII

19. E.J. Davis believed in the _____ of 1867.

    a. Reconstruction Act
    b. Civil Rights Act
    c. Wade-Davis Bill
    d. Government Liberty Act
    e. All of the above

20. Texas is the _____ most frequently amended state constitution.

    a. Third
    b. Fourth
    c. Fifth
    d. Sixth
    e. Seventh

21. The U.S. Constitution barely has _____ words.

    a. 3,000
    b. 4,000
    c. 5,000
    d. 6,000
    e. 7,000

22. The Bill of Rights is found in Article _____ of the Texas Constitution.
    a. I
    b. II
    c. III
    d. IV
    e. V

23. Counties are found in Article _____ of the Texas Constitution.
    a. VI
    b. VII
    c. VIII
    d. IX
    e. X

24. History has two major components: facts and:
    a. Fiction
    b. Social norms
    c. Principles
    d. Interpretation
    e. Folkways

25. Article _____ of the Texas Constitution is Railroads.
    a. VII
    b. VIII
    c. IX
    d. X
    e. XI

26. The Texas Constitution, like any other document, has both its general _____ and objectives.
    a. Laws
    b. Sovereignty
    c. Principles
    d. Limitations
    e. Powers

Name _____ Date _____

27. Which Texas Constitution was the most radical?

   a. 1869

   b. 1845

   c. 1861

   d. 1836

   e. 1876

28. The Texas Constitution must provide power to the _____ government which is subject to the U.S. Constitution's division of power.

   a. Local

   b. State

   c. County

   d. Special Districts

   e. City

29. Some have argued that E.J. Davis was a (an):

   a. Democrat

   b. Tyrant

   c. Socialist

   d. Radical

   e. Liberal

30. These are _____ Articles in the Texas Constitution.

   a. 13

   b. 14

   c. 15

   d. 16

   e. 17

Federalism: The National Government and the States

Who has more power, the federal government or states?
Among politicians this has caused numerous debates.

The Feds argue that they have the Supremacy clause;
therefore, the states cannot ignore their laws.

The states say that we have Amendment 10,
and if there is a conflict, we should win.

This argument over power between national government
and states has caused a negative disposition;
but states usually lose, even when they try to use
interposition.

The U.S. Constitution is Supreme Law of the Land.
This is something the state governments must truly
understand.

—The Bowtie Professor

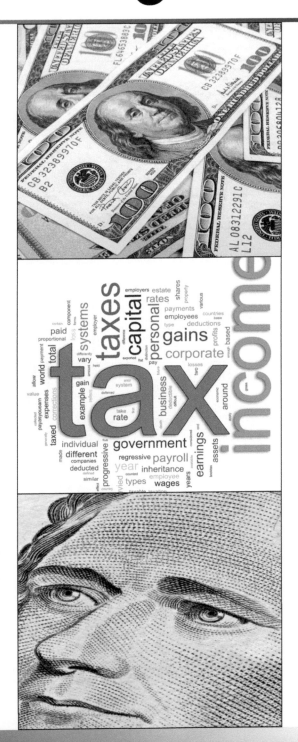

Name _____ **Date** _____

Explain:

_____

_____

_____

_____

_____

_____

_____

_____

_____

_____

_____

_____

_____

_____

_____

_____

_____

_____

In the beginning of the development of this nation, America's system of government was a Confederation, as we found out in Chapter 4. Today, the American political system is a federal system of government. **Federalism** is the sharing of power between the national government and the states. In the U.S. Constitution there is nothing in the main body which explicitly grants powers to the states, because the framers were trying to establish a national government which would perform only specified powers; all other governmental powers, except for a few restrictions listed in the constitution, would be held by the states. These powers are known as reserved powers and are found in the 10th Amendment of the Constitution. **Reserved powers** state that all powers that are not given to the U.S. Constitution are reserved to the people and the states.

Below are a few nations besides the U.S. which have federal systems of government:

1. Germany
2. Canada
3. Mexico
4. India
5. Brazil
6. Australia

By no means are the above countries conclusive. Nonetheless, the vast majority of world governments operate from a Unitary system. A **Unitary** form of government is one in which all power rests in the hands of the national government. Such countries as Ghana, France, Israel, Sweden, the Philippines, and Great Britain operate from this type of government. A **Confederation** is the exact opposite of a Unitary form of government, in which the central government is weak and the lower municipalities have the ultimate governmental authority. As stated earlier, America's first form of government was a confederation. Other confederations include:

1. Switzerland (a confederation of 23 states)
2. Commonwealth of Independent States (which consists of several republics of the former Soviet Union)
3. United Nations
4. NATO
5. Confederate States of America during the Civil War

So, we can see that there are three major systems of government around the world, and the U.S. chose the federal system of government because federalism:

1. Encourages policy innovation
2. Encourages experimentation
3. Protects liberties
4. Allows many functions to be worked out by the national government, and then it trickles down to the states.
5. Allows state governments to be training grounds for future leaders
6. Manages conflict
7. Increases political participation

8. Stops the notion of interposition
9. Disperses power
10. Keeps government closer to the people

Yet there are some arguments against federalism. First, a federal system can obstruct and block progress on the national level. Second, it can hinder the process of ethnic and minority groups. Third, it can expand national powers at the expense of state governments. Fourth, it can contribute to an unequal distribution of wealth by setting different levels of services in health, welfare, education, and other public areas. Fifth and finally, federalism cannot seem to eliminate urban poverty, declining infrastructures, and crime and violence.

Box 6-1 shows both the powers of federalism and the three major crises of our federal system of government in the United States.

BOX 6-1 A

THE POWERS OF FEDERALISM

1. **Delegated Powers**—Powers which are specifically spelled out in the Constitution for the national government only.
   Example: *The power to print or coin money or the power to declare war. Express powers are sometimes referred to as enumerated powers.*
2. **Concurrent Powers**—Powers both the national government and states share.
   Example: *Both the national government and the states can tax their citizens.*
3. **Reserved Powers**—The 10th Amendment powers which state that all powers not given to the U.S. Constitution are therefore reserved to the people and the states.
4. **Inherent Powers**—The national government's powers in foreign affairs.
   Example: *Making treaties with foreign nations.*
5. **Implied Powers**—Those powers which are not specifically spelled out in the U.S. Constitution but are yet possessed by the national government through the necessary and proper clause.

BOX 6-1 B

THE THREE MAJOR CRISES OF FEDERALISM

1. **Civil War**—The Civil War left the national government with control over banking, transportation, higher education, and land management.
2. **Industrialization Era**—This was a problem for the states because of businesses having a monopoly on the capital, engaging in price-fixing, and making it difficult for the states to regulate commerce. The federal government passed laws regulating the conduct of trade, as well as laws regulating food and drugs. The Justice Department also enforced Sherman Antitrust laws. The presidents during this period were Theodore Roosevelt (1901-09) and Woodrow Wilson (1913-21).
3. **Depression**—Franklin D. Roosevelt offered America the New Deal package. The purpose of the New Deal program was for America to have relief, recovery, and reform.

When one observes the powers of federalism, he or she must understand that there is no division of power between the national government or states in the U.S. Constitution. Certain powers, specifically for the central government, state governments, and powers in which both systems share, are set forth in the document. Table 6-1 gives a little enlightenment on such powers. Table 6-1 also shows powers which are denied by both the national government and the states.

TABLE 6-1	The Constitutional Powers of Government

The Central Government

Delegated / Expressed Powers
1. Can admit new states
2. Can conduct foreign policy
3. Can declare war
4. Can establish post offices
5. Can print and coin money
6. Can regulate interstate commerce
7. Can raise and support the military

The Central Government and the States

Concurrent Powers
1. Both can tax its citizenry
2. Both can regulate transportation
3. Both can regulate the Criminal Justice
4. Both can borrow money
5. Both can regulate health care
6. Both can regulate education

The State Governments

Reserved Powers
1. Can create local governments
2. Can conduct elections
3. Cannot require elected officials to take a religious test
4. Cannot make ex post facto laws

The Central Government and the States

1. Cannot deny one employment because of gender or race
2. Cannot deny one the right to vote because of race, gender, or color
3. Cannot permit slavery
4. Cannot grant titles of nobility
5. Cannot deny one access to public accommodations because of sexual preference

State Governments

1. Cannot admit new states
2. Cannot declare war
3. Cannot make foreign policy
4. Cannot print or coin money
5. Cannot establish post offices

Federal grants have played a major role in our system of government. These grants usually have mandates attached to them. They are designed to supply state and local governments with revenue; to establish minimum national standards for such things as safe drinking water and clean air; to equalize resources among state governments through federal taxes by taking money from the wealthy, through grants, and giving it to the poor; and finally, to attack national problems while at the same time minimizing the growth of bureaucratic agencies.

Federal grants usually fall within four major areas, **Categorical Formula, Project, Block**, and **General Revenue Sharing**. Each must adhere to **Federal Mandates**, requirements imposed by the national government as a condition in order to receive federal funding.

Below are brief descriptions of the major federal grants.

1. **Categorical Formula**—Congress appropriates funds for specific purposes such as welfare, school lunches, and the building of airports and highways (AFDC and Medicaid).
2. **Project**—Congress appropriates a certain sum, but the dollars are allocated to states and local units and sometimes nongovernmental agencies based on applications from those who wish to participate. Examples are grants by the National Science Foundation to universities and research institutes to support the work of scientists. Project grants can also go to both states and cities to support training and employment programs.
3. **Block**—Broad grants are provided to states for prescribed activities in the areas of education, social services, preventive health, and health services with only a few specific strings attached.
4. **Revenue Sharing**—Grants are given to the states and local government to be used at their discretion and subject only to very general conditions. Revenue sharing was terminated to the states in 1986 and to local government in 1987, by the Reagan administration.

Each U.S. president when dealing with the issue of federalism has a direction in which he intends to guide the country. Franklin D. Roosevelt's federalism was cooperative federalism in which the national, state, and local governments had to work together in order to pull America out of the Depression. Roosevelt's package was the **New Deal**. With the New Deal, Roosevelt came up with the second Bill of Rights:

1. The right of every family to a decent home.
2. The right to adequate medical care and the opportunity to achieve and enjoy good health.
3. The right to adequate protection from the economic fears of old age, sickness, accident, and unemployment.

4. The right of every businessman, large and small, to trade in an atmosphere of freedom from unfair competition and domination by monopolies at home and abroad.
5. The right of every farmer to raise and sell his products at a return giving him and his family a decent living.
6. The right to earn enough to provide adequate food and clothing and recreation.
7. The right to a useful and remunerative job in the industries, shops, farms, or mines of the nation.

President Harry Truman and Dwight Eisenhower basically continued the concept of cooperative federalism; however, Truman referred to his program as the **Fair Deal**, as he sought to desegregate the military. President John F. Kennedy pushed for a **New Frontier** which would usher federalism into the era of the Civil Rights movement.

Lyndon B. Johnson's era of federalism was probably the most controversial because he in many cases bypassed state governments and gave federal funds directly to city governments. Federalism was used to address problems in areas that had been neglected by the states. Johnson's program was called **Creative Federalism** under the theme **The Great Society War on Poverty**. Richard Nixon's federalism was General Revenue Sharing in which money and power were given back to the states with very little restriction on how it should be spent. Nixon's General Revenue Sharing was directed under the theme of **Law and Order**. President Carter attempted his concept of creative federalism by using categorical grants in related policy areas, into a single block grant. This was done under the theme of **New Foundations**. Ronald Reagan's federalism was known as the **New American Revolution**, which was broken down into three categories:

1. **Devolution**—Give power back to the states
2. **Decrementalism**—Cut federal social programs
3. **Deregulation**—Reduce the regulation of corporations (this is also known as new federalism)

George Bush continued former President Reagan's policies under the disguise of **A New Kinder and Gentler Nation**. Bill Clinton's federalism emphasized **Education for the 21st Century** in which he pushed for a better educational system within state governments.

President George W. Bush really did not have a guided theme concerning federalism when he entered the White House until September 11, 2001, when the twin towers were bombed by terrorists. After this devastating incident, Bush's theme focused on **The War on Terrorism**.

Box 6-2 shows other key terms and concepts which one will always come across when discussing our federal system of government.

BOX 6-2

1. **Necessary and Proper Clause**—The clause in Article I, Section 8 of the U.S. Constitution granting Congress the power to enact laws "necessary and proper" for carrying out its delegated powers. The necessary and proper clause is sometimes referred to as either implied powers or the elastic clause.
2. **Supremacy Clause**—One in which the national constitution is the supreme law of the land. The national government has power over the state and local governments.
3. **Interposition**—An argument, long rejected by the Supreme Court, that a state may place itself between its citizens and the national government to prevent the enforcement of a national law believed by the state to be unconstitutional.
4. **Preemption**—Total or partial federal assumption of power in a particular field and, thus, restricting the authority of the states.
5. **Interstate Compacts**—Agreements among the states. The constitution requires that most such agreements be approved by Congress.
6. **Full Faith and Credit**—Article IV, Section 1 requires that state courts enforce the civil judgments of the courts of other states and accept their public record as valid.
7. **Interstate Privileges and Immunities**—Article IV, Section 2 requires that states must extend to citizens of other states the privileges and immunities granted to their own citizens, including the protection of laws, the right to engage in peaceful occupations, access to the courts, and freedom from discriminatory taxes.
8. **Dual Federalism**—Both the national government and the states have their own powers and jurisdictions.

■ CONCLUSION

Our federal system of government has its shortcomings. Yes, it is true that we still face problems in the areas of education, health care, welfare, crime, transportation, water and sewage, and regional rivalries; nevertheless, federalism has improved the lives of many Americans, particularly in the areas of rights and liberties. At present, federalism is caught in a dilemma resulting from conflicting desires—to reduce national spending while at the same time maintaining federal assistance to the states.

Suggested Readings

Bok, Derek. *The State of the Nation.* Cambridge, Massachusetts: Harvard University Press, 1996.

Derthick, Martha. *The Influence of Federal Grants.* Cambridge, Massachusetts: Harvard University Press, 1970.

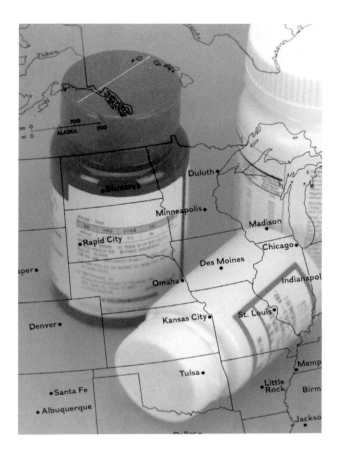

Donahue, John D. Disunited States: *What's at Stake as Washington Fades and the States Take the Lead.* Glenview, Illinois: Basic Books, 1997.

Dye, Thomas. *American Federalism: Competition Among Governments.* Lexington, Massachusetts: Lexington Books, 1990.

Elazar, Daniel J. American Federalism: A View from the Sates. New York: Harper and Row, 1984.

Elkins, Stanley, and Eric McKitrick. *The Age of Federalism.* New York: Oxford University Press, 1994.

Peterson, Paul E. *The Price of Federalism.* Washington, D.C.: The Brookings Institution, 1995.

CHAPTER 6
STUDY GUIDE

After reading and reviewing this chapter, one should be able to either explain, define, identify, or list the following:

1. What were the Bowtie Professor's views concerning federalism?

_____

2. Identify or define the following:
   a. Federalism

_____

   b. Reserved powers

_____

   c. Unitary system

_____

   d. Confederation

_____

   e. Delegated powers

_____

   f. Concurrent powers

_____

   g. Inherent powers

_____

Name _____   **Date** _____

3. Explain the four arguments against federalism.

_____

_____

_____

_____

4. List the 10 advantages of federalism.

_____

_____

_____

_____

_____

_____

_____

_____

_____

_____

5. Name and explain the powers of federalism.

_____

_____

_____

Name _____ **Date** _____

6. Name and explain the three crises of federalism.

_____

_____

_____

7. Give examples of the different powers of federalism.

_____

_____

_____

8. List at least six countries that have federal systems of government.

_____

_____

_____

_____

_____

9. Give at least four examples of confederations.

_____

_____

_____

_____

10. Give at least five examples of nations that have unitary systems.

_____

_____

_____

_____

_____

11. Name and explain the four major areas of federal grants.

_____

_____

_____

_____

12. List Franklin D. Roosevelt's 7-second Bill of Rights.

_____

_____

_____

_____

_____

_____

13. Identify the following:
   a. New American Revolution

_____

b. New Frontier

_____

c. Fair Deal

_____

d. Creative federalism

_____

e. New Deal

_____

f. Dual federalism

_____

g. Interposition

_____

h. Supremacy clause

_____

i. Necessary and proper clause

_____

j. Full faith and credit

_____

k. Interstate privileges and immunities

_____

14. What was the conclusion of this chapter?

_____

_____

_____

TRUE/FALSE MULTIPLE CHOICE SAMPLE TEST

1. Devolution is giving power back to the states.
   a. True
   b. False

2. Presidents Harry Truman and Dwight Eisenhower continued creative federalism.
   a. True
   b. False

3. Block grants are provided to states for prescribed activities in the areas of education and social services.
   a. True
   b. False

4. Decrementalism cuts federal social programs.
   a. True
   b. False

5. Federal grants have played a major role in our system of government.
   a. True
   b. False

6. There have been four major crises of federalism.
   a. True
   b. False

7. In the U.S. Constitution, there is no division of power between the national government or the states.
   a. True
   b. False

8. The power to print or coin money is a reserved power.
   a. True
   b. False

9. The Civil War left the national government with control over land management.
   a. True
   b. False

10. Reserved Powers are found in the 9th Amendment to the U.S. Constitution.
    a. True
    b. False

11. Federalism is the sharing of powers between national governments and the states.
    a. True
    b. False

12. Both the national government and the states can tax their citizens.
    a. True
    b. False

13. NATO is an example of a unitary system.
    a. True
    b. False

14. Federalism does not encourage policy innovation.
    a. True
    b. False

15. Concurrent powers are shared by both national government and the states.
    a. True
    b. False

16. The power to print or coin money would be an example of a(n) _____ power.
    a. Reserved
    b. Delegated
    c. Inherent
    d. Implied
    e. Concurrent

17. The state government can:
    a. Conduct elections
    b. Admit new states
    c. Establish post offices
    d. Regulate interstate commerce
    e. Raise and support

18. Making treaties with foreign nations would be an example of a(n) _____ power.
    a. Reserved
    b. Delegated
    c. Inherent
    d. Implied
    e. Concurrent

19. _____ is the cutting of social programs.
    a. Devolution
    b. Deregulation
    c. Dual federalism
    d. Decrementalism
    e. Delegated power

20. During the Industrialization Era, _____ was the U.S. President.
    a. George Washington
    b. James Madison
    c. Andrew Jackson
    d. Herbert Hoover
    e. Theodore Roosevelt

21. During the Industrialization Era, was the U.S. President.
   a. Abraham Lincoln
   b. John Q. Adams
   c. Lyndon B. Johnson
   d. James Polk
   e. Woodrow Wilson

22. The "New American Revolution" was the slogan of President:
   a. Johnson
   b. Truman
   c. Eisenhower
   d. Reagan
   e. Carter

23. Australia is an example of a(n) system.
   a. Federal
   b. Unitary
   c. Confederation
   d. Republic
   e. Socialist

24. The vast majority of world government are:
   a. Federal systems
   b. Unitary systems
   c. Confederations
   d. Republics
   e. Socialists

25. India would be an example of a(n) _____ system of government.
   a. Confederate
   b. Unitary
   c. Federal
   d. Republic
   e. Socialist

26. President Harry Truman and Dwight Eisenhower basically continued the concept of:
   a. Creative Federalism
   b. Fair Deal
   c. Cooperative Federalism
   d. Law and Order
   e. New Frontiers

27. Federal grants usually fall within _____ major areas.
   a. Four
   b. Two
   c. Five
   d. Three
   e. Six

28. America's type of government at the beginning of this nation was a(an):
   a. Unitary System
   b. Federal System
   c. Socialist Society
   d. Confederation
   e. Marxist Society

29. There are _____ major systems of government around the world.
   a. Six
   b. Five
   c. Four
   d. Three
   e. Two

30. _____ has a federal system of government.
   a. Switzerland
   b. France
   c. Australia
   d. Israel
   e. Ghana

Texas: The Local Governments

Local governments in Texas
are creations of the state.
This is what Texas politicians believe, and therefore,
it is not open to debate.

Some local entities are large,
while others are small.
Nonetheless, local government are those
which can truly include all.

It really does not take a lot of money,
to run a local campaign.
Especially if one is selfless,
and is not out for personal gain.

Local governments definitely
are closer to the masses.
Therefore their public policies
reach a broad range of classes.

One could go before the city councils,
and be heard loud and clear.
For local entities are not far off,
but are actually very near.

—The Bowtie Professor

Name _____ **Date** _____

Explain:

_____

_____

_____

_____

_____

_____

_____

_____

_____

_____

_____

_____

_____

_____

_____

_____

_____

_____

As pointed out by Professor Yecats, local governments are creations of the state. In fact, the relationship between the states and municipalities take on the form of a Unitary system. This has been known as the **Dillon Rule,** a principle which holds that local governments' powers and responsibilities are defined by the state, because they are creations of the state. This rule, when applied to local governments of the United States, became popular after Judge John F. Dillon of the Iowa Supreme Court included two of his 1868 decisions, based on the common law rule in his **Commentaries on the Law of Municipal Corporations.**

Local governments basically go into four major categories:

1. **General Law City**—A city allowed to exercise only those powers specifically granted to it by the legislature. General law cities have fewer than 5,000 residents.
2. **Home Rule**—A city with more than a population of 5,000 which can adopt any form of government residents choose, provided it doesn't conflict with the state constitution or statutes.
3. **Special District**—A unit of local government created by an act of the legislature to perform limited functions.
4. **Counties**—The chief governmental units created by the states to administer state law and business at the local level.

Historically, there have been four systems of local governments within the states. Each are described below:

1. **Strong-Mayor-Council Form**
   a. The form consists of a council composed of members elected from single-member districts.
   b. A mayor is elected at-large and given the power to appoint and remove department heads.
   c. Budgetary power is given to the mayor, with council approval.
   d. Veto power over council actions are given to the mayor.
2. **Weak-Mayor-Council Form**
   This model of local government gives limited administrative powers to the mayor, who is popularly elected along with members of the city council, some departmental heads, and other municipal officials. The council has the power to override the mayor's veto. The mayor's position is weak because the office shares appointive and removal powers over municipal government personnel with the city council.
3. **Council-Manager Form**
   Sometimes called the commission-manager form, the council manager form has the following characteristics:
   - City council members are elected at-large or in single-member districts.
   - A city manager is appointed and removable by the council and is responsible for coordination.
   - A mayor, elected at large, presides over the council.

4. **City Commission**
   A form of local government whereby each commissioner administers a department. This system does not provide a single executive, but relies on elected commissioners who constitute a policy-making board.

Note: Due to the Council-Manager form of government, the City Commission form of government is practically nonexistent.

The vast majority of the home rule cities in Texas use the Council-Manager form of government, with Dallas and San Antonio being the two largest cities in Texas who use this form. The home rule was established in 1912 by a state constitutional amendment, which consists of 290 cities; nineteen of those with populations above 5,000 have chosen to remain among the over 800 general-law cities. Out of the 290 home-rule cities, 251 use the Council-Manager form of government. The Strong-Mayor Council form is used by 39 cities in Texas, with Houston, El Paso, and Pasadena being the three largest cities who chose this form. Some strong mayor cities have borrowed a few elements from the council-manager system by allowing the mayor to appoint a professional city manager to run the daily activities of the city government. The weak-mayor-council form of government lacks the power of a strong mayor system. Most small cities in Texas use the weak-mayor form because with few people and little demand for services, small city governments can operate with low budgets and low or no taxes. In these small, relatively homogeneous communities, business is conducted on a friends-and-neighbors basis. The commission form of government in Texas was pioneered by Galveston after the disastrous 1900 hurricane. Because of its inherent weakness, however, the commission form of government has almost disappeared and there are no pure examples of this form in Texas.

Municipal governments have their electoral systems, just like the states and the national government. The one **At-Large Elections,** in which all candidates are elected jurisdiction-wide, such as in the entire city, county, or state. **District Elections** are those which require candidates to live in geographic areas whereby only voters in those areas can vote for them. The **Place System** is one in which all candidates are elected citywide, while each seat is designated place one, so that each candidate runs only against others who have filed for the same position. Local elections, however, are usually **Nonpartisan,** in which the candidates bear no party label, such as Republican or Democrat.

Another unit of local government is the **Special District.** The Special District is created by the Texas state legislature to perform limited functions. Below are examples of special districts:

- **School Districts**—over 1,000 independent school districts in the state
- **Junior/Community College Districts**—49 community/junior college districts
- **Non-School Districts:**
  1. 900 water or utility districts

2. 326 housing authorities
3. 210 soil and water conservation districts
4. 86 hospital districts
5. 46 hospital authorities and much more

The county government plays a vital role in local politics because it is the chief governmental unit created by the state to administer state law and business at the municipal level. The structure of the county government is as follows:

- **Commissioners Court**—The principal policy-making body for county government. It sets the county tax rate and supervises expenditures.
- **County Judge**—The presiding officer of a county commissioners court. This office has some judicial authority which is assumed by separate county courts—at law in most urban counties.
- **County Clerk**—The chief record-keeping officer of a county.
- **County Attorney**—An elected official who is chief legal officer of some counties. He or she also prosecutes lesser criminal offenses, primarily misdemeanors, in county courts.
- **District Attorney**—An elected official who prosecutes the more serious criminal offenses, usually felonies, before state district courts.
- **Tax Assessor-Collector**—An elected official who determines how much property tax is owed on the different pieces of property within a county, and then collects the tax.
- **Sheriff**—An elected official who is the chief law enforcement officer of a county.
- **Constable**—An elected law enforcement officer who is responsible primarily for executing court judgments, serving subpoenas, and delivering other legal documents.
- **County Auditor**—An appointed officer who is primarily responsible for viewing every bill and expenditure of a county to assure it is correct and legal.
- **County Treasurer**—An elected officer who is responsible for receiving and disbursing county funds.

County government serves all of Texas, but it is particularly important for Texans in rural and unincorporated suburban areas. For individuals who live in these areas, the county is usually the major source of local public services, such as law enforcement protection, roads, and hospitals. County governments, however, have relatively few implied powers. Unlike home-rule cities, county governments lack the basic legislative power of enacting ordinances.

City governments must deal with the issues of revenue and expenditures. They must deal with the following areas of concern:

- **Revenue Bonds**—Bonds that are used to finance the construction of a public facility and are repaid with income produced by the facility.
- **General Obligation Bonds**—Bonds requiring voter approval in which the city borrows money to pay for new construction projects such as

prisons, mental hospitals, or school facilities. General obligation bonds are repaid with tax revenues.

- **Infrastructure**—Streets, waste disposal systems, libraries, and other public facilities built and operated by governments.
- **Rollback Election**—An election in which local voters can nullify a property tax increase that exceeds 8 percent in a given year.
- **Regressive Taxes**—A tax system whereby the poor disproportionately pay more in taxes than the wealthy.
- **Homestead Exemption**—A tax reduction system that municipal governments grant on a taxpayer's home or place of residence.

Local governments in Texas must face the problems that go along with urbanization, just as other state municipalities. Problems such as racial conflict, crime, declining infrastructures, the "graying" of Texas cities, unemployment, class conflict, and state and federally mandated programs have taken their toll on Texas cities. Some have called for the following solutions in order to try and ratify the problems:

- **Privatization**—Government contracting with private companies to provide some public services.
- **Annexation Powers**—The authority of cities to add territory which would be subject to restrictions set by state law.
- **Exterritorial Jurisdiction**—The power of an incorporated city to control development within nearby unincorporated areas.
- **Metro Governments**—The consolidation of city and county governments to avoid the duplication of public services.

■ CONCLUSION

Local governments in Texas are creations of the state, and they possess powers which are only granted to them by the state constitution and statutes. City municipalities are most likely to have a daily impact on its citizens, and much of this effect is critical to the quality of life. One can easily get involved in his or her local environment by:

1. Registering to vote.
2. Once voter registration is completed, be sure to vote.
3. Attend neighborhood meetings and speak out.
4. Attend school board and city council meetings.
5. Volunteer to work on a local campaign.
6. Contact public officials and let them know about your concerns.
7. Encourage others in your neighborhood to become politically aware.

The above list is not conclusive; however, it does give one an idea of how to get involved in the political system.

Suggested Readings

Blodgett, Terrell. *Texas Home Rule Charters.* Austin: The Texas Municipal League, 1994.

Bridges, Amy. *Morning Glories: Municipal Reform in the Southwest.* Princeton: Princeton University Press, 1997.

Bullard, Robert D. Invisible Houston: The Black Experience in Boom and Bust. College Station.

Burns, Nancy. *The Formation of American Local Governments: Private Values in Public Institutions.* New York: Oxford University Press, 1994.

Jones, Lawrence, and Delbert A. Taebel. "Hispanic Representational Change in Texas Country Government." *Texas Journal of Political Studies.* 16 (Fall 1993): 321.

Miller, Charles, and Heywood T. Sanders, Ens. *Urban Texas.* College Station: Texas A&M University Press, 1990.

Norwood, Robert E., and Sabrina Strawn. *Texas County Government: Let the People Choose.* 2nd ed., Austin: Texas Research League, 1984.

Orum, Anthony M. *Power, Money and the People: The Making of Modern Austin.* Austin: Texas.

CHAPTER 7
STUDY GUIDE

After reading and reviewing this chapter, one should be able to either list, identify, explain, or define the following:

1. Explain the historical four systems of local governments.

_____

_____

_____

_____

2. Name and explain the four categories of local governments.

_____

_____

_____

_____

3. Explain the Bowtie Professor's views concerning local governments.

_____

_____

_____

_____

_____

_____

_____

_____

Name _____ **Date** _____

4. Name and explain the 10 components that make up the structure of the county government.

_____

_____

_____

_____

_____

_____

_____

_____

_____

5. List at least seven ways one could easily get involved in his or her local environment.

_____

_____

_____

_____

_____

_____

6. Name and explain the four major solutions that local governments have used in order to solve many of its problems.

_____

_____

_____

_____

7. Name and explain the different types of districts within local governments.

_____

_____

_____

8. Identify the following:
   a. John F. Dillon

_____

   b. Dillon rule

_____

   c. General law city

_____

   d. Counties

_____

   e. Home rule

_____

   f. District elections

_____

Name _____ Date _____

g. Nonpartisan

_____

h. Place system

_____

i. At-large elections

_____

j. Special district

_____

k. Rollback election

_____

l. Regressive taxes

_____

m. Infrastructure

TRUE/FALSE MULTIPLE CHOICE SAMPLE TEST

1. The county judge is the presiding officer of a county commissioners court.
   a. True
   b. False

2. There are about 900 water or utility districts.
   a. True
   b. False

3. County governments are *not* the chief governmental unit created by the state to administer state law and business at the municipal level.
   a. True
   b. False

4. City governments must deal with the issues of revenue and expenditures.
   a. True
   b. False

5. County governments do not serve all of Texas.
   a. True
   b. False

6. The vast majority of the home rule cities in Texas use the strong mayor system.
   a. True
   b. False

7. Local governments in Texas are creations of the county.
   a. True
   b. False

8. Municipal governments have their electoral system just like the states and national government.
   a. True
   b. False

9. The constable is an elected law enforcement officer.
   a. True
   b. False

10. There are only 800 independent school districts in the state of Texas.
    a. True
    b. False

11. The county government does not play a vital role in local politics.
    a. True
    b. False

12. At-large elections are those in which all candidates are elected internationally.
   a. True
   b. False

13. Local governments in Texas are creations of the Feds.
   a. True
   b. False

14. The "graying" of Texas cities has become a problem within Texas.
   a. True
   b. False

15. A general city law is one with fewer than 5,000 people.
   a. True
   b. False

16. According to the Bowtie Professor, local governments are creations of the:
   a. Feds
   b. County
   c. State
   d. People
   e. Politicians

17. A home rule city has more than _____ people.
   a. 5,000
   b. 10,000
   c. 15,000
   d. 20,000
   e. 25,000

18. The Dillon rule was named after:
   a. Judge Jack C. Dillion
   b. John F. Dillon
   c. Frank Dillon
   d. Joe Dillon
   e. Peggy Dillion

19. There have been, historically, _____ types of municipal governments.

    a. 2

    b. 3

    c. 4

    d. 5

    e. 6

20. _____ are the chief governmental units created by the states to administer state laws and business at the local level.

    a. Districts

    b. Municipal corporations

    c. Special districts

    d. Counties

    e. Commissioners

21. The _____ is a process in which all candidates are elected citywide.

    a. Nonpartisan system

    b. Special district

    c. At-large election

    d. District election

    e. Place system

22. There are about _____ water or utility districts in Texas.

    a. 500

    b. 600

    c. 700

    d. 800

    e. 900

23. Texas has about _____ housing authorities.

    a. 326

    b. 410

    c. 525

    d. 600

    e. 710

24. The _____ is created by the state to perform limited functions.
   a. District election
   b. Place system
   c. Special district
   d. At-large election
   e. Nonpartisan election

25. According to Yecats, local governments are closer to the:
   a. State
   b. County
   c. Council
   d. Masses
   e. Classes

26. Which of the following is not a solution for local governments?
   a. Privatization
   b. Metro Governments
   c. Exterritorial Jurisdiction
   d. Annexation Powers
   e. Revenue Bonds

27. City municipalities are most likely to have a daily impact on:
   a. Its Citizens
   b. Voter's Registration
   c. Elected Officials
   d. Metro Governments
   e. Annexation Powers

28. Small city governments can operate with low budgets and low or no:
   a. Federal Support
   b. County Involvement
   c. Taxes
   d. Funds
   e. Revenue Bonds

29. Local elections are usually
   a. Special Districts
   b. At-Large Elections
   c. Partisan
   d. Non-Partisan
   e. Place Systems

30. The principle policy-making body for county government is the:
   a. County Commissioner
   b. County Judge
   c. Sheriff
   d. Constable
   e. Commissioners Court

Public Opinion: Poli-ology

Public opinion in American politics
can project a certain type of perception.
For many politicians,
it is their most powerful weapon.

These opinion polls can predict which candidates
will be ahead, and which candidates will be behind.
It is enough to make the average voter
change his mind.

The opinion polls may show one thing today,
and something else next week.
But the truth is the only objective
the voter must seek.

Public opinion does influence us,
in more ways than one.
As an American citizen,
unless you vote, your job is still not done.

—The Bowtie Professor

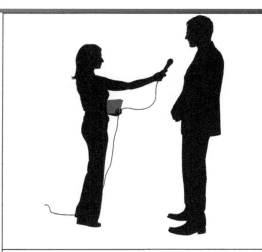

Name _____ **Date** _____

Explain:

_____

_____

_____

_____

_____

_____

_____

_____

_____

_____

_____

_____

_____

_____

_____

_____

_____

_____

_____

_____

Public opinion is the beliefs shared by significant numbers of citizens on issues of widespread importance. Public opinion, therefore, is of utmost importance to governmental decision-makers. A democratic form of government rests upon public support, and being cognizant of whether government is functioning in cooperation with or in opposition to the "will" of the people becomes a vital concern. No government can claim to be the legitimate voice of the people unless public opinion plays an integral role in the choice of the political leaders and the development of public policy. The philosopher Plato believed that public opinion should only reflect the will of the state and its rulers, whereas John Stuart Mill argued that public opinion should reflect the views of the people, and not just those groups in power. When studying the American political system, by far John Stuart Mill had the right idea. Public opinion can be:

- **Constant**—Public opinion issues that change little from day to day
- **Dynamic**—Public opinion issues that change according to political and social events
- **Intense**—Public opinion issues in which individuals believe in strongly and, thus, are willing to act on their beliefs.

Public opinion is measured by the use of opinion polling. Gallup, Roper, and Harris, and other types of polls have been periodically published in newspapers and magazines, or announced on television or the radio. The findings of these polls are studied by politicians and other governmental officials. Polls during an election year can indicate with accuracy which candidate, even before the election, will be the winner of practically any political office. The accuracy of public opinion polls are based on a method known as **Survey Research,** which is the gathering of data or information by questioning a representative sample of the population. If the sample is not representative of the population, then the validity of the survey research will be inaccurate, which was the case with the *Literary Digest* poll of 1936. In that presidential year, Alf Landon was a Republican nominee running against Franklin D. Roosevelt, the Democratic incumbent. The *Digest,* which was similar to today's *Newsweek, Time,* or *U.S. News & World Report* magazines, predicted that Alf Landon would win a landslide victory over Roosevelt. The opposite occurred, however, when FDR won the election by a landslide victory. The inaccuracy of the *Digest* polling was due to the fact that they used a **Bias Sample,** a sample which does not represent the population as a whole. The Literary Digest sampled only the wealthier groups in America's society by its own subscribers, from lists of automobile owners, from telephone books, and the like. Poll cards were mailed to these individuals across the country and those who were inclined to do so mailed them back with the name of the presidential candidate they preferred. Prior to this election, the *Digest* correctly predicted every presidential election from 1920 to 1932. Nevertheless, after the major setback of the 1936 prediction, the *Digest* in less than a year went bankrupt.

George Gallup, who is considered by many to be the father of public opinion in the U.S., like the *Digest* made a few mistakes as well, before he was known as a public opinion expert. In 1948, Gallup and many other pollsters incorrectly predicted that Thomas E. Dewey would defeat presidential Harry S. Truman. In many cases when public opinion polls are way off in their predictions, either a bias sample was used or a **Straw Poll,** which is a nonscientific method of measuring public opinion. By far, public opinion polls play a major role in politics because:

1. They provide leaders with accurate information about popular concerns.
2. They make it more difficult for political leaders to ignore public preferences.
3. They help define the mandate of elections by revealing the reasons why voters cast their ballot for one candidate over another.

Public opinion polls, however, can also have other shortcomings such as low levels of political knowledge by the respondents, the Halo Effect, inconsistencies, and instability. Nonetheless, public opinion polls overall have been pretty accurate, not just in the political arena but also in other walks of American life as well. Without public opinion polls, citizens would not have any say-so in shaping administrative decisions, and political leaders would not have accurate information about popular concerns, as well as why voters cast their ballots for one candidate over others.

There are six major factors which influence one's personal views concerning public opinion. They are:

1. Race
2. Education
3. Gender
4. Age
5. Religion
6. Occupation

Out of the six major factors which influence one's views concerning public opinion issues, one can gage which groups are active in the different forms of political participation, such as voting, campaigns, contacting public officials, protest movements, other group activities, or actually becoming elected officials. For example, when it comes to the issue of **Race,** Whites are more likely to vote than nonwhites. With regard to **Education,** highly educated people vote more than those who are less educated. Regarding **Gender,** men are more likely to vote than women; however, the voting gap between the sexes has been disappearing. As for **Age,** people in their mid-thirties to mid-fifties are more likely to vote than truck drivers, welders, and security officers. In general, people who vote on a regular basis are usually more established than those who do not vote; these people tend to not be established in certain areas of life.

Several political scientists argue that many people do not vote because of the following:

1. They did not register.
2. They do not like the candidates.
3. They are not interested in politics.
4. They are sick or disabled.
5. They are not U.S. citizens.
6. They are new residents in the area.
7. They are away from home.
8. They have no way to get to polls.

Even though the above reasons may be true, I believe most Americans do not vote because they are too preoccupied with their day-to-day lives, as shown in Figure 5, the Plate Theory of Non-Voting Participation.

I just explained those factors which help to shape one's personal view concerning public opinion; however, below are those elements that help to change the collective views of citizens concerning public opinion:

1. **Reference Group**—Refers to those groups or social categories that are especially important in shaping a person's beliefs, attitudes, and values.
2. **Propaganda**—The teaching of any unified body or doctrine, or the manipulation of ideas and the appeal to people's emotions and prejudices.
3. **Rumors**—Untrue or unverified reports that are informally communicated from person to person.
4. **Leak**—The deliberate release of information by an official to a journalist for a specific purpose.
5. **Opinion Leaders**—Persons who have a strong influence over public opinion.

Once individuals and groups have determined their opinions based on their ideologies and beliefs, then they will engage in the political process, based on those values and beliefs. As stated earlier, there are several different forms of political participation:

1. Voting
2. Campaigns
3. Contacting public officials
4. Protest movements
5. Other group activities
6. Becoming an elected official

Voting, quite naturally, is the most elementary form of political participation. When one casts a ballot for a candidate and understands the political philosophy of that particular candidate, one has voted as a **Political Logical Citizen**. The **Political Emotional Citizen** is one who votes for a candidate because

Plate Theory of Non-Voting Participation

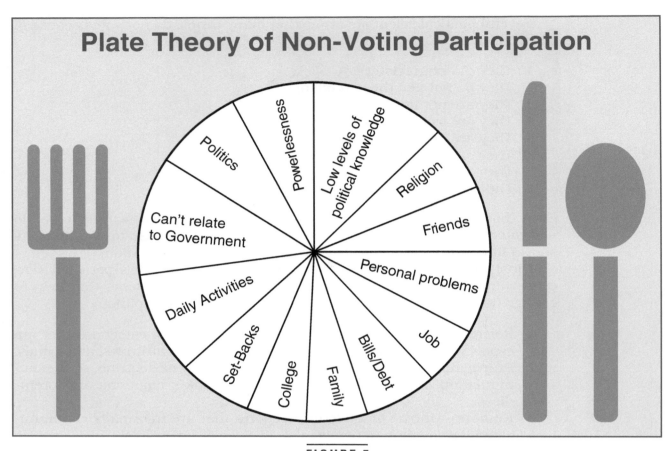

FIGURE 5

People do not vote because they are caught up with just day to day living.

she is a woman and the voter happens to be a woman, or one who votes for a particular candidate because he is Hispanic and the voter is Hispanic, or one may vote for a candidate from New York City because the voter is from New York City. **The Political Rhetoric Citizen** is one who is always complaining about the government but who never gets involved. This individual always claims to have solutions to solve many of the governmental problems, while at the same time hasn't even taken the time to go register to vote. Far too many of the American citizenry fall within this category.

Think for a moment. When it comes to voting, are you a:

- Political Logical Citizen?
- Political Emotional Citizen?
- Political Rhetoric Citizen?

Box 8-1 presents a moment of thought for the Political Emotional Citizen.

Public opinion and political participation are based on one's values and beliefs. **Political Socialization** is the process of learning the values, beliefs, and

---

BOX 6-1 B

Are you an individual who votes for someone because you are White and the candidate is White?

Are you an individual who votes for someone because you are Black and the candidate is Black?

Are you an individual who votes for someone because you are Hispanic and the candidate is Hispanic?

Are you an individual who votes for a woman just because you are a woman?

If the answer is yes to the above, you are the **Political Emotional Citizen**. There are four characteristics of the **Political Emotional Citizen**.

1. PEC's are always looking and hoping for so-called racial unity. One can observe them all the time in the media pushing for white power, black power, brown power, or Gender power. These individuals or groups are always jumping up and down screaming and hollering and uttering things about the political system they truly do not understand.

2. PEC's always see themselves as victims. It is usually someone else's fault if these individuals cannot experience the American dream. If I am white, "Blacks and Mexicans are taking my job through affirmative action." If I am black, "The white man is holding me down by keeping his foot on my neck." If I am a woman, "These male chauvinistic pigs are holding us women down."

3. PEC's fail to notice that there is also a class struggle in the U.S., and the reason for this is due to the fact that they cannot seem to think outside of race.

4. PEC's are not that educated, for the most part; therefore, politicians and other officials can manipulate them like puppets. The Political Emotional Citizen can become the Political Logical Citizen by reading political materials such as or Attending city council meetings would not be a bad idea, as well as engaging in other political educational endeavors.

---

opinions concerning the role of government and politics. These values and beliefs are sometimes known as an **Ideology,** which is the set of doctrines or body of opinions of a person, class, or group. Quite naturally, one's values and beliefs or ideology come from four elements of political socialization:

1. Family
2. Church
3. Schools/Education
4. Media

Below are the three learning theories of political socialization:

1. **Social Learning Theory**—The subtle rewards and punishments we learn through interaction with others.
2. **Transfer Theory**—Patterns of thinking and behavior developments which transfer to other figures.
3. **Cognitive Development Theory**—A theory which emphasizes the changes of an individual's capacity to learn over time.

Historically in the United States there have been some voting barriers which hindered others from participating in the political process, such as the following:

- White Primary
- The Poll Tax
- "Good Moral Character" Tests
- Literacy Tests
- Constitutional Interpretation Tests
- The Grandfather Clause
- Property Ownership
- Ku Klux Klan

The above voting barriers no longer exist, thanks to the fights and struggles of those who came before us.

■ CONCLUSION

Public opinion is essential to any Representative Democracy, and without it, the government is illegitimate. Public opinion has a great deal of influence in American politics, and individuals can exercise power in the political process through forms of political participation.

Suggested Readings

Asher, Herbert. *Polling and the Public: What Every Citizen Should Know.* 4th ed. Washington D.C. Congressional Quarterly, 1998.

Crespi, Irving. *Public Opinion, Polls and Democracy.* Boulder, Colorado: Westview Press, 1989.

Erikson, Robert S., and Norman Luttberg. *American Public Opinion: Its Origin, Content and Impact.* New York: Wiley, 1980.

Fishkin, James S. *The Voice of the People: Public Opinion and Democracy.* New Haven, Connecticut: Yale University Press, 1989.

Rubenstein, Sondra M. Surveying Public Opinion. Belmont, California: Wadsworth Publishing, 1994.

Stimson, James A. *Public Opinion in America: Moods, Cycles and Swings.* 2nd ed. Boulder, Colorado: Westview Press, 1998.

Zaller, John. *The Nature and Origins of Mass Opinions.* New York: The University Press, 1992.

CHAPTER 8
STUDY GUIDE

After reading and reviewing this chapter, one should be able to do the following:

1. Explain the Bowtie Professor's view concerning public opinion.

_____

2. Identify the following:

    a. Reference group

_____

    b. Public opinion

_____

    c. Survey research

_____

    d. Straw poll

_____

    e. Bias sample

_____

    f. Rumors

_____

    g. Leak

_____

    h. Propaganda

_____

    i. Opinion leaders

_____

3. Explain the three learning theories of political socialization.

_____

_____

_____

4. List the six different forms of political participation.

_____

_____

_____

_____

_____

_____

5. Explain Box 8-1.

_____

_____

_____

6. List the eight voting barriers that hindered others from participating in the political process.

_____

_____

_____

_____

_____

_____

_____

7. List the six factors that would help shape one's personal views concerning public opinion.

_____

_____

_____

_____

_____

_____

8. Explain the three major ways public opinion plays an important role in American politics.

_____

_____

_____

9. List the eight reasons why political scientists argue that people do not vote.

_____

_____

_____

_____

_____

_____

_____

_____

10. Explain the Plate Theory of Nonvoting Participation.

_____

_____

_____

11. Identify the following:

a. Gender

_____

b. Race

_____

c. Education

_____

d. Age

_____

e. Political rhetoric citizen

_____

f. Political logical citizen

_____

g. PEC

_____

h. Ideology

_____

    i. Political emotional citizen

_____

    j. Political socialization

_____

    k. John Stuart Mill

_____

TRUE/FALSE MULTIPLE CHOICE SAMPLE TEST

1. PEC stands for "political emotional citizen."
   a. True
   b. False

2. John Stuart Mill believed that public opinion should reflect only those in power.
   a. True
   b. False

3. Public opinion issues that change little from day to day are known as constant.
   a. True
   b. False

4. Public opinion issues that change according to political and social events are known as dynamic.
   a. True
   b. False

5. Public opinion issues in which individuals believe strongly are known as intense.
   a. True
   b. False

6. There are nine reasons why political scientists argue that people do not vote.
   a. True
   b. False

7. There are seven factors that help to shape one's personal views concerning public opinion.
   a. True
   b. False

8. Figure 5 is the Plate Theory of Nonvoting Participation.
   a. True
   b. False

9. Public opinion is *not* measured by the use of opinion polling.
   a. True
   b. False

10. Alf Landon was a Republican nominee.
    a. True
    b. False

11. A sample that does not represent the population as a whole is known as a straw poll.
    a. True
    b. False

12. A bias sample is a random of the entire population.
    a. True
    b. False

13. The *Literary Digest* sampled only wealthier groups.
    a. True
    b. False

14. In 1948, the Gallup polls predicted incorrectly that Thomas E. Dewey would defeat Harry S. Truman.
    a. True
    b. False

15. Race is a factor that can influence one's personal views concerning public opinion.
    a. True
    b. False

16. A political emotional citizen might vote for a candidate because the candidate is a woman and the voter happens to be a woman.

    a. True

    b. False

17. The white primary was a major voting barrier.

    a. True

    b. False

18. Box 8-1 focuses on the political rhetoric citizen.

    a. True

    b. False

19. Which of the following is *not* an element of political socialization?

    a. Media

    b. Church

    c. Campaigns

    d. Schools/education

    e. Family

20. There are _____ factors that influence one's personal views concerning public opinion.

    a. 3

    b. 4

    c. 5

    d. 6

    e. 7

21. Public opinion issues that change little from day to day are known as:

    a. Constant

    b. Dynamic

    c. Intense

    d. Social

    e. Economical

22. The Plate Theory of Nonvoting Participation is Figure:

    a. II

    b. III

    c. IV

    d. V

    e. VI

23. A sample that does not represent the population as a whole is known as a(n):

    a. Piece of survey research

    b. Straw poll

    c. Random sample

    d. Intensed sample

    e. Bias sample

24. Which of the following were *not* voting barriers?

    a. Campaigns

    b. Literacy tests

    c. Poll taxes

    d. Grandfather clauses

    e. Property ownerships

25. _____ in American politics can project a certain type of perception.

    a. Survey research

    b. Voters

    c. Public opinion

    d. Random samples

    e. Straw polls

26. Public opinion polls have shortcomings such as:

    a. Low Levels of Political Know

    b. Propaganda

    c. Rumors

    d. Leaks

    e. Education

27. Many _____ argue that people do not vote.
    a. Psychologists
    b. Sociologists
    c. Politicians
    d. Historians
    e. Political Scientists

28. The Plate Theory of non-voting participation does not include:
    a. Marriage
    b. Setbacks
    c. Religion
    d. Politics
    e. College

29. The "Literary Digest" of _____ did an inaccurate poll.
    a. 1950
    b. 1942
    c. 1936
    d. 1955
    e. 1948

30. _____ are always looking and hoping for so-called racial unity.
    a. Blacks
    b. Whites
    c. Hispanics
    d. Political Emotional Citizens
    e. Political Rhetoric Citizens

The Mass Media: The Fifth Branch

Chapter

9

Political Scientists in some cases, refer to the mass media as the fifth branch of government. It can be defined as any means of communication with the general public, which consists of television, newspapers, magazines, radio, books, recordings, motion pictures, articles in journals, and the Internet.

The mass media is a very powerful agent of political socialization and it has been able to produce a world of technological cowards. With Instagram, Face-Book, Twitter, and You-Tube, even the most extreme introvert can express his or her views. Also this powerful institution has produced a world of individuals who have become technological drones, which lack both interpersonal communication and social interaction skills.

The fifth branch of government, has produced a world of individuals who lack both analytical and critical thinking skills. If you think I am joking, how many people do you know that can speak correct standard English and hold a decent conversation without splitting verbs and using profanity?

—The Bowtie Professor

Name _____ **Date** _____

Explain:

_____

_____

_____

_____

_____

_____

_____

_____

_____

_____

_____

_____

_____

_____

_____

_____

_____

_____

_____

The **Mass Media** can be defined as any means of communication with the general public; it consists of television, newspapers, magazines, radio, books, recordings, motion pictures, articles in journals, and the Internet. Some political scientists have referred to the media as the fourth branch of government, while others have referred to it as the fifth branch. In this short chapter, the Mass Media will be referred to as the fifth branch of government. The federal bureaucracy is usually referred to as the fourth branch by social scientists in general. The media is referred to as a branch of government because of the impact that this institution has on American society as a whole. Unequivocally, the mass media is a powerful agent of political socialization. The media plays a major role in American politics in the following areas:

1. **News Making**—Deciding which information is worthy enough to gain the interest of the public and, therefore, reporting such topics and events.
2. **Agenda Setting**—Deciding on a list of topics or events which affect society as a whole, and how decision makers will address these issues.
3. **Muckraking**—The media's exposing of social and political evils, wrongdoings, or mismanagement in government, business, and other institutions of society. Muckraking historically consisted of a group of American journalists and novelists of the early 1900's who were noted for exposing corruption within our governmental system.
4. **Interpreting**—The media's ability to bring out the meaning of a topic, event, or presentation by construing it in a particular way.
5. **Negativism**—Journalists and reporters who bring out the dark side of American politics, such as political scandals, corporate fraud, and character assassination.
6. **Sensationalism**—The ability of the media to play on the emotions of the general public, which can trigger feelings of joy, grief, fear, love, hate, or anger, concerning a particular topic, event, or presentation which is given coverage in the news.

The question that one might ask is: "What type of topics or events make the news headlines?" First of all, the president of the U.S. makes the headlines on a daily basis because he is the most powerful politician in America. Secondly, major tragedies make the news headlines, such as the September 11, 2001 event, which was a series of attacks, one of them on the World Trade Center. Third, disasters make the news headlines; this could be a destructive fire, or an earthquake that causes much suffering or loss. Fourth, racial conflict seems to always make news headlines, especially if it is on a large scale. Fifth, if our nation is in a war, such as the Vietnam war or the war in Iraq, such topics will be given a great deal of coverage in the media. Sixth and finally, major sports figures and their events get more than their share of media attention. Whether it is the Super Bowl, the NBA Championship, or the World Series, professional sports is everywhere present in the mass media.

The media plays a very crucial role in campaigns and elections. The media engages in image-making, and by doing so, it can make a political candidate look strong and positive, or weak and negative.

The media goes through steps when dealing with campaigns and elections:

1. The media and candidate-voter linkage
2. The media and candidate selection
3. The media and the horse race
4. The media as campaign
5. The media and political bias
6. The media and the electoral victory

Box 9-1 gives a moment of thought on former president Bill Clinton and media politics.

The media has the potential to have a powerful impact on the American public because it plays a variety of roles inside and outside of politics. The mass media does the following:

1. Socializes the American citizenry
2. Identifies public problems and concerns
3. Reports the news in several different ways
4. Provides cultural entertainment
5. Provides political activities and forums
6. Makes large profits

BOX 9-1

The scandal concerning former president Bill Clinton and Monica Lewinsky became the headlines of the mass media all across this country. This event became one of the great media extravaganzas of all time. Many social scientists as well as the general American public felt that the media spent too much time on the Clinton/Lewinsky scandal, instead of on major policy issues in which the American citizenry seemed to be more interested, such as the growing crisis in the Balkans. The questions which should be raised are: "Were people such as the Republicans and other conservative groups attacking Bill Clinton for his infidelity?" "Or were these individuals attacking Bill Clinton for something else, and his infidelity was a doorway to trigger their attacks?" I believe that it is the latter. I do not believe that the conservative crowd came after Clinton because of his infidelity. They came after Bill Clinton because he was too Black. Every time one would look up, or turn around, he or she would notice how Bill Clinton had a tendency to surround himself with African Americans. Whether playing the saxophone on the Arsenio Hall show, or hugging civil rights activist Rosa Parks for her courageous efforts, Bill Clinton always seemed to support people of color, especially those of African American descent; and he was not afraid to do it publicly. If we as Americans start attacking politicians for their immorality, then we had better shut down Capitol Hill and all the lawmaking bodies within our state and local governments as well. By no means am I condoning the former president's action. Yes, I believe that infidelity is wrong because one should be faithful to his or her mate. Nonetheless, Kenneth Starr of the Independent Council and the Republicans just took the incident too far. It is just a moment of thought.

Professor Yecats

One major issue which has brought a lot of attention and debate over the past few decades is the issue of violence in the media. Politicians and other governmental officials, civic and community leaders, and the general public have raised the question: "Is there too much violence in the media?" Numerous studies have shown that violence on movies and on television increases violence in society, and that the entertainment industry must do more to alleviate the amount of animosity and chaos that comes across the screens. If not, then the government and the public must step in and deal with the problem by working together to reduce violence in the media. Not all agree, however, with the notion that there is too much violence in the media. Some have argued that television has become a scapegoat for those looking for a cause of America's high crime rate; and while there is violence on television and movie screens in the U.S., there are also high-quality television shows which educate and inspire, such as **The Learning Channel, The Discovery Channel, The History Channel,** and the **Public Broadcasting Station (PBS).**

Box 9-2 gives a content review of debates taken from the book, *Violence in the Media,* by Barbour, de Koster, and Lenore.

BOX 9-2

I. Does Media Violence Affect Society

Yes: Media Violence Harms Society

Media Violence Increases Violence in Society by Carl M. Cannon

Numerous studies have shown that violence in movies and on television increases violence in society. The entertainment industry has done nothing to address this problem, so the government and the public must work together to reduce violence in the media.

Media Violence Has Increased the Murder Rate by Susan R. Lamson

Many critics point to guns as the cause of America's high murder rate. But guns are not the problem—media violence is. The public must pressure the entertainment industry and government to reduce violence on television.

Violence in TV News Promotes Violence Against Women by Susan Douglas

Television news often reports specific, especially horrific incidents of violence against women and children. But this is only sensationalism. The broader, more important issue of violence against women is rarely covered. This neglect of women promotes violence in society.

No: Media Violence Does Not Harm Society

The Negative Impact of Media Violence on Society is Exaggerated by John Leonard

Television has become the scapegoat for those looking for a cause of America's high rate of violent crime. While there is violence on television, there is also high-quality television that educates and inspires.

BOX 9-2

Evidence Connecting Media Violence to Real Violence is Weak by Brian Siano
   Those who believe media violence causes violence in society cite numerous studies to back their claims. But these studies are inconclusive, and those who cite them exaggerate the connection between media violence and violence in society to justify censorship.

Media Violence May Not Harm Children by Patrick Cooke
   Many critics of television believe that it causes children to be violent. But there is not a proven connection between media violence and aggressiveness in children. In addition, these critics never consider the positive effect television may have on children.

II. What Should Be Done About Media Violence?
Addressing Media Violence: An Overview by Elizabeth Jensen and Ellen Graham
   Media violence, especially that on television, has been controversial for more than forty years. The government, the networks, and public interest groups have all proposed ways to reduce media violence, but no concrete, effective measures have been implemented.

Increased Government Regulation of Media Violence is Necessary by William S. Abbott
   The government, through the Federal Communications Commission, must increase its regulation of television to protect America's children from the harmful effects of media violence. Such regulations might include prohibiting violent programs between 6 a.m. and 10 p.m., developing a rating system, and warning viewers of upcoming violent programming.

Boycotts of Advertisers Could Reduce Media Violence by Daniel Schorr
   Some have suggested that censorship or increased government regulation is needed to reduce television violence. But these measures would meet with much opposition and would not be completely effective. Instead, consumers should boycott the products of those companies that advertise on violent shows. This economic incentive would dramatically reduce television violence.

High-Tech TV Locks Could Reduce the Negative Impact of Media Violence by Amitai Etzioni
   Television violence must be reduced to protect the nation's children. Some believe that the answer is for parents to simply increase and improve their monitoring of their children's viewing habits. This is difficult, however, when both parents work and when children have ready access to television. A new invention, the V-chip, would help "lock out" violent programs and protect children from television violence.

Media Literacy Education Can Effectively Combat Media Violence by Elizabeth Thoman
   Using media literacy education to teach the public to think critically about what is portrayed on television and in other forms of media is an effective way to combat the effects of media violence.

Media Violence Should Be Treated as a Public Health Problem by Anthea Disney
   Public health campaigns addressing the hazards of smoking and drunken driving have been very effective. A similar campaign should be organized to educate the public about the hazards of media violence.

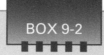

BOX 9-2

A Bipartisan, Moderate Approach to Media Violence is Needed by Philip Berroll
By taking an extreme anti-censorship, anti-regulation stance, liberals have lost public support for their views on media violence. A more moderate approach could unite conservatives and liberals to find creative, effective solutions to media violence.

A Variety of Measures Could Combat Media Violence by Suzanne Braun Levine
Parents have many ways to combat media violence. Some of these measures include boycotting advertisers, protesting, and educating children concerning media violence.

III. Does Music Promote Violence?
Yes: Music Promotes Violence
Heavy Metal Rock and Gangsta Rap Music Promote Violence by Barbara Hattemer and Robert Showers
Heavy metal rock and gangsta rap music are more violent than ever before. Much of this violence is sexually graphic and contributes to the rampant sexism and racism in America today. Children and teenagers should not be allowed to listen to the violent messages in this music.

Gangsta Rap Promotes Violence in the Black Community by Nathan McCall
Music has always been an influential force in the black community. Much of the black music of today—rap—is filled with violent and sexist messages that motivate some young blacks, especially those without positive role models, to commit violence.

Gangsta Rap Promotes Violence Against Women by Glamour
Some rap music, especially gangsta rap, describes women as sexual objects and details explicit and violent sexual acts. This promotes violence against women in society. Consumers must take action to regulate such music.

Rap Music Should Be Censored by Jonathan Alter
Those who defend offensive rap lyrics and oppose regulating such music do not understand or are unwilling to admit the difference between censorship and regulation. The government should not censor music. But record companies and the rap artists themselves have a responsibility to regulate music that might promote violence in listeners.

No: Music Does Not Promote Violence
Rap Music is Unfairly Blamed for Society's Violence by Tricia Rose
Rap music has become a scapegoat for society's violence. Most of those who wish to censor rap refuse to understand black culture and see how blacks are oppressed. Rap, even violent rap, is simply an expression of this oppression and poses no threat to society.

Rap Music Should Not Be Censored by Barbara Ehrenreich
Many critics of violent rap music support censoring or regulating it. Such measures would be wrong and unnecessary. Rap artists have a right to express their views. Censoring rap, not rap itself, is what would threaten society.

Rap Musicians Contribute Positively to Society by Mara Armoudian
Rap musicians are often criticized for the violent messages in their songs. But many rap songs expose society to the plight of poor blacks, and many rap artists contribute to society by working on behalf of social welfare organizations.

Source: Scott Barbour, Katie de Koster, Bruno Leone. *Violence in the Media,* San Diego, CA: Greenhaven Press, 1995, (Table of Contents), pp. 1-9.

Note: The V-Chip has been required by the government on all television networks. This is a rating for all T.V. shows which come across the screen.

Another controversial topic concerning the mass media is the issue of both image-making and projection. Some have argued that the media has a tendency to project the following groups in a negative way:

1. Small-town people
2. Poor white southerners
3. Hispanics
4. African Americans
5. Uneducated people
6. Fat people
7. Little people
8. Educators

Whether the above groups are seen as negative or positive, unequivocally, the mass media is a very powerful institution within itself, both in and outside of politics. Below are some of the major distributions of the mass media:

1. New York Times
2. The Wall Street Journal
3. USA Today
4. Christian Science Monitor
5. The Washington Post
6. ABC
7. CBS
8. NBC
9. FOX
10. CNN
11. Time
12. Newsweek
13. U.S. News & World Report
14. The World Wide Web

■ CONCLUSION

It is only through the media that the general public comes to know about political events, personalities, and issues. The media has always played a significant role in American politics, and its enormous power and influence have caused several political scientists to label it as the fifth branch of government. The mass media consists of the printed press, such as newspa-

pers, magazines, newsletters, journals, and the electronic media, such as television, radio stations, and networks, as well as computer information like the Internet. Whether one views the media as good or evil, the institution itself has transformed all aspects of American society, especially government and politics.

Suggested Readings

Bates, Stephen. *If No News, Send Rumors.* New York: St. Martin's Press, 1989.

Graber, Doris A. *Mass Media and American Politics.* 5th ed. Washington, D.C.: CQ Press, 1996.

Kerbel, Matthew R. *Remote and Controlled: Media Politics in a Cynical Age.* Boulder Colorado: Westview Press, 1995.

Leonard, Thomas C. *The Power of the Press: The Birth of American Political Reporting.* New York: Oxford University Press, 1986.

Ranney, Austin. *Channels of Power: The Impact of Television on American Politics.* New York: Basic Books, 1983.

Rubin, Richard L. *Press, Party, and Presidency.* New York: Norton, 1981.

Stephens, Mitchell. *A History of News: From the Drum to the Satellite.* New York: Viking Publisher, 1989.

CHAPTER 9
STUDY GUIDE

After reading and studying this chapter, one should be able to do the following:

1. Explain the Bowtie Professor's views concerning the mass media.

_____

_____

_____

_____

2. Explain the mass media's role when dealing with campaigns and elections.

_____

_____

_____

_____

3. Identify Box 9-1.

_____

_____

_____

_____

4. Explain the variety of roles the mass media plays inside and outside of politics.

_____

_____

_____

_____

5. Name and explain the six major roles the mass media plays in American politics as a whole.

_____

_____

_____

_____

_____

_____

6. List at least 10 major media outlets.

_____

_____

_____

_____

_____

_____

_____

_____

_____

_____

7. Identify Box 9-2.

_____

_____

_____

Name _____ Date _____

TRUE/FALSE MULTIPLE CHOICE SAMPLE TEST

1. Some have argued that some music has the tendency to promote violence.
   a. True
   b. False

2. Boycotts of advertisers could reduce media violence.
   a. True
   b. False

3. The V-chip has been required by the government on certain television networks.
   a. True
   b. False

4. Professor Yecats believe that the Bill Clinton and Monica Lewinsky scandal went too far.
   a. True
   b. False

5. African Americans are sometimes projected in a negative way in the mass media.
   a. True
   b. False

6. The mass media does not make large profits.
   a. True
   b. False

7. The mass media is considered by some as being the sixth branch of government.
   a. True
   b. False

8. The mass media does *not* have the candidate-voter linkage.
   a. True
   b. False

9. The mass media does have the candidate selection.
   a. True
   b. False

10. The federal bureaucracy is sometimes referred to as the fifth branch of government.
   a. True
   b. False

11. Muckraking started as early as the:
   a. 1800s
   b. 1700s
   c. 1900s
   d. 1600s
   e. 1500s

12. The media goes through steps when it comes to campaigns and elections.
   a. 3
   b. 4
   c. 5
   d. 6
   e. 7

13. The mass media is referred to as the branch of government.
   a. Fourth
   b. Fifth
   c. Sixth
   d. Seventh
   e. Eighth

14. According to the Bowtie Professor, the mass media is a very powerful agent of:
   a. Political socialization
   b. The people
   c. Political culture
   d. America's society
   e. All of the above

15. The media overplays the issue of:
   a. Class
   b. Politics
   c. Gender
   d. Negativism
   e. Race

16. _____ is the ability of the media to play on the emotions of the general public.
    a. Sensationalism
    b. Negativism
    c. Muckraking
    d. Interpreting
    e. News making

17. _____ is the media's ability to bring out the meaning of a topic or an event.
    a. Sensationalism
    b. Negativisim
    c. Muckraking
    d. Interpreting
    e. News making

18. Kenneth Starr was part of the:
    a. National Security Council
    b. Trusteeship Council
    c. Independent Council
    d. Council for Foreign Relations
    e. Social and Economic Council

19. Box 9-2 discusses the:
    a. Bill Clinton/Monica Lewinsky scandal
    b. V-chip for television shows
    c. Media and its campaigns
    d. NBC network
    e. Violence in media music

20. Bill Clinton played the _____ on the Arsenio Hall show.
    a. Drums
    b. Saxophone
    c. Piano
    d. Keyboard
    e. Horn

21. The fifth branch of government has produced a _____ of technological cowards.
 a. Nation
 b. World
 c. State
 d. System
 e. Country

22. _____ in some cases, refer to the mass media as the fifth branch of government.
 a. Political Scientists
 b. Sociologists
 c. Psychologists
 d. Historians
 e. Governments

23. Which of the following is not a part of the mass media:
 a. political socialization
 b. Twitter
 c. Articles
 d. Face-Book
 e. You-Tube

24. _____ has become a scapegoat for society's violence.
 a. The mass media
 b. Motion pictures
 c. Books
 d. Rap music
 e. Country and Western music

25. _____ said that the negative impact of media violence on society is exaggerated.
 a. Daniel Schoor
 b. Nathan McCall
 c. Philip Berroll
 d. Carl M. Cannon
 e. John Leonard

26. _____ said that gangsta rap promotes violence in the black community.
    a. Nathan Mc call
    b. Tricia Rose
    c. Patrick Cooke
    d. Carl M. Cannon
    e. Robert Showers

27. _____ said that heavy metal and gangsta rap music promotes violence.
    a. Jonathan Alter
    b. Barbara Daniel
    c. Glennell Glenn
    d. Robert Showers
    e. Bernice Williams

28. _____ said that violence should be treated as a public health problem.
    a. Anthea Disney
    b. Donna Johnson
    c. Juan Earl Williams
    d. Stoney Daniel
    e. Brenda Wright

29. The mass media is a very powerful agent of:
    a. our society
    b. Political Culture
    c. Political Socialization
    d. our governmental system
    e. all of the above

30. The federal bureaucracy is the _____ branch of government.
    a. Fourth
    b. Third
    c. Fifth
    d. Sixth
    e. Seventh

Campaigns and Elections

During election times,
voting has been a very powerful tool.
If one does not exercise this right,
he is practically a fool.

Whether one wins,
or whether one loses,
voting gives the individual
the opportunity to choose.

Voting alone does not give
one absolute power.
But it does give one the keys,
to the Ivory tower.

By voting one can
make a choice,
and others, too
can hear his voice.

However, when an individual does not vote,
he should not complain
When politicians pass laws
which he perceives to be insane.

—The Bowtie Professor

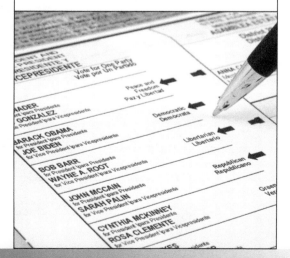

Name _____ **Date** _____

Explain:

_____

_____

_____

_____

_____

_____

_____

_____

_____

_____

_____

_____

_____

_____

_____

_____

_____

_____

_____

Political campaigns are at the heart of a representative democracy, and they serve a variety of objectives such as:

1. Providing a forum for new leadership by giving information to the voters
2. Mobilizing the voting population
3. Obtaining funds from supporters
4. Acquiring the party endorsement

Campaigns are the processes of individuals seeking to win political office by obtaining votes in and outside of a governmental system. The anatomy of a political campaign involves (1) the decision to run, (2) getting the nomination of the party, (3) acquiring the electoral victory, and (4) the post-election stage. The decision to run involves the politician considering all the consequences, both negative and positive, of running for political office. This usually involves selecting a theme, "defining" the opponent, using focus groups and polling, challenging the opponent, a planned media management strategy, paid advertising and free air time. Getting the nomination of the party consists of party leaders, and activists are courted to ensure that the candidate is nominated in primaries or conventions which involve the following:

1. Media "mentions"
2. Political experience
3. The decision to run
4. A strategy for the primaries
5. The New Hampshire primary
6. The front end strategy
7. Super Tuesday
8. Big state strategy
9. Convention showplace

Box 10-1 defines many of the key terms that are used in political campaigns.

The electoral victory is when the campaign appeals to the nation as a whole by engaging in electioneering, which involves image-making through the media, speeches and debates, campaign financing, and sometimes negative campaigning in which the candidate seeks to destroy his or her opponent's reputation. Finally, the post-election stage is when the candidate is elected into office; he or she must attempt to carry out the promises that he or she made to the voters.

Every candidate for public office is confronted with a basic set of problems. First, the candidate must gain name recognition. Second, the candidate must present a positive image. Third, the candidate must exemplify leadership abilities. Fourth, the candidate must know the issues. Fifth, the candidate must possess attractive personal qualities. And sixth, although not required, a political candidate must have some type of prior political experience, especially when trying to get elected on the national level.

BOX 10-1

Define the following concepts:

1. **Front End Strategy**—A presidential political campaign strategy in which a candidate focuses on winning early primaries to build momentum.
2. **Super Tuesday**—A cluster of presidential primaries held in early March that includes several important southern states.
3. **Big State Strategy**—A presidential political campaign strategy in which a candidate focuses on winning primaries in large states because of their high delegate counts.
4. **Electoral College**—The 538 presidential electors apportioned among the states according to their congressional representation (plus three for the District of Columbia) whose votes officially elect the President and Vice President of the United States.
5. **Spin Doctor**—A practitioner of the art of spin control or manipulation of media reporting to favor one's own candidate.
6. **Sound Bites**—Concise and catchy phrases that attract media coverage.
7. **Quid Pro Quo**—One thing in return for another.
8. **Mandate**—The perception of popular support for a program or policy based on the margin of electoral victory won by a candidate who proposed it during a campaign.
9. **Political Entrepreneurship**—The ability to sell one's self as a candidate for public office, including skills of organizing, fund raising, communicating, and publicizing.
10. **Incumbent**—A candidate currently in office seeking re-election.
11. **Political Action Committee (PAC)**—A corporation, union, or other interest group that pools contributions to support political candidates.
12. **Franking Privilege**—The free use of U.S. mails granted to members of Congress in order to promote communication with constituents.
13. **Casework**—Services performed by legislators and their staff on behalf of individual constituents.
14. **Focus Group**—In a political context, a small number of people brought together in a comfortable setting to discuss and respond to themes and issues, allowing campaign managers to develop and analyze strategies.
15. **Campaign Strategy**—A plan for a political campaign, usually including a theme, an attempt to define the opponent or the issues, and an effort to coordinate images and messages in news broadcasts and in paid advertising.
16. **Federal Election Commission**—Agency charged with enforcing federal election laws and disbursing public presidential campaign funds.
17. **Soft Money**—Political contributions to a party for activities such as party building or voter registration, not directly for campaigns.
18. **Photo Ops**—Staged opportunities for the media to photograph the candidate in a favorable setting.

Politicians who are currently in office and are seeking re-elections are known as **Incumbents.** When it comes to campaigns and elections, there are some major advantages of incumbency. Box 10-2 lists a few advantages of being an incumbent.

Political campaigns in the U.S. are lengthy and very expensive, and they have become more candidate-centered rather than party-centered in response to the advanced technological innovations in the mass media, thus decreasing party loyalty and identification. By far, the race for the U.S. Presidency is the most expensive and drawn-out campaign in America. The presidential campaign gets both the mass media and the general public's attention, more than any other campaigns in the U.S. When choosing a presidential candidate, the voters technically do not vote for the presidential candidate directly, but they choose a slate of presidential electors; and the slate that wins the most popular votes throughout the state gets to cast all the electoral votes for the state. The candidate who receives a majority (270) of the electoral votes becomes the president of the United States.

Many have argued that too much money is being spent on financing political campaigns, especially on the national level. Below are a variety of strategies that reformers have tried to use in order to prevent abuse in political contributions:

1. The Federal Campaign Acts of 1972 and 1974 instituted major reforms by limiting spending and contributions; the acts allowed political action committees (PAC's) to be set up by interest groups, labor unions, and corporations, to raise money for candidates.
2. Requires public disclosure of the sources and uses of political money.
3. Giving governmental subsidies to presidential candidates, campaigns, and parties, including incentive arrangements.

The right to vote is an essential feature of our Republic form of government and has been expanded throughout U.S. political history. In colonial times, white males who had property were the only ones who were allowed to vote.

BOX 10-2

1. Name recognition
2. Campaign finances
3. Office resources
4. Prior political electoral experience
5. Media access
6. Large staff to help with casework
7. More support from PAC's
8. Taking credit for monies that get allocated to their areas

Let it be known, however, that property did not just mean land, but also slaves, donkeys, cows, and other animals. Box 10-3 shows the evolution of voting in the United States.

The American electorate is not "homogenized." Major subgroups of voters often exhibit markedly different levels of voter turnout and substantially different patterns of voting behavior. Most people probably do not think of the way they vote as a product of their age, sex, race, income, and socio-economic status, education, religion, party identification, or what have you. Yet when one breaks down the total electorate into groups based on these kinds of factors, it is often found that voting within groups is too similar, and differences between these groups are too great to attribute to chance alone.

For example, highly educated individuals turn out to vote at significantly higher rates than those with less education. White males between the ages of thirty-five to forty-nine have the tendency to vote at significantly higher rates than other age, sex, and racial groups. Minority groups such as Blacks and Hispanics have supported Democratic party candidates in practically every election since the New Deal era. Wealthy whites have a tendency to vote in the Republican party on a regular basis, and overall, men still vote more than women.

Elections play a very important role in our democratic process because they give practical meaning to the notion of "consent." They allow the American citizenry to choose among candidates and parties and decide who will occupy public office. They give people the opportunity to pass judgment on current officeholders, either by re-electing them or not re-electing them; and they allow voters to direct the course of public policy by choosing between candidates or parties with different policy priorities.

Box 10-4 deals with short questions and answers concerning the electoral and voting process in Texas.

BOX 10-3

First   White males who possessed property were the only ones who were allowed to vote.

Second   White males in general were allowed to vote whether they owned property or not. In most states, the age was twenty-one.

Third   African American males were allowed to vote due to the 15th Amendment of the Constitution. The 15th Amendment was ratified in 1870.

Fourth   In 1920, women were allowed to vote due to the 19th Amendment of the Constitution. Women thought they would get the right to vote during the Abolition Movement in the 1840's but it did not happen until fifty years after black males were allowed to vote.

Fifth   The 26th Amendment of the U.S. Constitution allowed all American citizenry who have reached the age of 18 or older the right to vote. The 26th Amendment was ratified in 1972.

BOX 10-4

1. **What are the four qualifications in order to vote in Texas?**
   a. A U.S. citizen at least eighteen years old by election day
   b. A resident of the state and county thirty days before election day
   c. A resident of the election precinct on election day
   d. Registered to vote at least thirty days prior to election day
2. **What are the two ways to absentee vote?**
   a. County clerk's office
   b. By mail
3. **What is the present system of registration in Texas?**
   a. Voters may register in person or by mail.
   b. Registration remains in effect as long as the voter is qualified.
   c. Voters may register at any time.
4. **Why don't Texans vote?**
   a. The political socialization process in Texas does not encourage voting.
   b. One-day elections
   c. Poorly managed polling places
   d. The long ballot
   e. Long waiting lines
   f. The voting barriers of nonparticipation
   g. An uncompetitive political party system discourages a high voter turnout rate.
5. **What were some of the voting barriers used in Texas as well as other southern states, to keep Blacks and other minorities from voting?**
   a. White primary
   b. The poll tax
   c. "Good moral character" test
   d. Literacy test
   e. Constitutional test
   f. Grandfather clause
   g. Property ownership
   h. Ku Klux Klan
6. **What is the stake in social theory?**
   Only white adult male property owners could be trusted with the vote in Texas.
7. **Name and explain the three different standpoints concerning voting in Texas.**
   a. **Individual**—Voting is illogical, but many people vote nonetheless because they have been socialized to do so.
   b. **Candidate**—Voting provides the means of winning public office and exercising political power.
   c. **Political System**—Voting is crucial because it decreases alienation, confers legitimacy on officeholders, and—when done on a large scale—ensures the selection of the best candidate and prevents dishonesty in elections.

■ CONCLUSION

Campaigns and elections are the most prominent and dramatic occasion for interaction among voters, interest groups, political parties, politicians, candidates, and the mass media. Whether on the national level or the states', elections must serve as policy mandates whereby competing candidates would have to offer clear and precise policy alternatives to the problem at hand; the voters must then cast their ballots on the basis of these policy alternatives. The election results would have to reflect the voters' policy preferences and elected officials must carry out their campaign promises.

Suggested Readings

Bartels, Larry M. *Presidential Primaries and the Dynamics of Public Choice.* Princeton, NJ: Princeton University Press, 1988.

Burnham, Walter D. *Critical Elections and the Mainsprings of American Politics.* New York: Norton, 1970.

Carroll, Susan J. *Women as Candidates in American Politics.* Bloomington: Indiana University Press, 1994.

Conway, Margaret M. *Political Participation in the United States.* 2nd ed. Washington, D.C.: CQ Press, 1990.

Fenno, Richard F. *Senators on the Campaign Trail: The Politics of Representation.* Norman: University of Oklahoma Press, 1996.

Kern, Montague. *30-Second Politics: Political Advertising in the Eighties.* New York: Praeger, 1989.

Sorauf, Frank J. *Inside Campaign Finance.* New Haven, CT: Yale University Press, 1996.

CHAPTER 10
STUDY GUIDE

After reading and reviewing this chapter, one should be able to do the following:

1. Explain the Bowtie Professor's views concerning campaigns and elections.

   _____

   _____

   _____

2. Explain the four objectives of political campaigns.

   _____

   _____

   _____

3. Explain the anatomy of a political campaign.

   _____

   _____

   _____

4. List the nine elements that are involved when a candidate is being nominated in primaries or conventions.

   _____

   _____

   _____

   _____

   _____

   _____

   _____

5. Define the following concepts:

a. Campaigns

_____

b. Incumbents

_____

c. Photo ops

_____

d. Soft money

_____

e. Federal Election Commission

_____

f. Campaign strategy

_____

g. Focus group

_____

h. Casework

_____

i. Franking privilege

_____

6. List the eight advantages of incumbency.

_____

_____

_____

Name _____ **Date** _____

_____

_____

_____

7. Explain what reformers have tried to do in order to prevent abuse in political contributions.

_____

_____

_____

_____

8. Explain the evolution of voting in U.S. politics.

_____

_____

_____

_____

9. Explain the four qualifications of voting in Texas.

_____

_____

_____

_____

10. Explain the present system of voting in Texas.

_____

_____

_____

_____

11. Explain the two ways to absentee vote in Texas.

_____

_____

12. List the seven reasons why many Texans do not vote.

_____

_____

_____

_____

_____

_____

13. List the eight major voting barriers that were historically used in Texas as well as other southern states to keep blacks and other minorities from voting.

_____

_____

_____

_____

_____

_____

_____

14. Identify the concepts in Box 10-1.

_____

_____

_____

15. Name and explain the three different standpoints concerning voting in Texas.

_____

_____

_____

TRUE/FALSE MULTIPLE CHOICE SAMPLE TEST

1. The American electorate is homogenized.
   a. True
   b. False

2. One advantage of incumbency is no political experience.
   a. True
   b. False

3. Political campaigns in the United States are lengthy but not expensive.
   a. True
   b. False

4. An incumbent is a candidate who is currently in office but is seeking re-election.
   a. True
   b. False

5. Media access is an advantage of incumbency.
   a. True
   b. False

6. There are four major purposes of a political campaign.
   a. True
   b. False

7. Minority groups such as blacks and Hispanics have always supported the Democratic Party.
   a. True
   b. False

8. The Electoral College is used only in presidential elections.
   a. True
   b. False

9. The right to vote is an essential feature of the American republic.
   a. True
   b. False

10. Photo ops are not stage opportunities for the media.
   a. True
   b. False

11. Which of the following is *not* part of the anatomy of a campaign?
   a. Acquiring the electoral victory
   b. Getting the nomination of the party
   c. Obtaining funds from supporters
   d. Deciding to run
   e. The postelection stage

12. The candidate must know or have all the following *except:*
   a. Media mentions
   b. The issues
   c. How to gain name recognition
   d. Leadership abilities
   e. Political experience

Name _____ **Date** _____

13. When the political candidate attempts to carry out his or her promises, it is known as the:
    a. Electorate mobilization
    b. Postelection stage
    c. Party endorsement
    d. Promise keeping
    e. Electoral victory

14. Which of the following is *not* an advantage of incumbency?
    a. Photo ops
    b. Media access
    c. Name recognition
    d. Office resources
    e. Campaign finances

15. The Electoral College has a total of votes.
    a. 435
    b. 535
    c. 538
    d. 640
    e. 720

16. The District of Columbia has electoral votes.
    a. 7
    b. 6
    c. 5
    d. 4
    e. 3

17. Women got the right to vote in:
    a. 1940
    b. 1931
    c. 1929
    d. 1920
    e. 1971

18. Many women thought that they would get the right to vote in the:

    a. 1840s

    b. 1860s

    c. 1930s

    d. 1950s

    e. 1940s

19. The 26th Amendment to the U.S. Constitution was ratified in:

    a. 1925

    b. 1937

    c. 1949

    d. 1966

    e. 1972

20. One must be at least _____ years old in order to vote in Texas.

    a. 21

    b. 18

    c. 17

    d. 25

    e. 19

21. The right to vote is an essential feature of our _____ form of government.

    a. Democratic

    b. Republic

    c. Liberal

    d. Conservative

    e. Federal

22. The Federal Campaign Acts of 1972 and _____ instituted major reforms by limiting spending and contributions.

    a. 1976

    b. 1973

    c. 1974

    d. 1977

    e. 1975

23. The American electorate is not _____.
   a. unified
   b. incumbents
   c. quid pro quo
   d. mobilizing
   e. homogenized

24. The _____ is when the candidate is finally elected into office.
   a. campaign
   b. party endorsement
   c. decision to run
   d. post-election stage
   e. media mentions

25. _____ is when the campaign appeals to the nation as a whole.
   a. Super Tuesday
   b. Electioneering
   c. The Front End Strategy
   d. The Big State Strategy
   e. The Convention Showplace

26. Which of the following is not a part of the primaries or conventions?
   a. Providing a forum for new leadership
   b. Super Tuesday
   c. The Decision to run
   d. Convention Showplace
   e. Political Experience

27. Which is not a problem that a candidate must face?
   a. Name recognition
   b. A positive image
   c. Exemplify leadership skills
   d. Attractive personal qualities
   e. Mobilizing the voting population

28. African Americans got the right to vote in _____.

    a. 1972

    b. 1870

    c. 1929

    d. 1924

    e. 1959

29. Women got the right to vote about _____ years after the Abolition Movement.

    a. 30

    b. 40

    c. 50

    d. 60

    e. 60

30. The Abolition Movement was around:

    a. 1880's

    b. 1950's

    c. 1920's

    d. 1840's

    e. 1770's

Political Parties In American Government and Texas Politics

To many Americans,
the Democrat and Republican parties are the same.
All both parties do
is play the political game.

The Republicans claim to fight, for the man at the top,
whereas the Democrats claim to fight for the man down below.
Nevertheless, the objective of both parties
is to maintain the status quo.

When political problems arise,
each party blames one another.
Neither party is truly concerned,
about the middle class brother.

Both parties make promises
that they can't keep.
It is enough to make
a grown man weep.

The political parties must represent
U.S. citizens as a whole.
Anything less than this,
would be downright wicked and cold.

—The Bowtie Professor

Name _____ **Date** _____

Explain:

_____

_____

_____

_____

_____

_____

_____

_____

_____

_____

_____

_____

_____

_____

_____

_____

_____

_____

_____

_____

T he goal of a political party is to win political office. A **Political Party** can be defined as any group who organizes to win elective offices in order to control government policies. The evolution of U.S. political parties has been remarkably smooth, and the stability of the Democratic and Republican parties is a wonder, considering all the social and political chaos in American political history. America's political parties are among our most misunderstood and the least appreciated institutions. There are a few reasons for this. First, U.S. political parties have little or no constitutionally defined roles in government. In fact, there is no mentioning of political parties in the U.S. Constitution. Second, American political parties help to generate conflict and confusion. Unlike the British Parliament, our parties as organization can do little to resolve the conflict they promote. In the U.S., elected officials, not parties, govern. Finally, most Americans overestimate the extent to which major political parties can function as a cohesive national organization. It is at the state and local level where most electoral politics actually take place. The president and vice president are the only offices filled on the basis of national elections. Figure 6 shows the five major political parties which have held a competitive position in the U.S. politics in the last 200 years or so.

The Democratic and Republican parties have outlasted the other three major political parties; this has made the U.S. party system uniquely a two-party system. As a result, the two-party system in American politics has served as the mechanism we use to organize and resolve social and political conflict. Although it may seem that the two major political parties do not differ substantially on the issues, each has a different core group of supporters. The general shape of the parties' coalitions reflect the party divisions of Franklin D. Roosevelt's New Deal to Ronald Reagan's New American Revolution, to the 2008 coalition of Barack Hussein Obama's theme of "Change" as seen below:

■ THE NEW DEAL DEMOCRATIC COALITION OF 1932 CONSISTED OF:

1. Southern whites, who had provided the most loyal block of Democratic voters since the Civil War.
2. Poor people, who associated the New Deal with expanded welfare and social security programs.
3. Blacks, who ended their historic affiliation with the party of Lincoln to pursue new economic and social groups.
4. White ethnic groups, who had previously aligned themselves with Republican machines.
5. Working classes and union members, especially in large cities.

■ THE REAGAN COALITION OF THE 1980'S CONSISTED OF:

1. Internationalists and anti-communists who wanted the U.S. to maintain a strong military force and to confront Soviet-backed Marxist regimes around the world.

The Major American Parties

In the last 200 years, there have been only five political parties that have achieved and held a position in American politics for any amount of time. Of these five, only the Democrats and the Republicans hold such a position today.

1. *The Federalists.* This was the first American political party. Named after its leaders' outspoken defense of the federal Constitution during the ratification process, it had the support of merchants, landowners, and those of wealth and status in the Northeast and the Atlantic states. But it was limited by this narrow base and fell away before the successes of the next party, the Jeffersonians.
2. *The Jeffersonians.* This was a party of the small farmers, workers, and less wealthy citizens who were opposed to the nationalism of the Federalists and preferred the authority of the states.Its founder was Thomas Jefferson, and like him, it espoused many of the ideals of the French Revolution, such as the idea of direct popular self-government. (At times this party was also called the Anti-Federalists, the Republicans, and the Democratic-Republicans.)
3. *The Democrats.* This was the first really broad-based, popular party in the United States. It represented less privileged voters, welcomed new immigrants, and stood up to nativist opposition to immigration; it also opposed national banking and high tariffs. The Democrats grew from the Jacksonian wing of the Jeffersonian party.
4. *The Whigs.* This party had a short life, during which it was the representative of many interests, among them nativism, property, and business and commerce. It had its roots in the old Federalist Party and was formed in opposition to the strong presidency of Andrew Jackson.
5. *The Republicans.* This party grew out of northern opposition to slavery and came to power as the Civil War approached. It was the party of the Union, Lincoln, and the freeing of the slaves. From the Whigs it also took on a concern for business and propertied interests.

Source: Congressional Quarterly, Guide to Elections, 2nd ed. (Washington, D.C.: Congressional Quarterly, 1985), p.224.

FIGURE 6
The Major American Parties

2. Economic conservatives concerned about high taxes and excessive government regulation, including business and professional voters who had traditionally supported the Republican Party.
3. Social conservatives concerned about crime, drugs, and racial conflict, including many white ethnic voters and union members who had traditionally voted Democratic.
4. Religious fundamentalists concerned about issues such as abortion and prayer in schools.
5. Southern whites concerned about racial issues, including affirmative action programs.

THE OBAMA COALITION OF 2008 CONSISTED OF:

1. Poor people who associated Obama's theme of "change" with a better life which would expand the social welfare state.
2. Working and middle class Whites, Blacks, and Hispanics in large metropolitan areas.
3. Gays and Lesbian groups, and women who believed in pro-choice, union members and the elderly who all believed that their rights and privileges would be expanded on a larger scale.
4. Above middle class White, Blacks, Hispanics, and Asians who felt it was time for America as a nation to have its first person of color to hold the highest office in the land.
5. The Black, Hispanic, White and Asian underclass, which primarily consisted of a large block of new voters, saw Obama's presidency as a potential positive change for them.

There are several functions of political parties; however, throughout America's political history, the primary function of political parties has been to screen those who seek public office. The party nomination process has provided us with suitable candidates at all levels of government and has usually weeded out the undesirables.

Other functions of political parties are:

1. To bridge the separation of powers, and foster coordination and cooperation in our system of checks and balances.
2. To help organize government.
3. To translate public preferences into policy.z
4. To unify the electorate and moderate conflicts.
5. To determine who shall hold office and exercise legitimate power.
6. To simplify the choices facing the electorate.
7. To organize the competition within elections by registering and activating voters and by providing resources to candidates.

Box 11-1 is a moment of thought concerning the two-party system in the U.S. and the American citizenry.

BOX 11-1

It is amazing to me how Jim Bob claims to be a Republican, riding around in his red pick-up with twelve bloodhounds in the back with a Confederate flag posted in his back window. Does Jim Bob not know that Republicans, who are on the average upper class Anglos with money, would look at him with disdain? To them, an individual like himself would be an embarrassment within the party itself. Jim Bob, however, calls himself a Republican because he has internalized that Republicans as a whole are anti-Black and Hispanic; and since he considers himself a Redneck, he too is also anti-Black and Hispanic. Well, Jim Bob is truly being deceived.

It amazes me how both African Americans and Hispanics consistently vote for the Democratic Party without asking any serious questions about the party's views or beliefs. Instead, they are guided by the propaganda that is pushed by both the race and poverty pimps within the Democratic Party. The notion in the Black community is that if any African American does not vote in the Democratic Party, or chooses to vote in another political party, then he or she will be labeled as an "Uncle Tom" and a sellout. Hispanics also seem to face the same problem within their own group. Any Hispanic who deviates from the norm is labeled a "Coconut," meaning brown on the outside and white on the inside.

The point that I am making here is that the American citizenry should not vote for political parties blindly. Regardless of one's race, class, gender, religion, or ethnicity, one should make every attempt to see if the political candidates within these parties are practicing what they preach. Figure 7 shows both the Democrats' and the Republicans' beliefs. Please notice that Figure 7 only shows the general beliefs of both parties. For example, not every Democrat is pro-choice when it comes to the issue of abortion, and not every Republican is against affirmative action. Remember, liberals, moderates, and conservatives exist in both parties. This is why it is not wise to vote for party candidates blindly, or to vote straight ticket. I do believe that the masses are being deceived by many of the politicians. If the truth were to be told, neither party does anything to alleviate the tax burden of the so-called middle class American. The Democrats love to take from a man who is working, and give to a man who can work but won't. The Republicans' major problem is that they love to play the big Christian role, while at the same time helping the rich get richer, and the poor get poorer.

A moment of thought.

Professor Yecats

Below are key terms one will usually see in party politics:

- **Blanket Primaries**—A primary in which voters may cast in either party's primary, on an office by office basis.
- **Caucus**—A nominating process in which party leaders select the party's nominee.
- **Closed Primaries**—A primary election in which only a party's registered voters are eligible to vote.

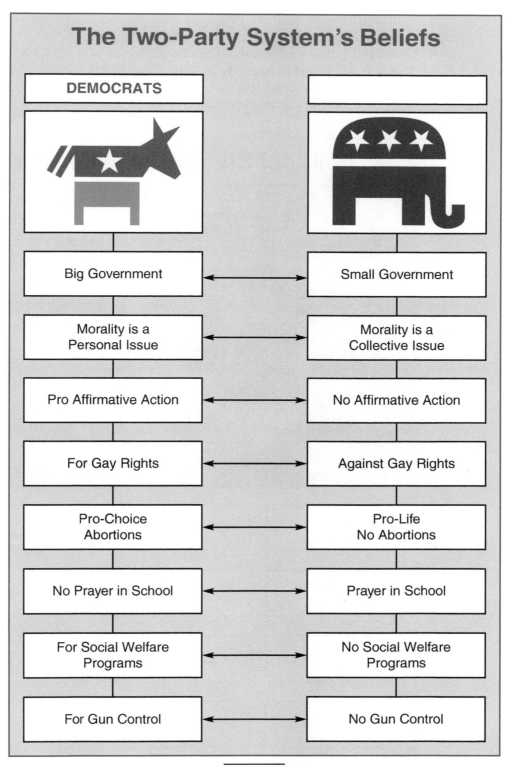

The Two-Party System's Beliefs

DEMOCRATS		
Big Government	⟷	Small Government
Morality is a Personal Issue	⟷	Morality is a Collective Issue
Pro Affirmative Action	⟷	No Affirmative Action
For Gay Rights	⟷	Against Gay Rights
Pro-Choice Abortions	⟷	Pro-Life No Abortions
No Prayer in School	⟷	Prayer in School
For Social Welfare Programs	⟷	No Social Welfare Programs
For Gun Control	⟷	No Gun Control

FIGURE 7

- **Convention**—A nominating process in which delegates from local party organizations select the party's nominee.
- **De-alignment**—Declining attractiveness of the parties to the voters and a reluctance to identify strongly with either party.
- **Delegate**—An accredited voting member of a party's national presidential nominating convention.

Political Education in America

Voting	National Lawmakers	County Governments
School Board Officials	Campaigns	Group Activities
Elected Officials	Letter Writing	Phone Calls
City Councils	Protest Movements	State Legislature

FIGURE 8

- **Nomination**—A political party's selection of its candidate for public office.
- **Nominee**—A political party's sole entry in a given political race.
- **Open Primaries**—Allow voters to choose on election day in which party primary they wish to participate.
- **Patronage**—Appointment to public office based on party loyalty.
- **Political Machine**—Tightly disciplined party organization, headed by a boss, that relies on material rewards which include patronage jobs to control politics.
- **Primary Elections**—Elections to choose party nominees for public office that may be open.
- **Realignment**—A long-term shift in social group support for various political parties that creates new coalitions in each party.

In order for political parties to be effective, they must possess money, jobs, workers, votes, and offices. The health of party organizations varies a great deal from state to state and from locality to locality. On the national level, however, party organizations have been in the decline for some time now, and some political scientists argue that the two-party system as a whole has lost a great deal of strength due to the following:

1. The breakdown of political machines
2. The civil service system
3. The rise of media politics
4. Political action committees (PAC's)
5. Personal campaign organizations
6. Single-issue interest groups
7. Social welfare programs
8. Declining party socialization

TABLE 11-1

Ross Perot	Reform Party	1996
John B. Anderson	Independent Party	1980
George C. Wallace	American Independent Party	1968
Robert M. LaFollette	Progressive Party	1924
Theodore Roosevelt	Bull Moose Party	1912
Eugene V. Debs	Socialist Party	1912
James B. Weaver	Populist Party	1892
John C. Breckinridge	Southern Democrat Party	1860
John Bell	Constitutional Union Party	1860
Millard Fillmore	Whig Party—American	1856
Martin Van Buren	Free Soil Party	1848
William Wirt	Anti-Masonic Party	1832

Source: Congressional Quarterly Weekly Report (October 18, 1980): 3147 (as adopted), and official election returns for 1992, 1996.

The evidence that there is a decline in the two-party system is declining party loyalty, ineffective organization, and political alienation. What we are seeing today in party politics are powerful interest groups in observable control, confusion in the electoral process, and the government not being responsible to the masses, which lack political education.

BOX 11-2

- **The Establishment**—In the day of the one-party system within the state, Democratic politics in Texas consisted of Anglo businessmen, oilmen, bankers, and lawyers who controlled state policy through the conservative wing of the Democratic Party.
- **One-Party System**—The domination of elections and governmental processes by a single party, which may be split into different ideological, economic, or regional factions. In Texas, the phrase is used to describe the period from the late 1870's to the late 1970's when the Democratic Party claimed virtually all elected partisan offices.
- **Bifactionalism**—The presence of two dominant factions organized around regional, economic, or ideological differences within a single political party. For much of the 20th century, Texas functioned as a one-party system within two dominant factions.
- **Realignment**—A major shift in political support or identification that usually occurs around a critical election. In Texas, this was a gradual transformation from a one-party system dominated by Democrats to a two-party system in which Republicans became competitive in elections.
- **Voting Rights Act**—A federal law designed to protect the voting rights of minorities by requiring the Justice Department's approval of changes in political districts and certain other electoral procedures. The act, as amended, has eliminated most of the most restrictive state laws that limited minority political participation.
- **Precinct**—A specific local voting area created by county commissioners court. The state election code outlines the detailed requirements for the drawing up of these election units.
- **Precinct Chair**—A local officer in a political party who presides over the precinct conventions and serves on the party's county executive committee. Voters in each precinct elect a chair in the party's primary election.
- **County Executive Committee**—A panel responsible on the local level for the organizational management of a political party's primary election. It includes the party's county chair and each precinct chair.
- **County Chair**—The presiding officer of a political party's county executive committee. He or she is elected countywide by voters in the party's primary.
- **State Executive Committee**—The statewide governing board of a political party. It includes a man and a woman elected by party members from each of the 31-state senatorial districts and the state chair and vice chair who are selected by delegates to the party's biennial state convention.
- **State Chair and Vice Chair**—The two top state leaders of a political party, one of whom must be a woman. They are elected every two years by delegates to the party's state convention.
- **Precinct Convention**—A meeting held by a political party in each precinct on the same day as the party primary. In presidential election years, the precinct conventions and the primaries are the first steps in selecting delegates to the major parties' national nominating conventions.

Political Education can take many forms, as seen in Figure 8. The average U.S. citizen votes infrequently, and does not engage in other political endeavors.

Third parties in the U.S. have played an interesting role in party politics. Third parties are those other than the traditional Democrat and Republican parties, whose members consist of groups of individuals who are dissatisfied with the two major parties. Third parties have three major characteristics:

1. They are for radical changes.
2. They address issues that the two major parties won't.
3. They have strong ideological foundations that are outside the mindset of the masses.

Table 11-1 shows examples of third parties in the American political system. Box 11-2 gives a short overview of Texas party politics.

■ CONCLUSION

Political parties are not mentioned in the U.S. Constitution, yet they have played a major role in American politics. Yet the future of parties may continue to be an ongoing debate. Political parties, according to some, have been both positive and negative in helping to shape public policy. In the case of Texas, between the late 1870's to the late 1970's the Democratic Party claimed virtually all elected partisan offices; this changed, however, during the period of realignment in which there was a gradual transformation from a one-party system dominated by Democrats to a two-party system in which Republicans become competitive in elections.

Suggested Readings

Aldrich, John H. *Why Parties? The Origin and Transformation of Party Politics in America.* Chicago: University of Chicago Press, 1995.

Fiorina, Morris P. *Divided Government.* Boston: Allyn and Bacon, 1996.

Epstein, Leon. *Political Parties in the American Mold.* Madison: University of Wisconsin Press, 1986.

Mayhew, David R. *Placing Parties in American Politics.* Princeton, NJ: Princeton University Press, 1986.

Price, David E. *Bringing Back the Parties.* Washington, D.C.: CQ Press, 1984.

Sorauf, Frank J. and Paul Allen Beck. *Party Politics in America.* 7th ed. New York: Harper/Collins, 1995.

Wattenburg, Martin P. *The Decline of American Political Parties, 1952-1994.* Cambridge, MA: Harvard University Press, 1996.

CHAPTER 11
STUDY GUIDE

After reading and reviewing this chapter, one should be able to do the following:

1. Identify the New Deal Coalition of 1932.

_____

_____

_____

2. Identify the Reagan Coalition of the 1980s.

_____

_____

_____

3. Explain the five major political parties that have gained a competitive position in U.S. politics.

_____

_____

_____

_____

_____

4. List the seven major functions of political parties.

_____

_____

_____

_____

_____

_____

5. Identify Box 11-1.

_____

_____

_____

6. Explain the beliefs of the current two-party system.

_____

_____

_____

7. Define the following:
   a. Patronage

_____

   b. Blanket primaries

_____

   c. Convention

_____

   d. Open primaries

_____

   e. Caucus

_____

   f. Closed primaries

_____

g. Delegate

_____

h. Political machine

_____

i. Nominee

_____

j. Primary elections

_____

k. Dealignment

_____

l. Re-alignment

_____

m. Nomination

_____

n. Precinct

_____

8. Identify Box 11-1.

_____

_____

_____

9. List at least seven third parties that have occurred in American politics.

_____

_____

_____

_____

_____

_____

_____

10. Identify Table 11-1.

_____

_____

_____

_____

11. Give examples of political education in America.

_____

_____

_____

_____

12. List the characteristics of third parties.

_____

_____

_____

_____

13. Explain the roles of political parties in Texas.

_____

_____

_____

_____

14. Explain the Bowtie Professor's views on political parties in American politics.

_____

_____

_____

_____

15. List the eight reasons why there appears to be a decline in the two-party system in the United States.

_____

_____

_____

_____

_____

_____

_____

_____

_____

TRUE/FALSE MULTIPLE CHOICE SAMPLE TEST

1. The Bowtie Professor believes that the two-party system in the United States does not benefit the middle class.
   a. True
   b. False

2. Democrats believe in big government.
- **a.** True
- **b.** False

3. Republicans believe that morality is a personal issue.
- **a.** True
- **b.** False

4. Yecats argues that African Americans who vote in any other party besides the Democratic Party are labeled as "Uncle Toms."
- **a.** True
- **b.** False

5. Republicans have a tendency to play the big Christian role.
- **a.** True
- **b.** False

6. Democrats have a tendency to help the wealthy.
- **a.** True
- **b.** False

7. Third parties have a tendency to address radical issues.
- **a.** True
- **b.** False

8. Political education can take only a few forms.
- **a.** True
- **b.** False

9. Box 11-2 shows examples of political education.
- **a.** True
- **b.** False

10. Ross Perot was a member of the Reform Party.
- **a.** True
- **b.** False

11. The Establishment controlled the conservative wing of the _____ party in Texas.
   a. Republican
   b. Democratic
   c. Socialist
   d. Whig
   e. Populist

12. _____ is the presence of two dominant factions in one political party that are organized around regional, economic, or ideological differences.
   a. Dealignment
   b. One-party
   c. Bifactionalism
   d. Realignment
   e. Convention

13. There are _____ major political parties that have gained a competitive position in American politics.
   a. 6
   b. 7
   c. 4
   d. 3
   e. 5

14. Social conservatives are concerned about all the following
   a. Crime
   b. Drugs
   c. Racial conflict
   d. Abortion
   e. All of the above

15. There are _____ functions of political parties.
   a. 4
   b. 5
   c. 6
   d. 7
   e. 8

16. Religious fundamentalists are concerned about:
   a. High taxes
   b. Government regulations
   c. Abortion
   d. Crime
   e. Drugs

17. The _____ was a party of small farmers.
   a. Federalists
   b. Whigs
   c. Democrats
   d. Republicans
   e. Jeffersonians

18. America has a _____ party system.
   a. Two-
   b. Three-
   c. Four-
   d. Five-
   e. Six-

19. The _____ see morality as a personal issue.
   a. Republicans
   b. Democrats
   c. Whigs
   d. Jeffersonians
   e. Federalists

20. The Reform Party of Ross Perot started around:
   a. 1979
   b. 1982
   c. 1996
   d. 2001
   e. 2005

21. _____ are not mentioned in the U.S. Constitution, yet they have played a major role in American politics.
    a. Precincts
    b. Political Parties
    c. State Chairs
    d. Elected Officials
    e. County Governments

22. Political Education includes all of the following except:
    a. Voting
    b. Campaigns
    c. Group Activities
    d. the civil service system
    e. Phone Calls

23. Theodore Roosevelt, was of the_____ party.
    a. Reform
    b. Bull Moose
    c. Independent
    d. Socialist
    e. Populist

24. The _____party grew from the Jacksonian wing of the Jeffersonian party.
    a. Republican
    b. Whigs
    c. Federalists
    d. Progressive
    e. Democratic

25. There are five political parties which have gained a competitive position in national politics in the past_____ years.
    a. 100
    b. 150
    c. 200
    d. 250
    e. 300

26. The Reagan coalition took place in the:
     a. 1970's
     b. 1980's
     c. 1990's
     d. 2010
     e. 2014

27. Economic conservatives are concerned about_____
     a. High taxes
     b. Prayer in public schools
     c. Drugs
     d. Crimes
     e. Abortion

28. The Obama coalition took place in:
     a. 2006
     b. 2008
     c. 2012
     d. 2014
     e. 2016

29. Martin Van Buren, was of the _____party.
     a. Free Soil
     b. Southern Democrat
     c. Progressive
     d. Anti-Masonic
     e. Bull Moose

30. James B. Weaver, was of the _____party.
     a. Reform
     b. American Independent
     c. Populist
     d. Whig
     e. Constitutional Union

Interest Groups: Inside and Outside of Government

Chapter 12

Interest groups are organizations,
at least of the middle class.
However, because of so many differences,
they usually don't last.

Some interest groups within themselves
have not made a name.
It is probably due to the fact
that they have not mastered the art of the political game.

Some have influence,
while others don't.
The way many are organized,
they won't.

Interest groups' objectives
must always be loud and clear.
So that others in the political arena
Can begin to hear.

—The Bowtie Professor

Name _____ **Date** _____

Explain:

_____

_____

_____

_____

_____

_____

_____

_____

_____

_____

_____

_____

_____

_____

_____

_____

_____

_____

Interest Groups are organizations that seek to influence government policy. The logical goal of interest groups is to try to influence the men and women who have the power to make political decisions and policies. These organizations can make demands on conversion structures at all three levels of American government (federal, state, and local), thereby permitting many citizens to express their wants, values, or complaints directly or indirectly through their designated group leadership. Direct techniques include such activities as rating legislators' voting records, making campaign contributions, testifying before committees and rulemaking agencies, and providing information to legislators. Indirect techniques consist of letter writing campaigns, campaigns to rally public sentiment, and the use of constituents to lobby for the group's interest. Table 12-1 shows examples of interest groups in America's political culture.

There is a major difference between public, private, and single-issue interest groups. Public interest groups are those that represent broad classes of people or the public as a whole, such as Common Cause, Human Rights Watch, and the American Civil Liberties Union. Private interest groups are those that represent narrow or small groups of individuals whereby the members benefit directly from the cause, such as the American Association of Retired Persons, the American Medical Association, and the American Bar

TABLE 12-1

Business Roundtable	Founded (1972)
U.S. Chamber of Commerce	Founded (1912)
American Civil Liberties Union	Founded (1920)
National Association for the Advancement of Colored People	Founded (1909)
Environmental Defense Fund	Founded (1967)
National Rifle Association of America	Founded (1891)
League of United Latin American Citizens	Founded (1929)
American Association of Retired Persons	Founded (1958)
National Organization for Women	Founded (1966)
Amnesty International U.S.A.	Founded (1961)
The American Society for the Prevention of Cruelty to Animals	Founded (1866)
Greenpeace	Founded (1971)
Planned Parenthood Federation of America, Inc.	Founded (1916)
Human Rights Watch	Founded (1978)
Handgun Control, Inc.	Founded (1974)
National Right to Life Committee, Inc.	Founded (1973)
Leadership Conference on Civil Rights, Inc.	Founded (1950)
National Urban League	Founded (1910)
National Gay and Lesbian Task Force	Founded (1973)
National Anti-Vivisection Society	Founded (1929)

Note: The above list is not conclusive.

Source: Foundation for Public Affairs, Public Interest Profiles 1995-1996. Washington, D.C.: Congressional Quarterly Press, 1995.

Association. Single-issue interest groups are those which focus on one major theme, such as the Human Control, Inc., the National Abortion Rights League, or the National Rifle Association of America. Below are examples of selective interest groups by categories:

- Age . . . American Association of Retired Persons/Meals on Wheels
- Agriculture . . . National Farmers Union/Farm Bureau Federation
- Business . . . United States Chamber of Commerce/Business Round-table
- Defense . . . Air Force Association/Army Association
- Environmental . . . Environmental Defense League/Greenpeace U.S.A.
- Ideological . . . People for the American Way/Amnesty International U.S.A.
- Professional . . . American Bar Association/American Medical Association
- Public Interest . . . Common Cause/ACLU
- Race . . . American Indian Movement/NAACP
- Religion . . . National Council of Churches/Southern Baptist Convention
- Single Issue . . . National Rifle Association/Handgun Control, Inc.
- Trade Associations . . . Home Builders Association/National Association of Manufacturers
- Unions . . . AFL-CIO/United Auto Workers
- Veterans . . . American Legion/Veterans of Foreign Wars
- Women . . . National Organization of Women/League of Women Voters

There are seven major functions of interest groups in American politics. The list and characteristics of each are:

1. **Political**—When an interest group tries to control or influence public policy. *Example: The NAACP using the judicial system to get laws passed.*
2. **Economic**—When an interest group tries to have some influence over the distribution of wealth and material products. They try to control economic policies. *Example: The American Medical Association trying to keep Bill Clinton's health program from being passed in Congress.*
3. **Social**—When an interest group is concerned with human beings and their relationships to one another. Social interest groups usually deal with living conditions and social problems of human beings. *Example: Common Cause fighting on behalf of the public.*
4. **Ideological**—The values and beliefs of an interest group. *Example: The National Rifle Association believes in the right to bear arms.*
5. **Symbolic**—The image the interest group portrays to the American public. *Example: The National Right to Life Committee image to the American public is the anti-abortion belief.*

6. **Informational**—When an interest group gives information to the American public concerning certain political issues. ***Example:*** *Common Cause gives Americans information concerning corruption in the government as well as in corporations.*

7. **Instrumental**—When an interest group is responsible for either getting a bill passed or for keeping a bill from being passed. ***Example:*** *The John Birch Society fought to keep the ERA Amendment from being passed.*

Students of government and politics often raise the question concerning the similarities and differences between interest groups and political parties. Interest groups and political parties are alike because:

1. They both represent their organizational interest to officeholders in all branches of government.
2. They both politicize their members and others.
3. They both mediate group conflict.
4. They both recruit political candidates and help finance their campaigns.
5. They both engage in electioneering.

Interest groups and political parties differ because:

1. Political parties try to gain political influence primarily by choosing candidates, running them in elections, and winning and holding public office.
2. Interest groups encourage and support certain candidates but do not try to win and hold public office.
3. Political parties try to be the government.
4. Interest groups try to influence government.
5. Political parties are organized around the electoral process and are fully active only in connection with elections.

Quite naturally in the United States we have had several different types of movements connected directly to interest group politics, such as the **Term Limitation Movement,** the **Civil Rights Movement,** the **Populist Movement,** the **Abolitionist Movement,** the **Anti-Vietnam War Movement,** the **Gay Rights Movement,** the **Moral Majority Movement,** the **Suffragist Movement,** the **Christian Coalition Movement,** and the list goes on. While some interest groups have been successful, others have not. There are, however, some factors that can determine whether or not an interest group will have success in America's political system. These factors will also determine whether or not the interest group will possess a great deal of power. Money, knowledge of political issues, leadership skills, legitimacy, prestige, organizational skills, and membership are the seven elements or factors that will determine the power and success of an interest group. Therefore it should be understood that interest groups differ markedly in their ability to achieve political success, and not all interest groups

BOX 12-1

- **Access**—Meeting and talking with decision-makers, a prerequisite to direct persuasion.
- **Bribery**—Giving or offering anything of value in an effort to influence government officials in the performance of their duties.
- **Coalition**—The uniting of interest groups (or individuals) to achieve a common goal.
- **Free Riders**—People who do not belong to an organization or pay dues, but nevertheless benefit from its activities.
- **Grass Roots Lobbying**—Influencing government decision-making by inspiring constituents to contact their representatives.
- **Ideological Organizations**—Interest groups that pursue ideological-based (liberal or conservative) agendas.
- **Interest Group**—Organization seeking to influence government policy.
- **Interest Group Entrepreneurs**—Leaders who create organizations and market memberships.
- **Iron Triangles**—Mutually supportive relationships among interest groups, government agencies, and legislative committees with jurisdiction over a specific policy area.
- **Lobbying**—Activities directed at government officials with the hope of influencing their decisions. The term arose from the practice of waiting in the lobbies of legislative chambers to meet and persuade legislators.
- **Lobbyist**—A person working to influence government policies and actions.
- **Policy Networks**—People who regularly interact in a common policy area, including lobbyists, elected officials, staff personnel, bureaucrats, journalists, and private sector experts.
- **Public Interest Groups**—Interest groups that claim to represent broad classes of people or the public as a whole.
- **Public Relations**—Building and maintaining good will with the general public.
- **Single Issue Group**—Organizations formed to support or oppose government actions on a specific issue.
- **Trade Associations**—Interest groups composed of business in specific industries.

possess the same resources, such as size of membership, leadership abilities, organizational skills, and political power. In any event, whether some interest groups are too powerful and others too weak, the fact remains that group activity and American politics are inseparable. Interest groups, whether public, private, or single issue, continue to pressure lawmakers in order to obtain their political objectives. Box 12-1 shows common terminology used by political scientists when dealing with the subject of interest group politics.

Interest group politics in Texas focuses on four major areas, which are economic organizations, religious organizations, public organizations, and private organizations. These groups in Texas politics are involved in the electoral activities and they encourage and support candidates. They also lobby and engage in litigation. Finally, interest groups in the Texas political process influence public opinion in more ways than one.

Box 12-2 shows a few interest groups in Texas politics, as well as the role of lobbyists in the Lone Star State.

BOX 12-2

1. Agricultural Groups
2. Business
3. Education
4. Governmental Lobbyists
5. Labor
6. Minority Interest Groups
7. Oil and Gas Industry
8. Professional Groups
9. Public Interest Groups
10. Religious Groups
11. Texas Good Roads and Transportation Association
12. Texas Railroad Commission
13. Texas Research League
14. Texas Trial Lawyers
15. Trial Lawyers

The role lobbyists play in the Lone Star State:
1. Lobbyists can influence the structure of the state government.
2. They can initiate or oppose government action.
3. Lobbyists can provide information for and to politicians.
4. They can help plan political strategies.
5. Lobbyists can provide new ideas and approaches to solving problems.

Many Texas political scientists would probably agree that the **Traditional Political Culture** in Texas controls the state's politics, and that the relationship between this culture and economic position concerning interest group politics in the state points to this elitist group. Its power gives it the ability to influence interest group politics and government policies in and outside the state. The Civil Rights Movement and the Reform Act of 1973, which made it possible to track campaign money, changed some of the political influence of the traditional political culture. But by and large, this group still controls interest group politics in Texas today.

■ CONCLUSION

In the last forty years, interest groups have grown tremendously, and single-issue interest groups have become more skillful. Interest groups exist to make demands upon government. The dominant groups are economic or occupational, but a variety of other groups have memberships that cut across the big economic groupings, thus causing their influence to be both reduced and stabilized.

Suggested Readings

Berry, Jeffrey M. *The Interest Group Society.* White Plains, New York: Longman, 1997.

Feingold, Russ "Lobbyists Rush for Bankruptcy Reform," *Washington Post.* June 7, 1999: A 19.

Lowi, Theodore J. *The End of Liberalism.* New York: Norton, 1969.

Sabato, Larry J. *Power: Inside the World of Political Action Committees.* New York: Norton, 1984.

Salisbury, Robert H. "An Exchange Theory of Interest Groups," *Midwest Journal of Political Science,* 13 (1969): 1-32.

Truman, David B. *The Governmental Process: Political Interest and Public Opinion.* New York: Knoff, 1951.

Walker, Jack L. "The Origins and Maintenance of Interest Groups in America," *American Political Science Review.* 77 (June 1983): 390-406.

CHAPTER 12
STUDY GUIDE

After reading and studying this chapter, one should be able to do the following:

1. Explain the Bowtie Professor's concerning interest groups.

_____

_____

_____

2. Explain the similarities and differences between interest groups and political parties.

_____

_____

_____

3. Define the following concepts:
   a. Access

_____

   b. Public relations

_____

   c. Policy networks

_____

   d. Lobbying

_____

   e. Trade associations

_____

Name _____   **Date** _____

    f. Iron triangles

_____

    g. Interest groups

_____

    h. Bribery

_____

4. Explain the differences between public and private interest groups.

_____

_____

_____

5. Identify at least 15 interest groups.

_____

_____

_____

_____

_____

_____

_____

_____

_____

_____

_____

_____

_____

_____

6. Name at least six interest group movements.

_____

_____

_____

_____

_____

_____

7. Name and explain the seven major functions of interest groups.

_____

_____

_____

_____

_____

_____

8. Identify the role lobbyists play in the Lone Star State.

_____

_____

_____

9. List at least 10 interest groups within the state of Texas.

_____

_____

_____

_____

_____

_____

_____

_____

_____

_____

10. Explain the difference between multi-interest groups and single-issue interest groups.

_____

_____

_____

11. Identify the following:
  a. Free riders

_____

Name _____ **Date** _____

   b. Grassroots lobbying

_____

   c. Ideological organizations

_____

   d. Interest group entrepreneurs

_____

   e. Lobbyist

_____

   f. Public interest groups

_____

   g. Single issue interest groups

_____

   h. Coalition

_____

12. Identify the traditional Texas political culture.

_____

_____

_____

13. Explain the Reform Act of 1973.

_____

_____

_____

TRUE/FALSE MULTIPLE CHOICE SAMPLE TEST

1. Lobbyists in Texas can influence the structure of the state's government.
   a. True
   b. False

2. The Civil Rights Movement was *not* a major interest-group activity.
   a. True
   b. False

3. Interest groups and political parties do *not* engage in electioneering.
   a. True
   b. False

4. One function of an interest group is that of symbolism.
   a. True
   b. False

5. The National Rifle Association would be an example of a single-issue interest group.
   a. True
   b. False

6. Interest groups in Texas are focused on three major areas.
   a. True
   b. False

7. Interest groups and political parties are pretty much the same.
   a. True
   b. False

8. Both interest groups and political parties politicize their members.
   a. True
   b. False

9. Whereas political parties mediate group conflict, interest groups do not.
   a. True
   b. False

10. The Civil Rights Movement made it possible to track campaign money in Texas.
    a. True
    b. False

11. The Reform Act of 1973 made it possible to track campaign money in Texas.
    a. True
    b. False

12. Public relations involves maintaining good images for elected officials only.
    a. True
    b. False

13. The Business Roundtable was founded around 1972.
    a. True
    b. False

14. In 1920, the ACLU was founded.
    a. True
    b. False

15. The Bowtie Professor believes that interest groups are of the middle class.
    a. True
    b. False

16. Organizations that seek to influence government policies are known as:
    a. Political parties
    b. Interest groups
    c. Lobbyists
    d. Civic organization
    e. Greenpeace

17. Interest groups in Texas focus on _____ major areas.
    a. 2
    b. 3
    c. 4
    d. 5
    e. 6

18. The Reform Act of _____ made it possible to track campaign money in Texas.

    a. 1973

    b. 1991

    c. 1986

    d. 1996

    e. 1967

19. Which of the following will *not* determine an interest group's power?

    a. Money

    b. Leadership skills

    c. Legitimacy

    d. Knowledge of political issues

    e. Votes

20. Box 12-1 shows:

    a. Common terminology used by political scientists

    b. Interest group behavior

    c. Trade association

    d. Symbolism

    e. Voters

21. Which interest group represents broad classes of people?

    a. Greenpeace

    b. Common Cause

    c. Business Roundtable

    d. NAACP

    e. Handgun Control

22. Table 12-1 shows:

    a. The seven functions of interest groups

    b. Yecats's moment of thought

    c. The difference between interest groups and political parties

    d. Examples of interest groups in America's political culture

    e. Interest group terminology

23. The National Organization of Women was founded in:
   a. 1920
   b. 1950
   c. 1946
   d. 1951
   e. 1966

24. Interest groups composed of businesses in specific industries are known as:
   a. Trade associations
   b. Public interest groups
   c. Policy networks
   d. Coalitions
   e. Iron triangles

25. A person who works to influence government policy is known as a(n):
   a. Politician
   b. Lobbyist
   c. Free rider
   d. Elitist
   e. Pluralist

26. The Handgun Control, Inc. was founded in:
   a. 1974
   b. 1929
   c. 1958
   d. 1912
   e. 1966

27. When an interest group portrays an image to the American public, it is fulfilling a _____ function.
   a. Ideological
   b. Symbolic
   c. Economic
   d. Social
   e. Instrumental

28. Amnesty International U.S.A., was founded in:
    a. 1955
    b. 1936
    c. 1961
    d. 1973
    e. 1999

29. The ACLU, was founded in:
    a. 1966
    b. 1965
    c. 1977
    d. 1920
    e. 1950

30. _____ are interest groups composed of business in specific industries.
    a. Public organizations
    b. Lobbyists
    c. Policy Networks
    d. Iron Triangles
    e. Trade Associations

Congress: The National Lawmakers

Chapter 13

Most members of Congress are in the back pockets of multinational corporations and big bankers. Both the Democrats and the Republicans adhere to the wishes of the Global elite. Quite nationally, it is hard for most American citizens to grasp this.

The vast majority of the U.S. citizenry really believe that there is a major difference between the two-party system. They fell to realize that the U.S. Congress and the two major political parties within it, are puppets used by the Global elite to push their agenda and the average "Joe Blow", really does not have any power. He only has the illusion of power. By power I mean, the ability or capacity to control or manipulate others whether they wish to be or not.

The U.S. Congress is not controlled by the American majority, but instead a limited minority. Article I of the U.S. Constitution, gives Congress its powers and duties, but the power elite gives them their orders.

—The Bowtie Professor!

Silhouette Collection : *Speech*   Vol: 30

Name _____ **Date** _____

Explain:

_____

_____

_____

_____

_____

_____

_____

_____

_____

_____

_____

_____

_____

_____

_____

_____

_____

_____

_____

By far the U.S. Congress is the number one lawmaking body in the United States. The Founding Fathers believed that the vast majority of power should be exercised by a national government in the hands of a legislature. The U.S. Constitution states that the national lawmaking body will consist of two chambers, and quite naturally this establishment came out of the Connecticut Compromise on 1789. The two houses of Congress—the Senate and the House of Representatives—are the lawmaking bodies. The House of Representatives consists of 435 members, and the Senate 100 members. The House membership is based on population and the Senatorial membership is based on equality of the states.

Article I of the U.S. Constitution spells out the powers of the U.S. Congress. These powers are known as **Enumerated** or **Delegated** powers and are those which are specifically spelled out for the national government. The first seventeen clauses of Article I Section 8 applies to the U.S. Congress.

The functions of Congress are the following:

1. To make laws
2. To provide the setting for debating issues
3. To oversee the federal bureaucracy
4. To develop the national budget
5. To give advice and consent to the President of the U.S.
6. Representation
7. Consensus building
8. Policy clarification
9. Investigation

One may ask himself the question, "How well does Congress carry out the above nine major functions?" Well, it probably depends on who you would ask. In general, most Americans have a negative view of Congress; however, the same individuals have a different viewpoint when it comes to his or her own individual representative. Part of the public's strange split on this issue is due to the fact that Congress has to play dual roles in which its members must combine and balance their roles as law and policy makers with their role as representatives to serve the best interests of their constituents back home.

There are three ways members of the U.S. Congress represent their constituents. The first is **Tellegate**. Tellegate is when the voters tell the congressperson how to vote on many issues. This is usually done by the wealthy. Secondly, **Serve-ship** is when the voters allow the congressperson to vote on his or her own conscience. Thirdly, **Telle-serve** is a combination of the theory of tellegate and serve-ship.

Table 13-1 gives a few facts concerning the U.S. Congress.

The **Committee System** is the mode of operation in the U.S. Congress. This is how members get things done. **Standing Committees** are permanent committees in Congress. **Subcommittees** are subsidiaries of standing committees. **Conference Committees** are those in which members of both chambers meet to reconcile their differences in determining whether or not a bill in

TABLE 13-1

1. The structure of Congress is:

   Bicameral (two-house legislature)
   435 House
   100 Senate

2. The qualifications to be in the U.S. Congress are:

House	*Senate*
U.S. citizen for 7 years	U.S. citizen of 9 years
Resident of state and district	Resident of the state
25 years old	30 years old

3. The leadership structure in Congress is:

House	*Senate*
Speaker	Vice President
Majority Leaders	President Pro Tempore
Minority Leader	Majority Leader
Majority Whip	Minority Leader
Minority Whip	Majority Whip

4. A Bill becomes law in the U.S. Congress as follows:
   a. A Bill is introduced in the House/Senate (placed in the hopper).
   b. First reading is given by the House/Senate clerk only by title and is assigned a number.
   c. Speaker of the House/Vice President of the Senate assigns the Bill to a committee.
   d. The committee considers the Bill and places it on the calendar and then files the bill.
   e. Second reading is conducted by the House/Senate clerk. The Bill is read in its entirety.
   f. Congress, friends, and foes debate the bill for a limited time. If the Bill passes the House/Senate, it goes to the third reading in title only. The vote is then taken in the entire House/Senate and, if it passes, the Speaker of the House signs the Bill. In the Senate, the Vice President signs the Bill.
   g. President line item vetoes the bill.
   h. President signs the Bill.
   i. President vetoes the Bill.
   j. President pocket vetoes the Bill.
   k. The Bill becomes law without the President's signature.
5. Members of the U.S. House of Representatives serve two-year terms in contrast to the senators who serve six-year terms. Historically, senators were chosen by state legislators; however, this changed with the ratification of Amendment 17 in 1913.
6. The U.S. Constitution requires that a census be taken every 10 years of all the American citizenry. The number of representatives in the House totaled 65 until the first census was taken. After that, each House member represented 37,000 people. In 1910, the U.S. House of Representatives expanded to 435 members. Finally, in 1929, the House number was fixed at 435.

both houses will become law. Ad Hoc Committees are emergency committees in the House or Senate. Once the problem is solved, the committee disbands. Below are a few standing committees in the U.S. Congress:

House	**Senate**
Ways & Means	Finance
Rules	Rules & Administration
Appropriates	Veterans Affairs
Foreign Affairs	Governmental Affairs
Armed Services	Foreign Relations
Commerce, Science, & Transportation	Budget
Education & Labor	Banking, Housing, & Urban Affairs
Banking, Finance, & Urban Affairs	

Note: The Ways and Means Committee is the most powerful committee in the U.S. Congress.

The tasks of a Congressperson are to legislate, know when to compromise, negotiate, reconcile differences, and mediate. **Logrolling** is bargaining agreements among legislators to support each other's favorite bills, especially projects that primarily benefit individual members and their constituents. The heart of the legislative task isn't so much creating legislation as it is weeding out, consolidating, and modifying legislation that involves compromise, negotiation, reconciliation, and mediation. Both chambers approach the legislative process through functional specialization through the committee system as mentioned earlier in this chapter. Each committee will have jurisdiction over bills introduced within its subject matter area. For example, if a bill has to do with education, it then goes to the Education Committee, or if the bill deals with foreign relations, then it goes to the Foreign Affairs Committee. Apart from the committee system, the legislative parties are the other institutional structures within which congresspersons can gain power and influence. Yet the exercise of power by party leaders is a complex business, and effective use of influence often requires many skills.

An average day in the life of a congressional member goes as follows:

1. In House/Senate chamber
2. In committee/subcommittee meeting
3. Talking with voters
4. Working with staff and reading staff papers
5. Making requests for government jobs
6. Helping with Social Security
7. Requesting appointments to military academies
8. Casework

Table 13-2 highlights a few major points concerning the national lawmakers.

The typical member of Congress is a white male, educated, at least of the upper middle class, and in his late 40's through mid 50's. Even the women and minorities in the U.S. Congress are educated and have incomes

TABLE 13-2

1. A congressperson's vote is influenced by the following:
   a. Interest group pressure
   b. Party ideology
   c. Informal groups in Congress
   d. Voter's desires
2. The conservative coalition is:
   A group of congressional members who have cut across party lines. The coalition consists of southern Democrats and Republicans who vote together against other Democrats.
3. The old Congress (1877-1954) was characterized by:
   a. Dominant committee chairpersons
   b. Closed committee meetings
   c. Power given to senior members
   d. Filibuster control
   e. Control of the House Rules Committee
4. What factors caused the downfall of the old Congress?
   a. The merge of the civil rights movement
   b. The election of President Kennedy
   c. The landslide victory of L.B. Johnson
   d. The Warren Court
5. The new Congress (1954-1981) was characterized by:
   a. Liberal legislation
   b. Open committee hearings to the public
   c. Stopped filibuster control
   d. More women and minorities
   e. More liberals on the House Rules Committee
6. A few of the informal groups in Congress:
   a. Wednesday Group, Moderate Republicans
   b. Democratic Study Group, Liberal Democrats
   c. Congressional Hispanic Caucus
   d. Congressional Black Caucus
   e. Congressional Clearing House on Women's Rights
   f. Conservative Democratic Forum ("Boll Weevils")
7. The powers of the House only:
   a. Originate tax bills
   b. Bring up impeachment charges
8. The powers of the Senate only:
   a. Get advice and consent to the President for treaties to be ratified.
   b. Confirm appointments to the Supreme Court and other federal courts. Also confirm ambassadors and cabinet candidates and other high executive posts.

far above the average American citizen. The vast majority of them are married and have children, and they are either Democrat or Republican. Nevertheless, some have criticized Congress for the following reasons:

1. They are inefficient.
2. They are unrepresentative.
3. They are unethical.
4. They lack collective responsibility.
5. They delegate too much to the executive branch.
6. They are too responsive to organized interests.

When reading the above criticisms, both "2" and "3" really do not have any validity. Congress being "unrepresentative" is a weak argument because if the average U.S. representative reflected the average American citizen, he or she would be poor and uneducated and thus could not get elected. Congress is "unethical" is also a weak argument because not everyone on Capitol Hill is engaging in unethical endeavors, and many of them do have a high sense of morality. It is very difficult, however, to defeat them once they have been in office for a while and, therefore, like the President of the United States, members of Congress should have term limitations. Incumbent members of Congress usually get re-elected because of the following:

1. Name recognition
2. Free mailing
3. Media access
4. Campaign money
5. Campaign experience
6. Large staff to help with casework
7. Their taking credit for federal monies that get allocated to their regions
8. Greater access to government research information

As stated earlier, 98% or more members of Congress are either Democrat or Republican. Within the two parties, they are either liberal, moderate, or conservative.

Box 13-1 provides a moment of thought on conservatives.

■ CONCLUSION

Members of Congress are largely driven by the desire to seek election and win re-election. Once elected, they are successful at staying in office. Much of what Congress does is in response to this motive. Members work hard to get favors for their districts, to serve the needs of constituents, and to maintain a high visibility in their districts or states.

Box 13-2 contains the address of the U.S. Congress.

BOX 13-1

When one observes the media when a candidate is either running for office for the first time or is trying to get re-elected, the media will emphasize that the new candidate or incumbent is a conservative. The notion is that if a candidate or incumbent is a conservative, he or she has high moral values. On the other hand, when a new candidate or incumbent is a liberal, it implies that he or she is amoral. As a result of this, one assumes that liberals have no moral values and conservatives are agents of righteousness.

The point that I would like to make here is that "conservative" doesn't mean "Christian," and since most Republicans claim to be conservatives, one would assume that they are God's agents of righteousness. When Republicans say that they are against abortion and homosexuality, they usually base their beliefs from a biblical viewpoint, and that is all right. These same conservatives, however, have a tendency to deviate from the Bible when it comes to the issue of race. When one studies their voting pattern, they always have a tendency to vote against any bill or legislation that would benefit people of color, or the less privileged classes in America. In my opinion, "Conservative" doesn't mean "Christian" because many of these conservatives are racists, and they only run to the Bible when it is in their interest to do so.

Just a moment of thought.

Professor Yecats

BOX 13-2

To write to your U.S. Congressperson, address correctly:

The Honorable John Doe
United States Senate
Washington, D.C. 20510

Dear Senator Doe:

The Honorable Mary Doe
United States House of Representatives
Washington, D.C. 20515

Dear Representative Doe:

Suggested Readings

Gill, Laverne McCain. *African American Women in Congress: Forming and Transforming History.* New Brunswick, N.J.: Rutgers University Press, 1997.

Gimpel, James G. *Legislating the Revolution: The Contract with America in the First 100 Days.* Needham, Massachusetts: Allyn and Bacon, 1996.

Hibbing, John R. and Elizabeth Theiss-Morse. *Congress as Public Enemy: Public Attitudes Toward American Political Institutions.* New York: Cambridge University Press, 1996.

Kluger, Richard. *Simple Justice.* New York: Vintage, 1975.

Mansbridge, Jane J. *Why We Lost the ERA.* Chicago: University of Chicago Press, 1986.

Mayhew, David R. *Congress: The Electoral Connection.* New Haven, CT: Yale University Press, 1986.

Price, David E. *The Congressional Experience: A View From the Hill.* Boulder, CO: Westview Press, 1995.

CHAPTER 13
STUDY GUIDE

After reading and reviewing this chapter, one should be able to do the following:

1. Explain the Bowtie Professor views concerning the U.S. Congress.

_____

_____

_____

2. Identify the nine major functions of the U.S. Congress.

_____

_____

_____

_____

_____

_____

_____

_____

3. Identify the three ways members of the U.S. Congress represent their constituents.

_____

_____

_____

Name _____ **Date** _____

4. Explain the structure of Congress and the leadership organization of Congress.

_____

_____

_____

5. Explain how a bill becomes law in the U.S. Congress.

_____

_____

_____

_____

6. Explain the committee system in the U.S. Congress.

_____

_____

_____

_____

7. Identify:
  a. The Connecticut Compromise of 1789

_____

  b. Enumerated or delegated powers

_____

  c. Article I, Section 8

_____

    d. The qualifications to be in the U.S. Congress

_____

8. Explain what goes on in the average day of a congressional representative.

_____

_____

_____

_____

9. List the six major criticisms concerning the U.S. Congress.

_____

_____

_____

_____

_____

_____

10. Identify which factors influence a congressperson's vote.

_____

_____

_____

11. Explain the Conservative Coalition.

_____

_____

_____

12. Explain the old and new Congress.

_____

_____

_____

13. Identify the informal groups in Congress.

_____

_____

_____

14. Explain the powers of the House only, and then explain the powers of the Senate only.

_____

_____

_____

15. Explain the importance of Box 13-1.

_____

_____

_____

16. Explain the eight reasons why incumbent members of Congress get re-elected.

_____

_____

_____

_____

Name _____ Date _____

_____

_____

_____

17. Identify Box 13-2.

_____

_____

_____

18. Identify the most powerful committee in the U.S. Congress.

_____

_____

_____

TRUE/FALSE MULTIPLE CHOICE SAMPLE TEST

1. One must be at least 25 years of age in order to run for the U.S. Senate.
   a. True
   b. False

2. Congress is a two-house or unicameral legislation.
   a. True
   b. False

3. Serveship is when the voters allow the congressperson to vote on his or her own conscience.
   a. True
   b. False

4. Members of the U.S. House of Representatives serve 2-year terms.
   a. True
   b. False

5. Article I spells out the powers of Congress.
   a. True
   b. False

6. U.S. senators serve 5-year terms.
   a. True
   b. False

7. There are 435 members in the U.S. Congress.
   a. True
   b. False

8. The committee system is the mode of operation in the U.S. Congress.
   a. True
   b. False

9. One function of Congress is to develop the national budget.
   a. True
   b. False

10. Delegated powers are not spelled out in the U.S. Constitution.
    a. True
    b. False

11. Conference committees are those in which members of both chambers meet to reconcile their differences.
    a. True
    b. False

12. Ad hoc committees are permanent committees in Congress.
    a. True
    b. False

13. Policy clarification is not a major function of Congress.
    a. True
    b. False

14. Table 13-1 gives a few facts concerning Congress.
 a. True
 b. False

15. One criticism of Congress is that they are inefficient.
 a. True
 b. False

16. One must be a U.S. citizen at least _____ years in order to be eligible to run for the U.S. Senate.
 a. 4
 b. 5
 c. 6
 d. 7
 e. 9

17. Box 13-1 explains:
 a. Thoughts on conservatives
 b. The role of Congress
 c. Congressional salaries
 d. The qualifications of congressional members
 e. All of the above

18. One power of the U.S. House of Representatives alone is to:
 a. Make laws
 b. Originate tax bills
 c. Oversee the federal bureaucracy
 d. Develop the national budget
 e. All of the above

19. Article _____ spells out the powers of Congress.
 a. I
 b. II
 c. III
 d. IV
 e. V

20. Members of the U.S. House of Representatives serve _____ terms.
   a. 2
   b. 3
   c. 4
   d. 5
   e. 6

21. The President has _____ options when determining whether or not a bill will become law.
   a. 3
   b. 3
   c. 4
   d. 5
   e. 6

22. Which committee is the most powerful committee in the U.S. Congress?
   a. Foreign Affairs
   b. Finance
   c. Ways and Means
   d. Armed Forces
   e. Budget

23. Box 13-2 shows:
   a. How a bill becomes law in Congress
   b. The addresses of congresspeople
   c. The leadership structure of Congress
   d. How conservatism does *not* mean "Christian"
   e. The functions of Congress

24. A combination of the theory of tellegate and serveship is known as:
   a. Ad hoc
   b. Delegation
   c. Trusteeship
   d. Politico
   e. Telle-serve

25. Enumerated powers are sometimes referred to as powers.
   a. Inherent
   b. Concurrent
   c. Implied
   d. Reserved
   e. Delegated

26. The average "Joe Blow" in America only has the _____ of power.
   a. notion
   b. illusion
   c. notion
   d. perception
   e. idea

27. Most members of _____ are in the back pockets of big bankers and multinational corporations.
   a. the U.S. House of Representatives
   b. the Senate
   c. the Supreme Court
   d. Committees
   e. Congress

28. There is really not a major difference between the_____in the U.S. Congress.
   a. Committee system
   b. Ad hoc committees
   c. two-party
   d. bureaucratic system
   e. economic

29. One major criticism of Congress is that:
   a. they delegate too much to the executive branch
   b. they are rich compared to the average American citizen
   c. they waste too much money
   d. they do not get things done in a timely manner
   e. all of the above

30. Apart from the committee system, _____ are the other institutional structures within Congress whereby its members can gain power and influence.

    a. informal groups

    b. open hearings

    c. campaign influence

    d. finances

    e. legislative parties

The Texas State Legislature: Tejas

The Texas State Legislature meets,
in odd-numbered years.
They all come together,
a total of 181 peers.

These politicians meet in regular sessions,
which last for 140 days.
When trying to make bills become laws,
they do it in a variety of ways.

These lawmakers do not have
a lot of time on their hands;
therefore, they must work tight schedules,
in order to complete their plans.

In committees they work day and night,
in hope that their legislation turns out all right.
Once the 140 days have passed,
Texas legislators have completed their task.

—The Bowtie Professor

Name _____ **Date** _____

Explain:

_____

_____

_____

_____

_____

_____

_____

_____

_____

_____

_____

_____

_____

_____

_____

_____

_____

_____

_____

Article III of the Texas Constitution places the legislative or law-making power of the state in the Texas Legislature, a body currently composed of 181 people serving in a Senate and the House of Representatives. The duties and functions of the state legislature are quite numerous and broad. Traditionally, the primary function has been to enact statutory laws and consider and pass bills designed to cope with various problems existing in the state.

Other functions include:

- To make constitutional law
- Reapportionment and redistricting
- To amend and ratify both the national and state constitutions
- To oversee the judicial functions
- Electoral function (political candidates)
- To oversee the state bureaucracy
- Investigatory function
- Impeachment

The structure of the Texas State Legislature is bicameral, 150 in the House of Representatives and 31 Senators. The senatorial districts are based on land area, and the representatives' districts are based on population. The formal qualifications to be in the Texas House are: resident of Texas, 21 years old, a qualified voter, and a one-year resident of the district that one hopes to represent. The Texas Senate requires one to be a legal resident of Texas for five years, 26 years old, a qualified voter, and a one-year resident of the senatorial district that one hopes to represent. Some of the historical informal qualifications to become a member of the state legislature have been: white, male, educated, Democratic conservative, about 40 years or more of age, a lawyer or businessman, and usually married with a family.

Note: *Members of the House serve two-year terms, and Senate members serve four-year terms.*

Since 1975, the salary of those in the state legislature is as follows:

- A small sum of $7,200 each year plus $95 per diem allowance when the legislature is in session. Note: The per diem allowance when in a regular session was $30 per day.
- When the legislators serve on state boards, they are allowed about $70 a day.
- The Lt. Governor and House Speaker receive the same salary, plus they are entitled to an apartment in the capitol.
- For operating and traveling allowance, legislators since 1985 have received $6,500 monthly for members of the House, and up to $13,500 monthly for members of the Senate. The operating and travel allow-

ance budget for members of the Texas Legislature requires that they must use these monies for postage as well.

The Texas State Legislature meets in regular sessions in odd-numbered years, the second Tuesday in January, and then these lawmaking bodies begin to mark up and "trash out" different pieces of legislation. In a regular session, the legislature could face up to 5,500 bills or more. This is why the lawmakers in Austin should meet every year instead of in odd-numbered years only. The subjects considered by the legislature are of an infinite variety, ranging from changing insurance laws to changing the type of evidence required for conviction in a rape trial, from whether $10,000 should be appropriated to increase the pension of retired judges, to whether $3 billion should be spent for public education. More than half of the bills passed by the lawmakers in Austin do not even apply to the state as a whole but rather are special bills pertaining only to particular cities and counties.

Table 14-1 gives a few facts concerning the state legislature.

As is the case with the U.S. Congress, the state legislature's mode of operation is the committee system. It is only through standing committees that any sort of detailed attention can be devoted to examining the hundreds of bills introduced in each session. In truth, only a small proportion of the bills introduced are studied and analyzed, and most bills when referred to a committee are shelved and never again see the daylight. Nearly all such bills, however, are basically ludicrous and undeserving of attention. An important bill in the Texas Legislature, such as the *Concealed Handgun Bill*,

TABLE 14-1

1. A bill becomes law in the Texas Legislature as follows:
   a. Bill introduced in the House/Senate in first reading.
   b. Bill is given a number and speaker/lt. governor assigns the bill to a committee.
   c. Committee places the bill on a calendar.
   d. Bill is debated at second reading.
   e. Bill is presented at third reading.
   f. Bill is voted on.
   g. If bill passes one chamber, it goes to the other chamber.
   h. Once bill has passed both houses, it goes to the governor.
   i. Governor signs the bill
   j. Governor line-item vetoes the bill (appropriations bills only).
   k. Governor vetoes the bill.
   l. Bill becomes law without the governor's signature in 10 days, excluding Sundays if the legislature is in session.
   m. Bill becomes law without the governor's signature in 20 days, excluding Sundays, if the legislature is out of session.

TABLE 14-1	*Continued*

2. The leadership structure in the Texas Legislature is as follows:

House	*Senate*
Speaker	Lt. Governor
Majority Leader	President Pro Tempore
Minority Leader	Majority Leader
Majority Whip	Minority Leader
Minority Whip	Majority Whip
	Minority Whip

3. The three major arms of the Texas Legislature are:

a. *Legislative Budget Board*

10-member House/Senate
Presiding officers
Governor

b. *Legislative Council*

5 members Senate
10 members House
Presiding officers

c. *Legislative Audit Committee*

Tax Committee Chairperson (House)
Appropriations Committee (House)
State Affair Committee (Senate)
Presiding officers

4. The procedural powers of the presiding officers are:
a. To appoint members of all standing committees.
b. To appoint members of all conference committees.
c. To appoint the chairpersons and vice-chairperson of all committees.
d. To determine the jurisdiction of committees through the referral of bills.
e. To interpret procedural rules when conflict arises.
f. To schedule legislation for floor action.
g. To recognize members who wish to speak or not to recognize members and thus prevent them from speaking.

5. The institutional powers of the presiding officers are to appoint members to the following:
a. Legislative Budget Board
b. Legislative Council
c. Legislative Audit Committee

will get careful attention and will be both studied and analyzed in the subject committee, and then sent to the Rules Committee to be placed on the calendar for floor action, and finally sent to the floor along with the subject committee's recommendation of "do pass or do not pass." The floor is where the total membership of the chamber votes, and they usually accept the committee's recommendation. If approved by the floor, then the bill goes through the same process in the other chamber.

Box 14-1 lists key terms of the legislature's process in Texas, as well as a few select standing committees.

BOX 14-1

1. Terms
   - **At Large District**—A legislative or other political district, sometimes called a multi-member district because two or more officials are elected from it.
   - **Bicameral**—A lawmaking body, such as the Texas Legislature, that includes two chambers.
   - **Bill**—A primary device for introducing a law or a change in a law.
   - **Bloc**—A group of legislators who act together for a common goal, regardless of party affiliation.
   - **Calendar**—The agenda or the list of bills to be considered by the House or the Senate on a given day.
   - **Calendars Committee**—A special procedural committee that schedules bills that already have been approved by other committees for floor debate in the House.
   - **Caucus**—A group of legislators who band together for common political or partisan goals, or along ethnic or geographic lines.
   - **Concurrent Resolution**—When both chambers have passed a resolution to allow a conference committee to add important language to a bill.
   - **Conference Committee**—A panel of House members and senators appointed to work out a compromise on a bill if different versions of the legislation were passed by the House and the Senate.
   - **Cloture**—A cloture stops a filibuster. It requires two-thirds vote of the senators.
   - **Division Votes**—Votes taken on the computerized voting boards in Texas, but erased without being permanently recorded.
   - **Filibuster**—An unlimited debate in the Senate to keep a bill from being passed.
   - **Institutionalization**—In the context of political science, the development of a legislative body into a formally-structured system with a stable membership, complex rules, expanded internal operations, and the delineation of staff functions.
   - **Interim Committees**—Those which work after the regular legislative session is over.
   - **Lt. Governor**—The presiding officer of the Senate.
   - **Record Vote**—A vote taken in the House or Senate of which a permanent record is kept, listing how individual legislators voted.

Continued

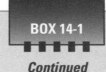

BOX 14-1

Continued

- **Regular Session**—The 140-day period in the odd-numbered years in which the Legislature meets and can consider and pass laws on any issue or subject.
- **Select Committees**—Special panels appointed to study major policy issues.
- **Single-Member District**—A system in which a legislator, city council member, or other public official is elected from a specific geographic area.
- **Speaker**—The presiding officer of the House of Representatives.
- **Special Session**—A legislative session that can be called at any time by the governor. This session is limited to 30 days and to issues or subjects designated by the governor.
- **Tag**—A rule that allows an individual senator to postpone a committee hearing on any bill for at least 48 hours, a delay that can be fatal to a bill during the closing days of a legislative session.
- **Two-Thirds Rule**—A rule under which the Texas Senate has traditionally operated that requires approval of at least two-thirds of the senators before a bill can be debated on the floor. It allows a minority of senators to block controversial legislation.

2. A few select standing committees in the Texas State Legislature:
- **Senate (13)**

  Criminal Justice
  Education
  Finance
  Health and Human Resources
  Natural Resources
  State Affairs

- **House (36)**

  Appropriations
  Corrections
  Economic Development
  Elections
  Higher Education
  Public Safety
  Ways and Means

■ CONCLUSION

The Texas State Legislature is atypical, especially when it is compared with the legislatures of other large urban states. Texas state lawmakers have numerous things to get done in such a short period of time. Nevertheless, they are able to accomplish the state's most major tasks.

Suggested Readings

Anderson, Arthur J. "Texas Legislative Redistricting: Proposed Constitutional and Statutory Amendments for an Improved Process," *Southwestern Law Journal.* 43 (October 1989): 719-757.

Bickerstaff, Steve. "State Legislative and Congressional Reapportionment in Texas: A Historical Perspective," Public Affairs Comment 37 (Winter 1991): 1-13.

Boulard, Garry. "Lobbyists as Outlaws," *State Legislatures.* 22 (January 1996): 20-25.

Deaton, Charles. *The Year They Threw the Rascals Out.* Austin: Shoal Creek Press, 1973.

Herskowitz, Mickey. *Sharpstown Revisited: Frank Sharp and a Tale of Dirty Politics in Texas.* Austin: Eakin Press, 1994.

Rosenthal, Alan. *Governors and Legislators: Contending Powers.* Washington, D.C.: Congressional Quarterly Books, 1990.

Texas Legislative Council. *Presiding Officers of the Texas Legislatures, 1946-1984.* Austin: Texas Legislative Council, 1982.

CHAPTER 14
STUDY GUIDE

After reading and reviewing this chapter, one should be able to do the following:

1. Explain the bowtie Professor's views concerning the Texas State Legislature.

_____

_____

_____

2. List the major functions of the Texas Legislature.

_____

_____

_____

3. Explain the salaries and fringe benefits of members of the state legislature.

_____

_____

_____

4. Explain both the formal and informal qualifications to be in the Texas Legislature.

_____

_____

5. Tell where the powers of the Texas state lawmakers are spelled out in the Texas Constitution.

_____

_____

_____

6. Explain when the Texas state lawmakers meet for regular sessions and for how long.

_____

_____

_____

7. Explain how a bill becomes law in the Texas State Legislature.

_____

_____

_____

8. Explain how the Texas Legislature is similar to the U.S. Congress.

_____

_____

_____

9. Describe how the Texas Legislature is different from the U.S. Congress.

_____

_____

_____

10. Explain the structure of the Texas State Legislature and its organizational leadership.

_____

_____

_____

11. Name the three major arms of the state legislature and their members.

_____

_____

_____

12. Explain both the institutional and procedural powers of the presiding officers.

_____

_____

13. Identify the following terms:

   a. Bill

_____

   b. Select committees

_____

   c. Interim committees

_____

   d. Concurrent resolution

_____

   e. Bloc

_____

   f. At-large district

_____

   g. Division votes

_____

h. Institutionalization

_____

i. Filibuster

_____

j. Cloture

_____

k. Record vote

_____

l. Caucus

_____

m. Regular sessions

_____

n. Special session

_____

o. Tag

_____

p. Two-thirds rule

_____

q. Single member district

_____

r. Conference committees

_____

    s. Calendar committees

_____

14. List a few standing committees in both the Texas House and Senate.

_____

_____

_____

15. Explain the committee system in the Texas Legislature.

_____

_____

_____

TRUE/FALSE MULTIPLE CHOICE SAMPLE TEST

1. There are about 36 standing committees in the Texas Senate.
    a. True
    b. False

2. A bill is only a primary device for making a change in a law.
    a. True
    b. False

3. A cloture stops a filibuster.
    a. True
    b. False

4. There is a thing such as the two-thirds rule in the state legislature.
    a. True
    b. False

5. Regular sessions last for 140 days in the state legislature.
   a. True
   b. False

6. The state legislature meets in odd-numbered years, the first Tuesday in January.
   a. True
   b. False

7. Members of the Texas House serve 2-year terms.
   a. True
   b. False

8. Members of the Texas Senate serve 6-year terms.
   a. True
   b. False

9. Article III spells out the powers of the state lawmakers in the Texas Constitution.
   a. True
   b. False

10. There are 35 senators in Texas.
   a. True
   a. False

11. One must be a qualified voter in order to run for the Texas Senate.
   a. True
   b. False

12. The Lt. Governor is entitled to an apartment in the capital.
   a. True
   b. False

13. The Texas Legislature is unicameral.
   a. True
   b. False

14. The Texas lawmakers meet for regular sessions in even-numbered years.
   a. True
   b. False

15. One must be at least 21 years old in order to be eligible to run for the Texas House.
  a. True
  b. False

16. There are _____ representatives in the Texas House.
  a. 435
  b. 150
  c. 100
  d. 181
  e. 535

17. There are _____ members in the Texas State Legislature.
  a. 435
  b. 150
  c. 100
  d. 181
  e. 535

18. Article _____ of the Texas Constitution spells out the powers and duties of the state lawmakers.
  a. I
  b. II
  c. III
  d. IV
  e. V

19. One must be at least _____ years old in order to run for the Texas Senate.
  a. 21
  b. 25
  c. 18
  d. 26
  e. 30

20. Since _____, the Texas lawmakers' salaries have been pretty much the same.
  a. 1965
  b. 2005
  c. 1995
  d. 1985
  e. 1975

21. Table 14-1 gives a few facts concerning the:
    a. Texas Legislature
    b. U.S. Congress
    c. Lt. Governor
    d. House Speaker
    e. All of the above

22. In a regular session, lawmakers in the state legislature could face up to _____ bills or more.
    a. 1,500
    b. 5,500
    c. 3,400
    d. 2,600
    e. 4,000

23. There are about _____ standing committees in the Texas House.
    a. 18
    b. 25
    c. 36
    d. 41
    e. 53

24. In the Texas Legislature, the presiding officers are the Texas Speaker of the House and the:
    a. Governor
    b. Majority Leader
    c. Minority Leader
    d. Lt. Governor
    e. President *Pro Tempore*

25. There are _____ major arms of the state legislature.
    a. 7
    b. 6
    c. 5
    d. 4
    e. 3

26. The_____is where the total membership of the chambers votes.
    a. floor
    b. committee
    c. special session
    d. Caucus
    e. Bloc

27. The Lt. Governor and the House Speaker receive the same_____.
    a. benefits
    b. salary
    c. traveling allowance
    d. per diem
    e. special session

28. Since_____members of the Texas House have received $6,500 per month for their traveling and operating allowance.
    a. 1965
    b. 1975
    c. 1985
    d. 1995
    e. 2005

29. Since_____the Texas Senate received up to $13,5000 for their traveling and operating allowance.
    a. 1955
    b. 1965
    c. 1975
    d. 1985
    e. 1995

30. The Legislative Audit Committee has the chairperson of the House:
    a. Rules Committee
    b. Budget Committee
    c. Ways and Means Committee
    d. Audit Committee
    e. Tax Committee

The Presidency: The National Executive

Chapter 15

The vast majority of Americans spend too much time focusing on the President of the United States, when they should focus on local civic engagement. Yes, the president is a very important and key figure in U.S. politics, but the office has its limitations.

The president has very limited time to accomplish his goals and objectives, especially if he ends up being a one term executive. He plays a variety of formal and informal roles. Negotiating and compromising with Congress, special interests, the mass media, and the general public is an everyday activity with the executive.

Candidates for this position must be strong and able to constantly be under tremendous pressure. To become President of the United States, one must be thick skinned and able to suffer a great deal of criticism on a daily basis. Without these attributes, very few can qualify for this position.

—The Bowtie Professor!

Silhouette Collection : *Speech*   Vol: 30

Name _____ **Date** _____

Explain:

_____

_____

_____

_____

_____

_____

_____

_____

_____

_____

_____

_____

_____

_____

_____

_____

_____

_____

The intent of the framers of the U.S. Constitution when creating the executive branch of government was to have a strong executive limited by checks and balances. The framers always wanted Congress to be stronger than the president.

The president of the United States is the central figure in American politics. He is the only official (along with the vice president) who is elected by the entire nation. While most Americans are relatively uninformed about politics, nearly everyone is aware of who the president is, his family, and his character, or lack of it. The chief responsibility of the president is to enforce or administer the laws, but the office carries other duties as well. Too often, the president is expected to solve all of our nation's problems with dispatch. Though not directly provided for in the constitution, through the interpretation of the constitution, the president may appoint officials to help fulfill the duties of the office. Through this custom, the president's cabinet and the federal bureaucracy have developed. Each of the fifteen cabinet departments is headed by a secretary, who reports directly to the president.

Article II of the U.S. Constitution spells out the qualifications, powers, and roles of the president of the United States. The formal qualifications to become president are that one must be a natural-born citizen, have U.S. residency for 14 years, and be 35 years old. Quite naturally it is the informal qualifications which carry more weight than the formal qualifications. The informal unspoken qualifications are:

- White male
- Wealthy
- Educated
- Religious background (within the realm of Christianity)
- Usually tall (for image-making)

Table 15-1 shows a few powers of the president and the roles he plays.

One major issue that has sparked a great deal of debate among political scientists and historians is the subject of presidential power. Has the office of the presidency become too powerful? Edwin Corwin in his book, *President, Office, and Powers,* argues that the U.S. president became so powerful after World War II because of the following:

1. The acceptance of the electorate of the national government in social welfare matters.
2. The breakdown of the doctrine of dual federalism as a restraint on the national government.
3. The weakened notion of both the doctrines of separation of powers and checks and balances.
4. Congress' inability to delegate power to the White House.
5. The enhancement of the president's role in international affairs.
6. The enhanced role of the president as Commander-in-Chief.

Arthur Schlesinger, Jr. also argues that presidential power has increased at a faster rate than the other two branches of government. In his book, *The Impe-*

TABLE 15-1

1. The powers of the president are:
   - **Covert Action**—A secret intelligence activity outside U.S. borders undertaken with specific authorization by the president. The acknowledgement of the U.S. sponsorship would defeat or compromise its purpose.
   - **Delegated Powers**—Those powers which are spelled out in Article II of the U.S. Constitution.
   - **Executive Order**—A formal regulation governing executive branch operations issued by the president.
   - **Executive Privilege**—The right of the president to withhold information from the other two branches of government and the American public. Yet the Supreme Court has only upheld the executive privilege in limited situations.
   - **Gridlock**—Political stalemate between the president and Congress, arising when one branch is controlled by one major political party and the other by the other party.
   - **Impoundment**—The refusal by the president to spend monies appropriated by Congress. This was weakened by the Impoundment Control Act of 1974.
   - **Inherent Powers**—Those powers that the president uses in foreign affairs.
   - **Pocket Veto**—The death of a bill when the President lets a bill lie on his desk 10 days (excluding Sundays).
   - **Prerogative Powers**—Powers used by the president without congressional collaboration. Prerogative powers are used in secret.
   - **Stewardship Powers**—Powers used by an assertive president at the time of emergencies within and outside the country. Stewardship powers are not spelled out under Article II of the U.S. Constitution. The restraining order theory argues that the only powers that the president has are those spelled out in the U.S. Constitution.
   - **Veto**—The power of the president to reject a bill.
2. The formal roles of the president are:
   - **Commander-in-Chief**
     - Command U.S. armed forces: "The president shall be Commander-in-Chief of the Army and Navy" (Article II, Section 2).
     - Appoint military officers.
   - **Chief of State**
     - "The executive power shall be vested in a President" (Article II, Section 1).
     - Grant reprieves and pardons (Article II, Section 2).
     - Represent the nation as chief of state.
     - Appoint federal court and Supreme Court judges (Article II, Section 2).
   - **Chief Executive**
     - Implement policy: "take care that the laws be faithfully executed" (Article II, Section 3).
     - Supervise executive branch of government.
     - Appoint and remove executive officials (Article II, Section 2).
     - Prepare executive budget for submission to Congress (by law of congress).
   - **Chief Legislator**
     - Initiate policy: "give to the Congress information of the State of the Union, and recommend to their consideration such measures as he shall judge necessary and expedient" (Article II, Section 3).
     - Veto legislation passed by Congress, subject to override by a two-thirds vote in both houses.

Continued

TABLE 15-1 *Continued*

- Convene special session of Congress "on extraordinary occasions" (Article II, Section 3).
- **Chief Diplomat**
  - Make treaties "with the advice and consent of the Senate" (Article II, Section 2).
  - Exercise the power of diplomatic recognition: "receive ambassadors" (Article II, Section 3).
  - Make executive agreements (by custom and international law).

3. The informal roles of the president are:
   - **Chief of Party**—The president is responsible for getting his party's views across.
     Example: George Bush and his anti-abortion policies.
   - **Chief Educator**—Leading the nation in the area of educational programs for the 21st century.
     Example: Bill Clinton's $1,500 tax credit program for college students.
   - **Leader of the People**—The sole spokesman for the American people.

rial Presidency, Schlesinger points out that this process began with Franklin D. Roosevelt. It was strengthened by the depression, World War II, the War in Korea, Vietnam, the Cold War, and by the fear of a nuclear war. The American president by the early 1970's had become on war and peace the most absolute monarch, according to Schlesinger. He lists the following proposals directed at the traditional constitutional role and structure of the presidency:

1. Change the current four-year-term of the president to a one six-year-term. Under this plan, a president could not run again for re-election. In other words, a president's maximum number of years in office would be reduced from eight years to six.
2. Replace the one-man president form with a six-man directorate with a rotating chairman, each member to serve for a year.
3. Give the president a *Council of State,* a body that he would be bound by the law to consult with, especially on very crucial matters.
4. Adopt a version of the British Parliamentary system. In other words, a president would be compelled at regular intervals to explain and defend his policies to key members of the political opposition. If Congress, by two-thirds or three-fourths vote, issues a vote of "no confidence," a new national election would have to be called within six weeks.

I agree partially with point "#1" made by Schlesinger. The four-year term should be changed to a one six-year term; however, I disagree with the point that a president cannot run for re-election. After a president's six-year term is up, he must sit out for six more years but should be allowed to run for the office once again. For example, former president Bill Clinton is still young enough to run again for the office of the presidency, but cannot because of term limitations. Also I think that the U.S. Congress are a bunch of hypocrites because they place term limitations on the president

TABLE 15-2

1. According to political scientists, some of the great presidents were:
   - Abraham Lincoln
   - George Washington
   - Franklin D. Roosevelt
   - Woodrow Wilson
   - Thomas Jefferson
   - Andrew Jackson
   - Theodore Roosevelt

2. The salaries of the U.S. presidents, past and present:
   - $25,000

George Washington	John Tyler
John Adams	James K. Polk
Thomas Jefferson	Zachary Taylor
James Madison	Millard Fillmore
James Monroe	Franklin Pierce
John Quincy Adams	James Buchanan
Andrew Jackson	Abraham Lincoln
Martin Van Buren	Andrew Johnson
William H. Harrison	Ulysses S. Grant

   - $50,000

Ulysses S. Grant (second term)	Grover Cleveland
Rutherford B. Hayes	Benjamin Harrison
James Garfield	William McKinley
Chester Arthur	Theodore Roosevelt

   - $75,000

William H. Taft	Herbert Hoover
Woodrow Wilson	Franklin D. Roosevelt
Warren G. Harding	Harry S. Truman
Calvin Coolidge	

   - $100,000

Harry S. Truman (second term)	John F. Kennedy
Dwight D. Eisenhower	Lyndon B. Johnson

   - $200,000

Richard Nixon	Ronald Reagan
Gerald Ford	George H. Bush
Jimmy Carter	Bill Clinton

   - $400,000

     George W. Bush

Note: The Constitution forbids any change in the president's salary during the period for which he shall have been elected. From Truman's second term, presidents have been given expense allowances of $50,000 a year, taxable from 1953, for which they do not have to account. Since 1909, they have also received a traveling allowance, currently $100,000, though most of their travel costs, like most of the non-personal costs of the White House, are met from other budgets.

TABLE 15-3

1. The Succession Acts are as follows:
   - **Succession Act of 1886**—Made the Secretary of State next in line after the Vice President if something were to happen to the President.
   - **Succession Act of 1947**—Made the Speaker of the House next in line after the Vice President if something were to happen to the President.
2. The line of succession to the President of the United States:
   1. Vice President
   2. Speaker of the House of Representatives
   3. President Pro Tempore of the U.S. Senate
   4. Secretary of State
   5. Secretary of Treasury
   6. Secretary of Defense
   7. Attorney General
   8. Secretary of the Interior
   9. Secretary of Agriculture
   10. Secretary of Commerce
   11. Secretary of Labor
   12. Secretary of Health and Human Services
   13. Secretary of Housing and Urban Development
   14. Secretary of Transportation
   15. Secretary of Energy
   16. Secretary of Education
   17. Secretary of Veteran's Affairs
   18. Secretary of Homeland Security
3. Twenty-fifth Amendment
   An amendment to the U.S. Constitution adopted in 1967 that establishes procedures for filling vacancies in the two top executive offices and that makes provisions for situations involving presidential disabilities. This amendment was used by Richard Nixon's vice president, Spiro Agnew, who resigned in 1973 because of his alleged receipt of construction contract kickbacks during his tenure as governor of Maryland. When Richard Nixon resigned on August 9, 1974, Vice President Gerald Ford became president and he nominated Nelson Rockefeller. For the first time in America's political history, both the president and vice president were individuals who were not elected.

but not on themselves. I do not agree with point "#2" made by Schlesinger concerning the six-man form because there would be no accountability. Each individual could blame the other if things did not go well within our country. Point "#3" is also a no-no because it would put too many constraints on the president and his role would be reduced merely to a managerial position, therefore no *Council of State*. Finally, I agree with point "#4," especially the part whereby the president would have to explain and defend his policies.

Table 15-2 gives some basic information concerning presidents.

Note: The Constitution forbids any change in the president's salary during the period for which he shall have been elected. From Truman's second term, presidents have been given expense allowances of $50,000 a year, taxable from 1953, for which they do not have to account. Since 1909, they have also received a traveling allowance, currently $100,000, though most of their travel costs, like most of the non-personal costs of the White House, are met from other budgets.

Table 15-3 deals with the issue of succession and vacancies.

■ CONCLUSION

The American presidency is potentially the most powerful office in the world. As head of state, the president symbolized national unity and speaks on behalf of the American people to the world. During the 20th century, the responsibilities of world leadership and the growth of the government led to enormous changes in the American presidency. The office changed from being that of a basic "managerial position" to being a leader of the most powerful military force in the Western world and the chief operating officer of a huge organization that affects the lives of all the American citizenry.

Suggested Readings

Barber, James D. *The Presidential Character: Predicting Performance in the White House.* 4th ed., Englewood Cliffs, NJ: Prentice Hall, 1992.

Corwin, Edwin S. *The Presidential Office and Powers.* 4th ed., New York: New York University Press, 1957.

Kellerman, Barbara. *The Political Presidency.* New York: Oxford University Press, 1986.

Kernell, Samuel. *Going Public: New Strategies for Presidential Leadership.* 3rd ed., Washington, D.C.: CQ Press, 1997.

Nelson, Michael, ed. *The Presidency and the Political System.* 6th ed., Washington, D.C.: CQ Press, 2000.

Neustadt, Richard E. *Presidential Power and the Modern Presidency.* New York: Free Power, 1991.

Ragsdale, Lyn. *Vital Statistics on the Presidency: Washington to Clinton.* Washington, D.C.: CQ Press, 1995.

CHAPTER 15
STUDY GUIDE

After reading and studying this chapter, one should be able to do the following:

1. Explain the Bowtie Professor's view concerning the U.S. presidency.

_____

_____

_____

2. Explain both the formal and informal qualifications to become President of the United States.

_____

_____

3. Name and explain both the formal and informal roles of the U.S. President.

_____

_____

4. Identify the six major reasons political scientist Edwin Corwin gave concerning the growth of the President after World War II.

_____

_____

_____

_____

_____

_____

5. Identify historian Arthur Schlesinger, Jr., and his alternative to the U.S. presidency.

_____

_____

_____

6. Identify the 11 key terms in Table 15-1.

_____

_____

_____

_____

_____

_____

_____

_____

_____

_____

_____

_____

7. Name the seven great presidents according to political scientists.

_____

_____

_____

_____

_____

_____

_____

8. Explain the line of succession of the President of the United States.

_____

_____

_____

9. Explain the 25th Amendment to the U.S. Constitution.

_____

_____

_____

10. Name both the President and Vice President who were not elected by the American people.

_____

_____

11. Identify the similarities between Abraham Lincoln and John F. Kennedy in Box 15-1.

_____

_____

_____

TRUE/FALSE MULTIPLE CHOICE SAMPLE TEST

1. Since 1909 presidents have received a traveling allowance.
   a. True
   b. False

2. "Chief Educator" is a formal role of the U.S. President.
   a. True
   b. False

3. Article II spells out the powers the U.S. President.
   a. True
   b. False

4. One must be at least 38 years old in order to be eligible to run for the U.S. presidency.
   a. True
   b. False

5. One must have U.S. residency for 15 years in order to be eligible to run for the U.S. presidency.
   a. True
   b. False

6. "Chief Diplomat" is a formal role of the U.S. President.
   a. True
   b. False

7. Richard Nixon resigned from the presidency in 1974.
   a. True
   b. False

8. Theodore Roosevelt was considered by many political scientists to be a great president.
   a. True
   b. False

9. The Constitution does *not* forbid any change in the President's salary during the period for which he or she shall have been elected.
   a. True
   b. False

10. The President has a formal role of "Chief of Party."
    a. True
    b. False

11. The Succession Act of 1886 made the U.S. Secretary of State next in line after the Vice President if something were to happen to the President.
    a. True
    b. False

12. George W. Bush is the first President to make $400,000 a year.
    a. True
    b. False

13. John Adams was *not* considered to be a great president according to many political scientists.
    a. True
    b. False

14. There are 13 members that make up the U.S. President's cabinet.
    a. True
    b. False

15. Arthur Schlesinger wrote the book *President, Office, and Powers.*
    a. True
    b. False

16. The _____ of the United States is the central figure in American politics.
    a. President
    b. Chief Justice
    c. Congress
    d. Media
    e. Vice President

17. The only chief responsibility of the President is to enforce or administer:
    a. Checks and balances
    b. Laws
    c. Pardons
    d. Court actions
    e. Gridlocks

18. The U.S. President has _____ formal roles.

    a. 3

    b. 4

    c. 5

    d. 6

    e. 7

19. When the U.S. President initiates policies, he or she is fulfilling the role of:

    a. Chief Diplomat

    b. Chief of State

    c. Commander-in-Chief

    d. Chief Legislator

    e. Chief Educator

20. When the U.S. President makes treaties with foreign nations, he or she is fulfilling the role of:

    a. Chief Legislator

    b. Chief of State

    c. Chief Executive

    d. Chief of Party

    e. Chief Diplomat

21. A formal regulation governing executive branch operations issued by the U.S. President is known as an Executive:

    a. Privilege

    b. Order

    c. Agreement

    d. Action

    e. Power

22. Which of the following is an informal role of the U.S. President?

    a. Chief of Party

    b. Chief of State

    c. Chief Executive

    d. Commander-in-Chief

    e. Chief Legislator

23. The President of the United States serves a _____ -year term.
    a. 2
    b. 3
    c. 4
    d. 5
    e. 6

24. Table 15-2 gives some basic information concerning:
    a. The Secretary of State
    b. The Succession Act of 1947
    c. Informal presidential roles
    d. The U.S. President
    e. All of the above

25. The U.S. President has _____ informal roles.
    a. 2
    b. 3
    c. 4
    d. 5
    e. 6

26. Most Americans spend too much time focusing the_____.
    a. Mass media
    b. General public
    c. Congressional sessions
    d. Supreme Court
    e. U.S. Presidency

27. Executive agreements are made by custom and:
    a. the C.I.A.
    b. the Cabinet
    c. the U.S. Congress
    d. International Law
    e. Foreign Policy

28. Which of the following does the president not have to negotiate with?

   a. Special Interests

   b. the Supreme Court

   c. Congress

   d. the General public

   e. the Mass media

29. A secret intelligence activity outside the U.S. borders without compromise is known as:

   a. Impounded

   b. Gridlock

   c. Covert Action

   d. Prerogative Powers

   e. Pocket Veto

30. _____ argued that presidential power has increased at a faster rate than the other two branches of government.

   a. Arthur Schlesinger

   b. Edwin Corwin

   c. Herman Pritchett

   d. Thomas Patterson

   e. James Wilson

The Governor: The State Executive

Chapter 16

There has never been a governor of Texas
who was non-white.
If you are a minority and decide to run for that office,
you better be ready for a fight.

This political position is for someone
who is humble and meek.
For the office itself
is definitely constitutionally weak.

The governor of Texas
plays a very powerless role.
The lt. Governor, believe it or not,
has a lot more control.

Yet the governorship of Texas
is still a leadership position,
Even though he or she may not get
the political recognition.

The only official that the governor appoints
Is the Texas Secretary of State.
The framers who wrote the Texas constitution
by no means made a mistake.

—The Bowtie Professor

Name _____ **Date** _____

Explain:

_____

_____

_____

_____

_____

_____

_____

_____

_____

_____

_____

_____

_____

_____

_____

_____

_____

_____

The governorship of Texas is a weak executive model due to the Texas Constitution of 1876. This constitution was adopted at the end of Reconstruction, and it is a highly restrictive and anti-governmental document drafted by Texans reacting to the abuses of the radical Reconstructionists and the oppressive administration of Governor E.J. Davis. Tight restrictions were placed on the governorship, the legislature, and other state officials who today inhibit the ability of the state government to respond to the complex needs of what is now a growing urban state. Nevertheless, the governor is still the most important person in Texas politics, and no other state government official is as widely known and recognized as the Texas governor. The governor serves as the *Head of State*, which is the formal representation of Texas. As such, he or she welcomes visiting dignitaries and acts as spokesperson for the state in dealings with other states and the national government. The governor of Texas has his or her own army, the National Guard, which he or she may call out for emergencies, such as natural disasters and civil disorders.

The qualifications to be governor of Texas are spelled out in Article IV of the Texas Constitution. A candidate for the governorship of Texas must be a citizen of the United States, must be at least 30 years old, and must have been a resident of Texas five years immediately preceding the election. These qualifications also include the lieutenant governor. Article IV also mandates that the governor "shall be installed on the first Tuesday after the organization of the legislature, or as soon thereafter as practicable." Article III gives the state legislature the power to settle any disputes that might arise concerning the election of the governor.

The formal qualifications to become governor of Texas allow practically any Texan to run for the office. The informal qualifications, however, carry more weight. The political, economic, and social realities of the state dictate that personal characteristics not stated in Article IV help to determine who will become the Texas governor. Texas tradition dictates that the successful candidate for governor will be a white male, politically conservative, involved in civic affairs, educated, married, and wealthy. These characteristics are similar to but are even more stringent than those for members of the state legislature.

Box 16-1, a moment of thought, explores whether "conservative" means racist.

The governor of Texas is elected by popular vote in a statewide election during even numbered off years when there is not a presidential election. Historically, the governorship of Texas was a two-year term; however, the term was extended to a four-year term in 1974 for the following reasons:

1. The four-year term gives the governor more time to learn the details of the office and to develop policy plans.
2. The four-year term makes it possible to delay campaigning for re-election. In the past, governors typically began their next campaigns immediately upon taking office.
3. The longer term permits the governor greater independence from the substantial financial campaign support of special interests.

BOX 16-1

In chapter 13, about the U.S. Congress, I raised the question concerning the idea of "conservatism." The question was: "Does conservative mean Christian?" I pointed out that just because someone says that he or she is a conservative does not mean that he or she is a Christian. I raised the question because it is assumed in America's political culture that if someone claims to be a conservative, then that person is a God-fearing Christian and he or she is an agent of righteousness.

The question I would like to raise now is: "Does conservative mean racist?" In order for someone to be a racist, he or she does not have to be conservative, even though if one were to study the voting patterns of conservatives on every level of government, one would definitely notice that such individuals have a tendency to vote against any policies that would benefit people of color and others of the less privileged classes in America. Yet there are those who do not exhibit the conservative viewpoint but who exemplify the same voting behavior. Does conservative mean racist? I think not.

—Professor Yecats

---

4. Finally, the four-year term allows elections to be held in even numbered off years, thus minimizing the effects of national political campaigns.

Below are the formal and informal rules of the governor:

Formal

- **Chief Executive**
  1. Appointments
  2. Removal
  3. Budgeting
  4. Planning
  5. Supervising
- **Chief Legislator**
  1. Message Power—The governor's means of formally establishing his or her priorities for legislative action.
  2. Session Power—The governor can call the legislature into special session and set the agenda of items to be considered during that session (called session).
  3. Veto Power—The governor's ability to stop legislation.
- **Chief Judicial Officer**
  The governor fills vacancies that occur in judgeships.
- **Commander-in-Chief**
  The governor is over all the police forces in the state.
- **Chief of State**
  The governor performs ceremonial functions.
- **Chief of Intergovernmental Diplomacy**

This is the governor's role when dealing with the national government and states.

Informal

- **Chief of Party**—The governor is leader of his or her party.
- **Leader of the People**—the people of Texas see the governor as the sole leader of the state.

The Texas governor plays a variety of roles and has many important functions to perform, yet these functions are limited by the following:

1. The state bureaucracy is largely controlled by multimember boards and commissions, resulting in a fragmented state administration.
2. The governor's power to remove appointed officials other than personal staff is still restricted in spite of recent statutory increases in the removal power.
3. The state has both a legislative and an executive budget.
4. Not only do statutes limit what appointments to boards and commissions the governor may take, but also senatorial confirmation of appointees requires a two-thirds vote.
5. There are five other elected executives, an elected state policy board, and an elected regulatory commission.

Even though the above factors have limited gubernatorial power, the Texas governor does have some constitutional and statutory strengths, by having: (1) effective control over regional planning and federal grant applications; (2) a line-item veto over appropriations and a general veto over legislation that because of timing is often absolute; (3) party, personal, and ceremonial leadership opportunities; and (4) the power of the address, whereby the governor requests the legislature to remove a district or appellate judge from office. A two-thirds vote of both Houses is required. The gubernatorial powers have increased substantially with the New Federalism concept of federal funding for state programs and the subsequent prominence of the governor's role in planning and interstate problem solving.

Table 16-1 lists the Texas governors and their terms of office, under the Constitution of 1876.

There are five other elected officials within the executive branch of Texas besides the governor, and they are:

- **Lt. Governor**—The presiding officer of the Senate, who also takes the place of the governor in his or her absence.
- **Attorney General**—The chief law officer and legal counsel of the state of Texas. He or she is responsible for legal matters, both criminal and civil, but primarily civil.
- **Comptroller of Public Accounts**—Responsible for the administration of the state tax system and also for performing pre-audits of state ex-

TABLE 16-1	RICK PERRY 2000–2015 GREG ABBOTT 2015 TO THE PRESENT		
Richard Coke*	1874–1876	Ross S. Sterling	1931–1933
Richard B. Hubbard	1876–1879	Miriam A. Ferguson	1933–1935
Oran M. Roberts	1879–1883	James V. Allred	1935–1939
John Ireland	1883–1887	W. Lee O'Daniel*	1939–1941
Lawrence S. Ross	1887–1891	Coke R. Stevenson	1941–1947
James S. Hogg	1891–1895	Beauford H. Jester*	1947–1949
Charles A. Culberson	1895–1899	Allan Shivers	1949–1957
Joseph D. Sayers	1899–1903	Price Daniel	1957–1963
S.W.T. Lanham	1903–1907	John Connally	1963–1969
Thomas M. Campbell	1907–1911	Preston Smith	1969–1973
Oscar B. Colquitt	1911–1915	Dolph Briscoe	1973–1979
James E. Ferguson†	1915–1917	William (Bill) Clements	1979–1983
William P. Hobby	1917–1921	Mark White	1983–1987
Pat M. Neff	1921–1925	William (Bill) Clements	1987–1991
Miriam A. Ferguson	1925–1927	Ann Richards	1991–1995
Dan Moody	1927–1931	George W. Bush	1995–2000
		Rick Perry	2000-present

*Coke and O'Daniel resigned from the governorship to enter the U.S. Senate. Jester died in office.
†Ferguson was impeached and convicted.
Source: Adapted from the *Texas Almanac and State Industrial Guide,* 1978–1979 (Dallas: A.H. Belo, 1977), 623.

penditures by state agencies; is also the state's banker and the custodian of all public monies and of the securities that the state invests in, or that it holds in trust.

- **Commissioner of the General Land Office**—Guardian of all the public land in Texas. For example, he or she must supervise the leasing of all state-owned land for such purposes as oil and gas production, mineral development, and grazing.
- **Commissioner of Agriculture**—Responsible for both the regulation and promotion of the agribusiness industry in Texas, as well as consumer protection.

Note: *The State Treasurer's office was abolished in 1995.*

Box 16-2 gives a few facts on the governorship of Texas.

CONCLUSION

The Texas governor has the advantage of a four-year term and is paid fairly well; however, the office itself is constitutionally weak due to the plural executive.

BOX 16-2

RICK PERRY 2000-2015 GREG ABBOTT 2015 TO THE PRESENT

The fringe benefits enjoyed by the governor of Texas are:

- Mansion
- Travel and operating budget
- Limousine
- Jet
- Offices
- Professional staff
- Executive assistant

The Republican governors of Texas:

- E.J. Davis (during Reconstruction)
- William (Bill) Clements (1979–1983, 1987–1991)
- George Bush, Jr. (1995–2000)
- Rick Perry (2000 to the present)

Two women have been governors of Texas:

- Miriam A. Ferguson (1925–1927, 1933–1935)
- Ann Richards (1991–1995)

Suggested Readings

Connally, John B. *In History's Shadow: An American Odyssey.* New York: Hyperion, 1993.

Davis, J. William. *There Shall Also Be a Lieutenant Governor.* Austin: Institute of Public Affairs, University of Texas, 1967.

DeBoer, Marvin E., ed. *Destiny by Choice: The Inaugural Addresses of the Governors of Texas.* Fayetteville: University of Arkansas Press, 1992.

Gantt, Fred, Jr. *The Chief Executive in Texas: A Study in Gubernatorial Leadership.* Austin: University of Texas Press, 1964.

Hendrickson, Kenneth E. *Chief Executives of Texas: From Stephen F. Austin to John B. Connally, Jr.* College Station: Texas A&M University Press, 1995.

Morris, Celia. *Storming the Statehouse: Running for Governor with Ann Richards and Dianne Feinstein.* New York: Scribner's Sons, 1992.

Welch, June R. *The Texas Governors.* Dallas: Yellow Rose Press, 1998.

CHAPTER 16
STUDY GUIDE

After reading and studying this chapter, one should be able to do the following:

1. Explain the Bowtie Professor's view concerning the Texas governorship.

_____

_____

_____

2. Explain both the formal and informal qualifications to become Governor of Texas.

_____

_____

3. Name and explain both the formal and informal roles of the Governor of Texas.

_____

_____

4. Explain why the governorship of Texas was extended to a 4-year term.

_____

_____

_____

5. Explain why the governorship of Texas is a weak executive model.

_____

_____

_____

Name _____   **Date** _____

6. Identify where the qualifications and the powers of the governor are spelled out in the Texas Constitution.

_____

_____

_____

7. Identify Box 16-1 concerning "conservatism."

_____

_____

_____

8. Explain those five areas that limit the gubernatorial functions.

_____

_____

_____

_____

_____

9. Identify the Texas governor's four statutory and constitutional strengths.

_____

_____

_____

10. Identify a few Texas governors as outlined in Table 16-1.

_____

_____

_____

Name _____   **Date** _____

11. Identify the five other elected officials within the executive branch of Texas besides the Governor.

_____

_____

_____

_____

_____

12. List the fringe benefits of the Governor of Texas.

_____

_____

_____

13. Identify the two women governors of Texas.

_____

_____

14. List those Republicans who have been governors of Texas since the Reconstruction Era.

_____

_____

_____

TRUE/FALSE MULTIPLE CHOICE SAMPLE TEST

1. The formal representation of the Texas Governor is "Head of State."
   a. True
   b. False

2. Article IV of the Texas Constitution spells out the powers of the governorship of Texas.
   a. True
   b. False

3. The Governor of Texas serves a 2-year term.
   a. True
   b. False

4. Box 16-1 explores the roles of the Texas Governor.
   a. True
   b. False

5. The Governor is installed on the second Tuesday after the organization of the state legislature.
   a. True
   b. False

6. The Governor of Texas is elected by popular vote in a statewide election.
   a. True
   b. False

7. Due to the Texas Constitution of 1876, the Texas Governor is constitutionally weak.
   a. True
   b. False

8. The formal qualifications to become Governor of Texas allow practically any Texan to run for the office.
   a. True
   b. False

9. The Texas governor does *not* have message power.
   a. True
   b. False

10. The Texas governor does *not* have session power.
    a. True
    b. False

11. Governor Beauford Jester died while in office.
   a. True
   b. False

12. Governor James Ferguson was impeached and convicted.
   a. True
   b. False

13. Ann Richards was the first woman governor of Texas.
   a. True
   b. False

14. Miriam Ferguson was the second woman governor of Texas.
   a. True
   b. False

15. The Lt. Governor is the presiding officer of the Texas Senate.
   a. True
   b. False

16. Which of the following is an informal role of the governor?
   a. Chief of State
   b. Chief of Party
   c. Chief Judicial Officer
   d. Chief Legislator
   e. Chief Executive

17. In Texas, there are _____ elected officials within the executive branch besides the governor.
   a. 2
   b. 3
   c. 4
   d. 5
   e. 6

18. Box 16-1 deals with the:
   a. Governorship
   b. Lt. Governor
   c. Issue of conservatism
   d. State bureaucracy
   e. Fourth Article

19. Which of the following is an informal role of the governor?
   a. Commander-in-Chief
   b. Chief Executive
   c. Chief of Intergovernmental Diplomacy
   d. Leader of the People
   e. Chief Judicial Officer

20. Article _____ of the Texas Constitution spells out the powers of the governorship.
   a. I
   b. III
   c. II
   d. V
   e. IV

21. The governor of Texas serves a _____ -year term.
   a. 2
   b. 3
   c. 4
   d. 5
   e. 6

22. The "Reconstruction Governor" of Texas was:
   a. E.J. Davis
   b. Miriam Ferguson
   c. Rick Perry
   d. Ann Richards
   e. William Clements

23. The state Treasurer's office was abolished in:
    a. 2006
    b. 2005
    c. 2001
    d. 1999
    e. 1995

24. The governorship is under the Texas Constitution of:
    a. 1827
    b. 1836
    c. 1845
    d. 1869
    e. 1876

25. In Texas, there are _____ elected officials within the executive branch besides the governor.
    a. 2
    b. 3
    c. 4
    d. 5
    e. 6

26. The state bureaucracy is largely controlled by _____ boards and commissions, resulting in a fragmented state administration.
    a. personal and ceremonial
    b. gubernatorial
    c. legislative
    d. senatorial
    e. multimember

27. The Texas governor does have some constitutional and _____ strengths.
    a. political
    b. ceremonial
    c. economic
    d. statutory
    e. bureaucratic

28. The gubernatorial powers have increased due to the _____.

    a. Creative Federalism

    b. Cooperative Federalism

    c. New Federalism

    d. Revenue Sharing

    e. Program Federalism

29. Charles A. Culberson was governor of Texas during _____.

    a. 1874–1876

    b. 1895–1889

    c. 1917–1921

    d. 1927–1931

    e. 1931–1933

30. Thomas M. Campbell was the governor of Texas during _____.

    a. 1907–1911

    b. 1947–1949

    c. 1883–1887

    d. 1887–1891

    e. 1889–1903

The U.S. Supreme Court: The Interpreters

The United States Supreme Court
is the highest judiciary in the land.
Through judicial review,
they attempt to bring justice to every man.

To many, some of the Court's landmark decisions
have made America more of a Democracy,
While to others these same court decisions
were full of political hypocrisy.

Yet the Supreme Court continues to make rulings,
which are politically bold.
These landmark cases do affect
America's society as a whole.

—The Bowtie Professor

Name _____ **Date** _____

Explain:

_____

_____

_____

_____

_____

_____

_____

_____

_____

_____

_____

_____

_____

_____

_____

_____

_____

_____

_____

_____

While only the U.S. Supreme Court is named specifically in the Constitution, Article III gives congress the authority to establish and abolish lower federal courts. Congress has established district courts, courts of appeals and specialized courts that hear certain types of cases. Article III section 1 also limits the jurisdiction of the federal courts to cases involving:

- A federal question—which is a question based, at least in part, on the U.S. Constitution, a treaty, or federal law; and
- Diversity of Citizenship—which arises when a lawsuit is between parties of different states or involved in a foreign citizen or government.

The lowest level of the federal court system is the district courts. The are ninety-four courts at this level and each state has at least one, and some of the more populous states, such as California, New York, and Texas, have as many as four district courts. Let it be known, however, that the number of judicial districts can vary over time, primarily owing to population changes and corresponding case loads.

The Courts of Appeals were created by congress in 1891 to help take the caseload off the U.S. Supreme Court. There are thirteen of these courts distributed throughout the U.S. These Courts are also referred to as U.S. Circuit Courts of Appeals. Finally, the United States Supreme Court is the highest judiciary in the land. It is composed of a chief justice and eight associate justices. When the Supreme Court came into existence in 1789, it had five justices. In the following years more justices were added, and since 1837 there have been nine justices on the Court. The president nominates all federal judges, but they must be confirmed by the U.S. Senate. Once the federal judges are confirmed by the senate, they can serve for life. Table 17-1 shows which type of cases can be heard by each federal court as well as the nine justices on the U.S. Supreme Court.

Several other federal courts have been created by Congress to hear certain types of cases such as the **Court of Claims,** the **Court of Customs and Patent Appeals and Trademarks,** the **United States Tax Court, Territorial District Courts,** the **Court of the District of Colombia,** and the **U.S. Court of Military Appeals.** The Court of Claims was created by Congress in 1855 to hear cases in which individuals who have complaints and claims against the federal government could sue. In 1909 the Court of Customs and Patent Appeals was created to review disputes over tariffs, patents, and trademarks. The United States Tax Court was created in 1969 to act as a court of appeals in all federal tax cases, and the Territorial District Courts govern the territories of the United States such as Guam, the Virgin Islands, and Puerto Rico. The Courts of the District of Columbia were created by Congress to serve as the court system for the nation's capital. Finally the U.S. Court of Military Appeals was created to serve as the final appellate court in court-marital cases. Below are key terms, which are used in our judicial system of government:

- **Appeal**—in general, a request that a higher court review a case decided at a lower level. In the Supreme Court certain cases are designated

---

TABLE 17-1

I. **The three levels of federal courts are:**
   A. Supreme Court—nine Justices
      1. **Appellate Jurisdiction** (one court)
         a. Lower federal courts
         b. Highest state courts
      2. **Original Jurisdiction**
         a. Two or more states
         b. The U.S. and a state
         c. Foreign ambassadors and other diplomats
   B. U.S. Courts of Appeals—13 circuit courts and over 100 circuit judges
      1. Hear appeals from lower courts
      2. Have no original jurisdiction
   C. Federal District Courts—94 courts and about 600 or more judges
      1. **Original Jurisdiction**
         a. Cases involving federal crimes
         b. Civil suits under federal law

II. **The nine U.S. Supreme Court Justices are:**
   A. John G. Roberts, Jr.
   B. Antonin Scalia
   C. Anthony M. Kennedy
   D. Clarence Thomas
   E. Ruth Bader Ginsburg
   F. Steven G. Breyer
   G. Samuel Anthony Alito, Jr.
   H. Sonia Sotomayor
   I. Elena Kagan

---

as appeals under federal law, and therefore must be heard by the court.

- **Appellate Jurisdiction**—refers to a particular court's power to review a decision or action of a lower court.
- **Concurring Opinion**—an opinion by a member of the court that agrees with the result reached by the court in the case but disagrees with or departs from the court's rationale for the decision.
- **Constitutional Law**—statements interpreting the U.S. Constitution that have been given Supreme Court approval.
- **Defendant**—the party against whom a criminal or civil suit is brought.
- **Dissenting Opinion**—an opinion by a member of a court that disagrees with the result reached by the court in the case.
- **Judicial Activism**—the making of new law through judicial interpretations of the Constitution.
- **Judicial Review**—the power of the courts, especially the Supreme Court, to declare laws of Congress and the states and actions of presidents unconstitutional and invalid.

- **Judicial Self-Restraint**—self-imposed limitation on judicial power by judges deferring to the policy judgments of elected branches of government.
- **Jurisdiction**—the power of a court to hear a case in question.
- **Litmus Test**—in political terms, a person's stand on a key issue that determines whether that individual will be appointed to public office or supported in electoral campaigns.
- **Majority Opinion**—an opinion in a case that is subscribed to by a majority of the judges who participated in the decision.
- **Original Intent**—a judicial philosophy under which judges attempt to apply the values of the founders to current issues.
- **Original Jurisdiction**—refers to a particular court's power to serve as the place where a given case is initially argued and decided.
- **Plaintiff**—a party initiating a suit and claiming damages.
- **Rule of Four**—when four justices decide to hear a case, that case will be heard.
- **Stare Decisis**—the judicial precept that the issue has already been decided in earlier cases and that the earlier decision need only be applied in the specific case before the bench. The rule comes from the Latin for "the decision stands."
- **Statutory Laws**—laws made by acts of Congress or the state legislatures, as opposed to constitutional laws.
- **Writ of Certiorari**—a writ issued by the Supreme Court, at its discretion, to order a lower court to prepare the record of a case and send it to the Supreme Court for review. Most cases come to the Supreme Court this way.
- **Writ of Habeas Corpus**—a court order directing a public official who is holding someone in detention to bring the prisoner into court and explain the reasons for holding the person in confinement.
- **Writ of Mandamus**—a court order requiring a public official to carry out his/her duties.

Throughout its history the U.S. Supreme Court has issued key decisions which have affected or greatly changed the course of American political history and society. By far, the Supreme Court is at the apex of our judicial system, and its decisions are closely monitored by political scientists, lawyers, judges, bureaucrats, executives, and legislators, as well as by the media. The American Citizenry learns the latest opinions of the Court from newspapers, television, and other forums of the mass media.

The Supreme Court hears three types of cases (see Table 17.1). First are those cases which have original jurisdiction or those which immediately go to the Court, involving the representative of another nation or a state as one of the parties. Secondly, are those cases which are appeals from lower federal courts, and thirdly, those cases which are appeals from the highest appeals courts within the states.

The Supreme Court begins its annual term on the first Monday in October and usually adjourns in late June or early July of the next year. A

special session may be held, but this is rarely the case. The court's decision to review a case is influenced by many factors including the significance of the parties and issues involved and whether the solicitor general is pressing the Court to take the case. Below are the seven major efforts of the U.S. Supreme Court in America's political history:

1. Define the life-or-death issue of capital punishment.
2. Define the rights of criminal defendants, prevent unlawful services, limit the questioning of suspects, and prevent physical or mental intimidation of subjects.
3. Ensure equality of representation, and require legislative districts to be equal in population.
4. Define the limits of free speech and free press, and decide about obscenity, censorship and pornography.
5. Determine the personal liberties of women and decide about abortion.
6. Ensure separation of church and state, and decide about prayer in public schools.
7. Eliminate racial segregation and decide about affirmative action.

Box 17-1 gives an overview of the Supreme Court throughout U.S. history and politics.

The Judiciary act of 1789 established the basic federal court system we have today, but it was the Marshall Court (1801-1835) which gave the Supreme Court its most powerful weapon, **Judicial Review,** the ability of the court to declare acts of both Congress and the president unconstitutional. There are not any major formal qualifications to be a Supreme Court Justice; however, Article III does emphasize a high sense of morality and integrity. Supreme Court Justices have been and still are:

BOX 17-1

a. **Marshall Court (1801-1835)**
  Marbury v. Madison (1803)
    judicial review
    Federal Judiciary Act (1789) unconstitutional
  McCulloch v. Maryland (1819)
    implied powers
    necessary and proper clause
    supremacy clause, Article VI
  Gibbons v. Ogden (1824)
    interstate commerce
b. **Taney Court (1836-1864)**
  Dred Scott v. Sanford (1857)
c. **Enlargement of Judicial Power (1865-1890)**
  1. power for the states
  2. the 10th amendment
  3. Slaughter House cases of 1873
  4. privileges or immunities clause
d. **Judicial Self-Confidence Court (1890-1937)**
  1. Plessy case (1896)
  2. anti-communist court
  3. court threatened by FDR
e. **New Deal Court (1937-1953)**
  1. New Deal interpretations
  2. beginning of protection of civil rights
  3. *Sweatt v. Painter* (1950)
f. **Warren Court (1953-1969)**
  1. Browns cases
  2. voting rights protected
  3. *Cooper v. Aaron* (1957)
  4. strong civil right action
g. **Burger Court (1969-1986)**
  1. *Roe v. Wade* (1973)
  2. Bakke case (1978)
h. **Rehnquist Court (1986-2006)**
  1. *Webster v. Reproductive Health Service* (1989)
  2. *Planned Parenthood of Pennsylvania v. Casey* (1992)
i. **John G. Roberts, Jr. (2006-present)**

1. Highly educated
2. Wealthy
3. Lawyers
4. Have held other political positions before being appointed to the Court
5. Married

TABLE 17-2

1. **The anatomy of a court case is as follows:**
   - Facts
   - Amendments, laws, statutes, and acts
   - Individuals involved in the case
   - Ruling in the case
   - Significance of the case
   - Civil liberties, civil rights, constitutional question
2. **Terms**
   - **Adversarial System**—the method of decision making in which an impartial judge or jury or decision-maker hears arguments and reviews evidence presented by opposite sides.
   - **Amicus Curiae**—a friend of the court. A person, private group or institution, or government agency that is not a party to the case but that participates in the case (usually through submission of a brief) at the invitation of the court or on its own initiative.
   - **Brief**—a document submitted by an attorney to a court, setting out the facts of the case and the legal arguments in support of the party represented by the attorney.
   - **Civil case**—a noncriminal court case proceeding in which a plaintiff sues a defendant for damages in payment for harm inflicted.
   - **Circuit Courts**—the 12 appellate courts that make up the middle level of the federal court system.
   - **Class Action Suits**—cases brought into court by individuals on the behalf of not only themselves, but of all other persons "similarly situated".
   - **Contingency Fee**—an agreement in which the attorney agrees to represent the plaintiff in a civil suit and receive in compensation an agreed set amount of funds if any were to be awarded.
   - **Grand Jury**—a jury called to hear evidence and decide whether a defendant should be indicted and tried.
   - **Petit (regular) Jury**—a jury called to determine guilt or innocence.
   - **Plea Bargaining**—the process in which defendants agree to a lesser charge and usually get a shorter sentence in return for giving up their rights to a full trial.
   - **Sovereign Immunity**—the legal doctrine that individuals can sue the government only with the consent of the government.
   - **Standing**—a requirement that a party who files a lawsuit have a legal stake in the outcome.

The above are informal qualifications to become a member of the U.S. Supreme Court.

Several legal and extra-legal factors affect how the court arrives at a decision, which include judicial philosophy, the original intent of the framers, and precedent. Extra-legal factors include public opinion and the behavior characteristics and ideology of the nine justices. Table 17-2 gives the anatomy of a court case as well as other key terms used in our judicial system of government.

The American legal system consists of the police, courts, and prisons. The law must give meaning through the American system of courts and

BOX 17-2

1. *United States v. Nixon* (1974): There is no constitutional absolute executive privilege that would allow a president to refuse to comply with a court order to produce information needed in a criminal trial.
2. *Roe v. Wade* (1973): The Supreme Court found that a woman's right to an abortion was protected by the right to privacy that could be implied from specific guarantees found in the Bill of Rights and the Fourteenth Amendment.
3. *Plessy v. Ferguson* (1896): Plessy challenged a Louisiana statute requiring that railroads provide separate accommodations for blacks and whites. The court found that separate but equal accommodations did not violate the equal protection clause of the Fourteenth Amendment.
4. *New York Times Co. v. Sullivan* (1964): Supreme Court decision ruling that simply publishing a defamatory falsehood is not enough to justify a libel judgment. "Actual malice" must be proved to support a finding of libel against a public figure.
5. *Miranda v. Arizona* (1966): The Fifth Amendment requires that individuals arrested for a crime must be advised of their right to remain silent and to have counsel present.
6. *McCulloch v. Maryland* (1819): Supreme Court upheld the power of the national government and denied the right of a state to tax the bank. The court's broad interpretation of the necessary and proper clause paved the way for later rulings upholding expansive federal powers.
7. *Marbury v. Madison* (1803): Supreme Court case in which the court first asserted the power of judicial review in finding that a congressional statute extending the Court's original jurisdiction was unconstitutional.
8. *Immigration and Naturalization Service v. Chadha* (1983): Legislative veto ruled unconstitutional by the Supreme Court.
9. *Gibbons v. Ogden* (1824): The court upheld broad congressional power over interstate commerce.
10. *Civil Rights Cases* (1875): Name attached to five cases brought under the Civil Rights Act of 1875. In 1883 the Supreme Court decided that discrimination in a variety of public accommodations, including theatres, hotels, and railroads, could not be prohibited by the act because it was private and not state discrimination.
11. *Brown v. Board of Education* (1954): U.S. Supreme Court decision holding that school segregation is inherently unconstitutional because it violates the Fourteenth Amendment's guarantee of equal protection; marked the end of legal segregation in the United States.

the judges who preside over those courts at every level of government. The American citizenry expect the U.S. Supreme Court as well as lower courts to provide fair hearings with all parties to the dispute, giving the chance to speak or not to speak, to call witnesses, and to have the evidence considered in an atmosphere of justice. The United States Supreme Court is the highest judiciary in the land and once the court makes its rulings, there is no other to which one can appeal.

Box 17-2 gives a few landmark Supreme Court cases.

■ CONCLUSION

Great power is lodged in the Supreme Court of the U.S. and the federal judiciary. A continuing concern of major importance is the reconciliation of the role of judges, independent and fair dispensers of justice for the parties before them with their vital role as the interpreters of the Constitution.

Suggested Readings

Abraham, Henry. "A Bench Happily Filled," *Judicature.* 66 (February 1983): 284.

Baum, Lawrence. *The Supreme Court.* 6th ed., Washington, D.C.: CQ Press, 1996.

Biskupic, Joan, and Elder Witt. *The Supreme Court and Individual Rights.* Washington, D.C.: CQ Press, 1996.

Epstien Lee, et al. *The Supreme Court Compendium: Data, Decisions, and Developments,* 2nd ed., Washington, D.C.: CQ Press, 1996.

O'Brien, David M. *Storm Center: The Supreme Court in American Politics.* 5th ed., New York: Norton, 1999.

Provine, Doris M. *Case Selection in the United States Supreme Court.* Chicago: University of Chicago Press, 1980.

Sunstien, Cass R. *One Case at a Time: Judicial Minimalism on the Supreme Court,* Cambridge: Harvard University Press, 1999.

CHAPTER 17
STUDY GUIDE

After reading and reviewing this chapter, one should be able to do the following:

1. Identify the Bowtie Professor's views concerning the U.S. Supreme Court.

_____

_____

_____

2. Identify the Supreme Court's role in the U.S. Constitution.

_____

_____

_____

3. List the other federal courts that have been created by the U.S. Congress.

_____

_____

_____

4. Explain the seven major efforts of the U.S. Supreme Court in America's political history.

_____

_____

_____

_____

5. Explain the formal qualifications of federal judges.

_____

_____

_____

6. Explain the informal qualifications of federal judges.

_____

_____

_____

7. Trace the history of the U.S. Supreme Court in America's society as outlined in Box 17-1.

_____

_____

_____

8. Identify the following terms:
   a. Judicial review

_____

   b. Statutory laws

_____

   c. Constitutional law

_____

   d. Litmus test

_____

e. Jurisdiction

_____

f. Rule of Four

_____

g. Plaintiff

_____

h. *Stare decisis*

_____

i. *Writ of certiorari*

_____

j. *Writ of habeas corpus*

_____

k. *Writ of mandamas*

_____

9. Identify some of the current U.S. Supreme Court justices.

_____

_____

_____

10. Explain the three major levels of federal courts as outlined in Table 17-1.

_____

_____

_____

Name _____   **Date** _____

11. Identify a few landmark U.S. Supreme Court cases.

_____

_____

_____

12. Explain the anatomy of a U.S. court case.

_____

_____

_____

13. Explain when the U.S. Supreme Court begins and ends its annual term.

_____

_____

_____

14. Identify the following:
   a. Adversarial system

_____

   b. *Amicus curiae*

_____

   c. Original jurisdiction

_____

   d. Original intent

_____

e. Majority opinion

_____

f. Jurisdiction

_____

g. Judicial activism

_____

h. Judicial self-restraint

_____

i. Defendant

_____

j. Concurring opinion

_____

k. Brief

_____

l. Grand jury

_____

m. Petit jury

_____

n. Plea bargaining

_____

o. Contingency fee

_____

p. Sovereign immunity

_____

q. Standing

_____

TRUE/FALSE MULTIPLE CHOICE SAMPLE TEST

1. There are 10 Justices on the U.S. Supreme Court.
   a. True
   b. False

2. By far, the U.S. Supreme Court is at the apex of the nation's judicial system.
   a. True
   b. False

3. The Dred Scott decision was decided by the Taney Court.
   a. True
   b. False

4. The U.S. Supreme Court begins its annual term on the first Tuesday in October.
   a. True
   b. False

5. The Judiciary Act of 1789 established only the U.S. Supreme Court.
   a. True
   b. False

6. The U.S. Supreme Court is named specifically in the U.S. Constitution.
   a. True
   b. False

7. Article III gives U.S. Congress the authority to establish and abolish lower federal courts.
   a. True
   b. False

8. The U.S. Supreme Court came into existence in 1789 with seven justices.
   a. True
   b. False

9. The lowest level of the federal system is the district courts.
   a. True
   b. False

10. U.S. Supreme Court justices are usually highly educated.
    a. True
    b. False

11. The American legal system consists of the police, courts, and prisons.
    a. True
    b. False

12. Article III spells out the powers of the federal court system.
    a. True
    b. False

13. The U.S. Supreme Court is *not* the highest judiciary in the land.
    a. True
    b. False

14. *Plessy v. Ferguson* (1896) established integration.
    a. True
    b. False

15. *Gibbons v. Ogden* (1824) struck down the "Separate but Equal Doctrine."
    a. True
    b. False

16. The circuit courts are made up of _____ appellate courts.
  a. 6
  b. 8
  c. 9
  d. 12
  e. 14

17. Article _____ spells out the powers of the federal courts.
  a. I
  b. II
  c. III
  d. IV
  e. V

18. The *Marbury v. Madison* decision took place in:
  a. 1803
  b. 1829
  c. 1840
  d. 1855
  e. 1865

19. The U.S. Supreme Court begins its annual term in the month of:
  a. August
  b. July
  c. September
  d. January
  e. October

20. The U.S. Supreme Court came into existence in:
  a. 1619
  b. 1820
  c. 1729
  d. 1800
  e. 1789

21. In 1891, the U.S. _____ was created.
    a. Court of Claims
    b. Court of Appeals
    c. Court of Customs
    d. Tax Court
    e. District Court

22. The United States Tax Court was created in:
    a. 1905
    b. 1969
    c. 1951
    d. 1936
    e. 1889

23. The U.S. Supreme Court started out with _____ justices.
    a. 5
    b. 6
    c. 7
    d. 8
    e. 9

24. The U.S. Supreme Court hears _____ types of cases.
    a. 2
    b. 3
    c. 4
    d. 5
    e. 6

25. The power of the courts to hear a case in question is known as:
    a. Jurisdiction
    b. Judicial review
    c. Judicial activism
    d. Judicial self-restraint
    e. Original jurisdiction

26. The _____ Courts govern the territories of the United States such as Guam.
  a. Territorial Districts
  b. United States Customs
  c. Tax
  d. Appeals
  e. Trademarks

27. The _____ were created by Congress to serve as the court system for the nation's capital.
  a. Courts of Claims
  b. Courts of the District of Columbia
  c. Federal District Courts
  d. Courts of Appeals Courts
  e. Appellate Courts

28. A person's stand on key issues will determines whether or not he or she will be elected is known as:
  a. Stare Decisis
  b. Judicial Review
  c. the Litmus Test
  d. the Plaintiff
  e. Original Intent

29. One major effort of the U.S. Supreme Court, is to eliminate racial segregation and decide about _____.
  a. Judicial Review
  b. Constitutional Law
  c. Statutory Law
  d. Affirmative action
  e. Stare Decisis

30. Which concept below means "the decision stands"?
  a. Writ of Habeas Corpus
  b. Writ of Certiorari
  c. Writ of Mandamus
  d. Judicial Activism
  e. Stare Decisis

The Texas Court System: Justice

Chapter 18

Texans know that abiding by the law is something of a must,
because justice in Texas means "just us."

There is something many Texans also know, and that is
"system maintenance" is in the interest of the status quo.

For a person who does not have any money
and cannot afford bail, I am here to let you know
my friend you are going to spend
a lot of time in jail.

For outsiders who come to the state,
you must be serious and do not play.
"Don't mess with Texas," we will lock
the prison doors and throw the keys away.

Texas is a state that does not go for a lot of tricks and games,
such as cursing out peace officers and calling them ugly names.

Don't mess with Texas means more than throwing trash on the ground,
because if you mess up, you will certainly be taken downtown.

—The Bowtie Professor

Name _____ **Date** _____

Explain:

_____

_____

_____

_____

_____

_____

_____

_____

_____

_____

_____

_____

_____

_____

_____

_____

_____

_____

_____

_____

A rticle V of the Texas Constitution spells out the powers of the judicial system, which has four distinctive features:

1. It created six types of courts and two supreme courts.
2. Different trial court levels are given concurrent jurisdiction.
3. Judges are elected and not appointed.
4. The article is overly specific and includes such features as the requirement that each county have an elected sheriff.

Texas has a **Bifurcated Court System** which is very unique within itself. The bifurcated court system in the state allows the existence of two state supreme courts at the highest level of the state judiciary. This bifurcated court system consists of the **Texas Supreme Court,** which is a nine-member court with final appellate jurisdiction over civil lawsuits, and the **Texas Court of Criminal Appeals,** which is a nine-member court with final appellate jurisdiction over criminal cases. The Texas Supreme Court will hear a case under the following conditions:

1. When there has been a disagreement among members of a court of appeals on a material question of law.
2. When a court of appeals renders a decision that conflicts with a decision of the Supreme Court or of another court of appeals.
3. When an act of the legislature has been held unconstitutional.
4. When the state revenues are involved.
5. When the Railroad Commission is a party.
6. When it appears that an error of substantive law affecting the judgment has been made by a court of appeals, except when the legislature has conferred final jurisdiction on those courts.

The Court of Criminal Appeals hears cases from the Court of Appeals or those that fall in line with **Original Jurisdiction,** the authority of a court to try or resolve a civil lawsuit or a criminal prosecution being heard for the first time. Below are examples of other courts of the judicial system in Texas, as well as a few terminologies:

1. **Appellate Jurisdiction**—The authority of a court to review the decisions of lower courts to determine if the law was correctly interpreted and legal procedures were correctly followed.
2. **Civil Lawsuit**—A noncriminal legal dispute between two or more individuals, businesses, governments, or other entities.
3. **Concurrent Jurisdiction**—Two or more different types of courts have authority to hear the same type of case.
4. **Constitutional County Court**—A court created by the state constitution, which is presided over by the county judge.
5. **Court of Appeals**—An intermediate-level court that reviews civil and criminal cases from the district courts.
6. **District Court**—The primary trial court in Texas. It has jurisdiction over criminal felony cases and civil disputes.

7. **Judiciary**—A collective term referring to the system of courts, its judges, and other personnel.
8. **Justice of the Peace Court**—A low-ranking court with jurisdiction over minor civil cases.
9. **Municipal Court**—A court of limited jurisdiction that hears cases involving city ordinances and primarily handles traffic tickets.
10. **Penal Code**—A body of law that defines most criminal offenses and sets a range of punishments that can be addressed.
11. **Statutory Court**—A court which exercises limited jurisdiction over criminal and civil cases. The jurisdiction of these courts varies from county to county.
12. **System Maintenance**—Perpetuating the status quo of the political system in general and of the courts, in particular, rather than carrying out its stated function of dispensing equal justice for all.

The major purposes of the Texas judicial system are to interpret and apply state law to resolve conflicts. To resolve conflicts by interpreting and applying the law is fundamentally political within itself because this is what politics is all about. The Texas courts then are political bodies and, just as the legislative and executive branches, are involved in conflicts, engage in compromise, allocate values, and determine who gets what, when, and how. What makes the judiciary different from the legislative and executive are the procedures the courts use in policy-making. Courts are passive and must wait for problems to come to them. Although the courts make great attempts to appear nonpolitical, objective, and neutral, they still are involved in the settlement of such major political questions as: how public schools should be organized and financed; whether abortions will be allowed; should same-sex marriages be permitted; and the list could go on. The Texas court system, of course, settles such questions as whether a certain individual should be found guilty of a particular crime, and whether one person's actions have damaged the interests of another.

Table 18-1 is the Texas system of graded penalties and the qualifications for judges in the state.

One can see after observing Table 18-1 that the grading penalties in Texas can range from execution to a simple Class "C" misdemeanor. In the Texas justice system there are six crimes that could lead to capital punishment and they are as follows:

1. Murdering two or more persons (serial murders) during the same criminal transaction or during different transactions pursuant to the same scheme or course of action.

TABLE 18-1

The Texas system of graded penalties is as follows:

Offense	Maximum Punishment	Examples
Capital felony	Execution	Capital murder
First-degree felony	5-99 years or life; $10,000 fine	Aggravated sexual assault; theft of property valued at $200,000 or more
Second-degree felony	2-20 years; $10,000 fine	Tampering with a consumer product; theft of property valued at $100,000 or more but less than $200,000
Third-degree felony	2-10 years; $10,000 fine	Drive-by shooting without injury; theft of property valued at $20,000 or more but less than $100,000
State jail felony	180 days to 2 years; $10,000 fine	Credit card or debit card abuse; theft of property valued at $1,500 or more but less than $20,000
Class A misdemeanor	1 year; $4,000 fine	Burglary of a vehicle; abuse of a corpse; theft of property valued at $500 or more but less than $1,500
Class B misdemeanor	180 days; $2,000 fine	Silent or abusive calls to a 911 service; prostitution; theft of property valued at more than $20 but less than $500
Class C misdemeanor	$500 fine	Assault without bodily injury; attending a dog fight; theft of property valued at less than $20

The qualifications for judges in Texas are as follows:

Court	Term of Office	Salary, 1998	Qualifications
Municipal courts	2 or 4 years, varies by city	Set by city, highly variable	Determined by the city
Justice of the Peace courts	4 years	Set by county, highly variable	None
Constitutional county courts	4 years	Set by county, highly variable	Must be "well informed in the law"
County courts at law	4 years	Set by county, highly variable	25 years of age, county resident for two years, served as judge or practiced law four years
District courts	4 years	$101,700, may be supplemented by the county	Citizen, district resident for two years, licensed attorney in Texas, practicing lawyer or judge for four years
Courts of appeal	6 years	Chief Justice: $107,850 Justices: $107,350, may be supplemented by counties in the district	Citizen, 35 years of age, practicing attorney or judge of a court of record for ten years
Texas Court of Criminal Appeals	6 years	Presiding judge: $115,000 Judges: $113,000	Same as courts of appeal
Texas Supreme Court	6 years	Chief Justice: $115,000 Associate Justices: $113,000	Same as courts of appeal

2. While incarcerated in a penal institution, murdering another who is employed in the operation of the penal institution.
3. Committing a murder while escaping or attempting to escape from a penal institution.
4. Committing a murder for pay or the promise of pay or employing another to commit a murder for pay or promise of pay.
5. Murdering someone in the course of committing or attempting to commit kidnapping, burglary, robbery, aggravated sexual assault, or arson.
6. Murdering a peace officer or fire fighter who is acting in the lawful discharge of an official duty and who the person knows is a peace officer or fire fighter.

Victims in Texas also have rights. Just as the criminals or the accused have due process of the law, victims within the state are given certain due processes as well. Victims have the following rights:

1. To be treated with fairness and respect for the victim's dignity and privacy.
2. To be reasonably protected from the accused.
3. To be notified of court proceedings.
4. To receive restitution.
5. To receive information concerning conviction, sentencing, imprisonment, and release of the accused criminal.
6. To confer with a representative of the prosecutor's office.
7. To be present at all public court proceedings, unless a judge decides that testimony by the victim might be materially affected.

Box 18-1 gives a few facts concerning jurors and jury duty, and also includes other terminologies used in the Texas judicial system.

There are five methods how judges are chosen by state governments and they are:

1. **Partisan Elections**—Judges are chosen in elections in which political parties participate freely.
2. **Election by Legislators**—The state legislature chooses the judges, although the governor often influences the choice.
3. **Appointment by the Governor**—The governor appoints judges sometimes with the consent of the legislature.
4. **Merit Plan**—The governor makes appointments from a list submitted by a nominating committee.
5. **Nonpartisan Election**—Judges are chosen in elections from which political parties are formally excluded.

Quite naturally, "#1" is the method used in Texas. Judges are chosen in elections in which political parties freely participate. A better method would be judges being nominated by the governor and confirmed by the Texas Senate for one seven-

---

BOX 18-1

The qualifications to be a juror are:

1. Citizen of the U.S. and the state of Texas.
2. 18 years of age or older.
3. Of a sound mind.
4. Able to read and write.
5. Not convicted of a felony or under indictment for a felony.

Persons who are exempted from jury duty are:

1. Those who are 65 years old or older.
2. Those who have legal custody of a child or children under age ten.
3. Those who are enrolled as full-time college or secondary school students.

Terms:

- **Capital Murder**—Murder committed under certain circumstances for which the death penalty or life in prison must be imposed.
- **De Nova**—In a civil lawsuit or criminal trial, evidence that is presented again before an appellate court because no record was kept of the evidence presented to the trial court.
- **Felony**—A serious criminal offense that can be punished by imprisonment or a fine.
- **Misdemeanor**—A minor criminal offense punishable by a fine or a short sentence in the county jail.
- **Ordinances**—Local laws enacted by a city council.
- **Parole**—The early release of an inmate from prison, subject to certain conditions.
- **Probation**—A procedure under which a convicted criminal is not sent to prison if he promises to behave himself and meet certain conditions, such as restrictions on where he travels and with whom he associates.
- **Tort Reform**—Changes in state law to put limits on personal injury lawsuits and damage judgments entered by the courts.
- **Veniremen**—Members of a panel from a petit or trial jury is chosen.
- **Writ of Error**—A primary means by which cases reach the Texas Supreme Court.

---

year term, and they should not be allowed to run again until they set out seven years. This way, Texans would not have the same individuals winning over and over again. Term limitations are needed for every aspect of government.

CONCLUSION

The Texas judiciary is a model of democratic accountability. Yet because judges run in partisan elections, how effective are they when allocating justice among the Texas citizenry? The dependence on political contributions from special interests may cloud the decision making of the Texas judiciary. As a result, justice in Texas may mean "Just Us."

Suggested Readings

Hill, John. "Taking Texas Judges out of Politics: An Argument for Merit Election." *Baylor Law Review.* 40 (Summer 1988): 340-66.

Parrish, James R. *A Two-Headed Monster: Crimes and Texas Prisons.* Austin: Eakin, 1989.

Reamy, Gerald S. *Criminal Offenses and Defenses in Texas.* Norcross, Georgia: Harrison, 1987.

Sharp, John. *Texas Crime, Texas Justice.* Austin: Comptroller of Public Accounts, 1992.

Texas Judicial Council. *Office of Court Administration: Texas Judicial System, 69th Annual Report.* Austin: Texas Judicial Council, 1997.

Texas Research League. *The Texas Judiciary: A Structural-Functional Overview.* Report 1. Austin: Texas Research League, 1990.

Texas Research League. *Texas Courts: A Proposal for Structural-Functional Reform.* Report 2. Austin: Texas Research League, 1991.

CHAPTER 18
STUDY GUIDE

After reading and studying this chapter, one should be able to do the following:

1. Identify the concepts below:
   a. System maintenance

   _____

   b. Municipal court

   _____

   c. Justice of the peace court

   _____

   d. Court of appeals

   _____

   e. Constitutional county court

   _____

   f. Civil lawsuit

   _____

   g. Original jurisdiction

   _____

   h. Statutory court

   _____

   i. Penal code

   _____

j. Judiciary

_____

k. District court

_____

l. Concurrent jurisdiction

_____

m. Appellate jurisdiction

_____

n. Bifurcated court system

_____

2. Explain the four distinctive features of the Texas court system.

_____

_____

_____

_____

3. Identify where the powers of the Texas judicial system are spelled out in the Texas Constitution.

_____

_____

_____

4. List the six reasons the Texas Supreme Court will hear a case.

_____

_____

_____

_____

_____

_____

5. List the six crimes that would lead to capital punishment in the Texas judicial system.

_____

_____

_____

_____

_____

_____

6. List the seven rights of victims in the Texas criminal justice system.

_____

_____

_____

_____

_____

_____

_____

7. Explain the five methods by which judges are chosen by Texas state government.

_____

_____

_____

_____

_____

8. List the five qualifications to become a juror in Texas.

_____

_____

_____

_____

_____

9. List those persons who are exempted from jury duty in Texas.

10. Identify the following:

   a. Ordinances

_____

   b. Parole

_____

   c. Probation

_____

   d. Tort reforms

_____

   e. Veniremen

_____

   f. Write of error

_____

   g. Misdemeanor

_____

h. Felony

_____

i. _De nova_

_____

j. Capital murder

_____

11. Explain the major purposes of the Texas judicial system.

_____

_____

_____

12. Identify the qualifications and terms of office for judges in Texas as outlined in Table 18-1.

_____

_____

_____

13. Explain the bifurcated system in the Texas judicial system.

_____

_____

_____

14. Explain the Bowtie Professor's views concerning the Texas court system.

_____

_____

_____

TRUE/FALSE MULTIPLE CHOICE SAMPLE TEST

1. Texas has a bifurcated court system.
   a. True
   b. False

2. Article IV of XX spells out the powers of the Texas court system.
   a. True
   b. False

3. There are six factors that inspire the Texas Supreme Court to hear a case.
   a. True
   b. False

4. Texas has five types of courts and one Supreme Court.
   a. True
   b. False

5. According to Yecats, justice in Texas includes everyone.
   a. True
   b. False

6. "System maintenance" is in the interest of the status quo.
   a. True
   b. False

7. There are five distinctive features of the Texas judicial system.
   a. True
   b. False

8. The Texas Court of Criminal Appeals is a nine-member court.
   a. True
   b. False

9. The Texas Supreme Court is a nine-member court.
   a. True
   b. False

10. Each county in Texas does *not* have to have an elected sheriff.
   a. True
   b. False

11. Judges in Texas are appointed and *not* elected.
   a. True
   b. False

12. There are six crimes that could lead to capital punishment in Texas.
   a. True
   b. False

13. The major purposes of the Texas judicial system are to interpret and apply state law to resolve conflicts.
   a. True
   b. False

14. Table 18-1 is the Texas statutory system.
   a. True
   b. False

15. There are five methods of selecting judges in state governments.
   a. True
   b. False

16. There are _____ major exemptions from jury duty.
   a. 3
   b. 2
   c. 5
   d. 4
   e. 6

17. The Texas governor makes appointments from a list submitted by a nominating committee known as the:
   a. Election by legislators
   b. Nonpartisan election
   c. Governor ppointment
   d. Partisan election
   e. Merit plan

18. _____ have rights in Texas, just like the criminals.
    a. Victims
    b. Legislators
    c. Judges
    d. Citizens
    e. Police officers

19. _____ gives a few facts concerning jurors and jury duty.
    a. Box 17-1
    b. Table 18-1
    c. Box 18-1
    d. Table 17-1
    e. Box 18-2

20. Texas has created _____ types of courts.
    a. 2
    b. 3
    c. 4
    d. 5
    e. 6

21. Texas has _____ Supreme Court(s).
    a. 1
    b. 2
    c. 3
    d. 4
    e. 5

22. Different trial level courts in Texas are given _____ jurisdiction.
    a. Original
    b. District
    c. Appellate
    d. Concurrent
    e. Municipal

23. The term "_____" means to perpetuate the status quo.
   a. System maintenance
   b. Appellate
   c. Venireman
   d. *De nova*
   e. Write of error

24. Article _____ of the Texas Constitution spells out the powers of the Texas judicial system.
   a. I
   b. II
   c. III
   d. IV
   e. V

25. There are _____ qualifications to become a juror in Texas.
   a. 2
   b. 3
   c. 4
   d. 5
   e. 6

26. The Texas judiciary is a model of democratic_____.
   a. maintenance
   b. power
   c. transactions
   d. justice
   e. accountability

27. In a lawsuit or criminal trial, evidence that is presented again before an appellate court because no record was kept of the evidence presented to the trial court, is known as:
   a. Tort Reform
   b. Capital Murder
   c. Felony Recall
   d. De Nova
   e. Systems Theory

28. _____ is changes in state law to put limits on personal injury lawsuits.
    a. System Maintenance
    b. Bifurcation
    c. Tort Reform
    d. De nova
    e. Concurrent Jurisdiction

29. The _____ is the primary trial court in Texas.
    a. Court of Criminal Appeals
    b. District Court
    c. Texas Supreme Court
    d. Constitutional County Court
    e. Commissioners Court

30. _____ is primary means by which cases reach the Texas Supreme Court.
    a. Writ of Error
    b. De Nova
    c. Justice
    d. Bifurcation
    e. Ordinances

Civil Liberties: The People

Civil liberties are those rights
which protect us from government intrusion.
However, government has become large and powerful,
one may wonder if they are a delusion.

These liberties are known
as the Bill of Rights.
And they did not come easy,
but through hard work, and constant political fights.

Many Americans do not appreciate these rights,
and are politically insincere.
However, as government grows larger,
most of us truly live in fear.

The Bill of Rights
could be easily taken away.
Because so many citizens do not understand
the political way.

If these liberties are to remain,
we as Americans must become politically aware.
Because in our present culture,
no one seems to really care.

—The Bowtie Professor

Name _____ **Date** _____

Explain:

_____

_____

_____

_____

_____

_____

_____

_____

_____

_____

_____

_____

_____

_____

_____

_____

_____

_____

_____

_____

Civil Liberties are those rights which protect us from an overbearing government. They are the first ten Amendments of the U.S. Constitution, which are also known as the Bill of Rights. The first ten Amendments are as follows:

Amendment 1	Freedom of speech, press, petition, assembly, religion
Amendment 2	Right to bear arms
Amendment 3	No quartering of troops
Amendment 4	No searches and seizures without a warrant
Amendment 5	Due process of law, no self-incrimination, right to a fair trial
Amendment 6	Right to have a lawyer in criminal cases
Amendment 7	Right to have a jury trial in certain civil cases
Amendment 8	No cruel and unusual punishment, no excessive bails and fines
Amendment 9	Enumerated powers, the protection of liberties not spelled out in the other amendments
Amendment 10	Reserved powers given to the states

Originally, the Bill of Rights was limited to the national government, as the Supreme Court ruled in *Barron v. Baltimore* (1833). Gradually, however, the Court accepted the selective incorporation theory, which emphasized that the Bill of Rights also applied to the state governments. Table 19-1 gives a few terminologies that are used when discussing the subject of civil liberties.

The First Amendment seems to be the most heavyweight amendment when it comes to the Bill of Rights because it appears to be the most controversial with its five major elements:

Freedom of

- Speech
- Press
- Petition
- Assembly
- Religion

The following are some gospel cases that have dealt with the First Amendment. All cases went to the U.S. Supreme Court.

When it comes to religion and freedom of expression, the U.S. Supreme Court has used the **Lemon Test,** a Court-devised test designed to measure the constitutionality of state laws that appear to further a religion. Accordingly, to be constitutional, a law affecting religious activity:

1. Must have a secular purpose
2. As its primary effect, must neither advance nor inhibit religion
3. Must not foster an excessive government entanglement with religion

It is really interesting to hear politicians, intellectuals, and others who claim that religion and politics are separate. Such individuals argue that one cannot

TABLE 19-1

- **Bad Tendency Test**—A test devised by the Supreme Court that allows the suppression of the freedom of speech if it might promote animosity and chaos.
- **Clear and Present Danger Test**—A standard used by the courts to determine whether speech may be restricted. An individual's speech can be restricted by the courts if it creates a clear and present danger threat to society.
- **Commercial Speech**—Advertising communications given only partial protection under the First Amendment to the Constitution.
- **Compelling Interest Test**—A test used by the Supreme Court to carefully scrutinize laws alleged to infringe on religious practices. The court disregarded the compelling interest test in *Employment Division v. Smith* (1990).
- **Espionage Act (1917)**—Made it a crime to try to hinder the enlistment of young men in the armed forces.
- **Free Exercise Clause**—A phrase in the First Amendment to the U.S. Constitution that prohibits the federal government from restricting religious beliefs and practices.
- **Freedom of Expression**—Collectively, the First Amendment's rights to free speech, press, and assembly.
- **New Judicial Federalism**—Contends that the U.S. Constitution should set minimum, not maximum, standards to protect our rights.
- **No Establishment Clause**—A phrase in the First Amendment to the U.S. Constitution that requires a separation of church and state.
- **Preferred Position**—Refers to the tendency of the courts to give preference to the First Amendment rights to speech, press, and assembly when faced with conflicts.
- **Sedition Act (1918)**—Made it a crime to speak or write against Congress or the president with the intent to defame or bring either in contempt.
- **Symbolic Speech**—Actions other than speech itself that are protected by the First Amendment because they constitute the clear sending of a message covered by that amendment.

legislate morality, but what they fail to realize is that morality dictates legislation. Every law that we have on every level of government came out of someone's religious beliefs. As stated earlier in Chapter 3 on America's political culture, **Religion** is a system of values and beliefs; it is not necessarily synonymous with **God**. America as a nation was founded on Judeo-Christian Western principles. The documents which are the backbone of America's civilization are:

1. The Bible
2. Federalist Papers #10 and #51
3. The Declaration of Independence
4. The U.S. Constitution

It is the Christian values and beliefs that made the U.S. a great nation. Unfortunately, America has detoured from **God** and from the Christian principles in which she once claimed to believe. As a result of this, we have a

BOX 19-1

I. **First Amendment Cases**
   A. *Schenck v. United States* (1919)
     1. First Amendment
     2. Convicted under the Espionage Act (1917)
     3. Ruling: Schenck lost the case
     4. Significance: Established the clear and present danger doctrine
     5. Type case: Civil liberties
   B. *Abrams v. United States* (1919)
     1. First Amendment freedom of speech
     2. Convicted under the Sedition Act (1918)
     3. Ruling: Abrams lost the case
     4. Significance: Sedition Act upheld
     5. Type case: Civil liberties
   C. *Gitlow v. New York* (1925)
     1. First Amendment freedom of speech
     2. Convicted under the New York Criminal Act (1902)
     3. Ruling: Gitlow lost the case
     4. Significance: New York Criminal Code upheld
     5. Type case: Civil liberties
   D. *Dennis v. United States* (1951)
     1. First Amendment freedom of speech
     2. Convicted under the Smith Act (1940)
     3. Ruling: Dennis lost the case
     4. Significance: Upheld the Smith Act (1940)
     5. Type case: Civil liberties
   E. *Yates v. United States* (1957)
     1. First Amendment freedom of speech
     2. Was not convicted under the Smith Act
     3. Ruling: Yates won the case
     4. Significance: Reversed the Smith Act (1940)
     5. Type case: Civil liberties

II. **The First Amendment and symbolic speech and the issue of obscenity**
   A. *United States v. O'Brien* (1968)
   B. *Tinker v. Des Moines ISD* (1969)   **Symbolic Speech**
   C. *Texas v. Johnson* (1989)
   D. *Roth v. United States* (1957)
   E. *Miler v. California* (1973)
     1. The First Amendment does not protect obscenity. It has upheld a group of obscenity convictions.

III. **The three levels of pornography are:**
   A. Light—*Playboy*
   B. Medium—Brutal forms
   C. Hard-core—The firm unyielding central party

nation that is going down the tube of immorality. Politicians and civic leaders want the blessings of God, but they do not want **God**. Below is a list of examples of how this nation has lost its morality:

1. We have too many politicians who do not stand for something and, therefore, they will go for anything.
2. We took prayer out of public schools and replaced it with sex education.
3. We condone abortions and kill unborn babies on a regular basis.
4. We live in a society whereby men do not want to be men and women don't want to be women; instead, some men want to be women, and there are some women who want to be men.
5. We live in a society in which children tell parents what to do, and parents have relinquished their authority.
6. We live in a society in which there is no respect for authority; kids today talk to older adults as if they are talking to their own peers.
7. We condone homosexuality and as a nation we debate whether or not gays can get married and adopt children.
8. We live in a society in which individuals no longer want to work, individuals who are lazy and expect the government to give them everything.
9. We live in a generation of proud boasters, despiteful, unmerciful, unforgiving, and deceitful individuals whose attitude is: "The world owes me something just for existing."

By no means am I trying to paint a dark picture of America; however, some things just need to be brought out. The U.S., with all of its social ills, is still the best country in the world.

Historically, the Judeo-Christian principles have been embedded in America's society in the following ways:

1. The U.S. Congress and state legislators pray before they start their new sessions.
2. On our money, we have "In God We Trust."
3. One used to have to swear on the Bible in court.
4. Many states had blue-laws, meaning one could not shop on Sundays.
5. The president lets a bill lie on his desk ten days excluding Sundays, and the bill dies or becomes law without his signature. Sunday is the day I am emphasizing here to show the Christian principle.
6. God is in our "Pledge of Allegiance." Quite naturally, the above list is not conclusive; but it does give one an idea of our nation's basic beliefs.

Table 19-2 shows a few other civil liberties cases as well as other terminologies.

In the Miranda case, as seen in Table 19-2, the Supreme Court held that criminal suspects, prior to interrogation by the law enforcement personnel, must be informed of certain constitutional rights, including the

TABLE 19-2

1. Civil Liberties Cases
   - *Engel v. Vitale* (1962)—The Supreme Court declared unconstitutional a nondenominational prayer written by the New York Board of Regents for use in state public schools.
   - *Reynolds v. United States* (1879)—The court ruled that polygamy was unconstitutional. The law had been challenged by the Mormon Church, which encouraged its members to practice polygamy in the name of its religious beliefs.
   - *Loving v. Virginia* (1967)—The court struck down a law banning interracial marriages.
   - *Bowers v. Hardwick* (1986)—Supreme Court upheld Georgia sodomy law.
   - *Roe v. Wade* (1973)—Supreme Court upheld a woman's right to have an abortion. These three cases dealt with the Ninth Amendment.
   - *Miranda v. Arizona* (1966)—The Supreme Court ruled that one's rights had to be read immediately after his or her arrest.
   - *John Doe v. University of Michigan* (1989)—The U.S. Supreme Court ruled that political correctness does violate the First Amendment.
   - *Gideon v. Wainwright* (1963)
     1. Denied his rights in the Fifth, Sixth, and Eighth Amendments.
     2. Sentenced by the judge to go to prison.
     3. Ruling: Supreme Court reversed the decision of lower court in Florida, and Gideon won the case.
     4. Significance: Upheld one's right to have a lawyer in criminal cases as well as to have due process under the law.
     5. Civil liberties case.
2. Terms
   - **Exclusionary Rule**—A rule of law that evidence found in an illegal search or resulting from an illegally obtained confession may not be admitted at trial.
   - **Gag Order**—An order by a judge banning discussion or reporting of a case in order to ensure a fair and impartial trial.
   - **Immunity from Prosecution**—A grant by the government to an individual of freedom from prosecution on a particular charge in return for testimony by that individual that might otherwise be self-incriminating.
   - **Prior Restraint**—Government actions to restrict publication of a magazine, newspaper, or book on grounds of libel, obscenity, or other legal violations, prior to actual publication of the work.
   - **Shield Laws**—Laws in some states that give reporters the right to refuse to name their sources or to release their notes in court cases.
3. The U.S. Supreme Court dealt with the issue of prior restraint in the following areas:
   - Film censorship
   - Radio and television censorship
   - The record industry

The Court has used prior restraint to protect the above; however, this does not mean that publishers and others are exempt from subsequent punishment for libelous, obscene, or other illegal publications.

right to remain silent and the right to counsel. As stated in a previous chapter, the three networks of the criminal justice system are the police, courts, and the prisons. If one commits a crime or is accused of a crime, the steps go as follows:

1. **Investigation by Law Enforcement Officers**
   Expectation that the police act lawfully.
2. **Arrest**
   Arrest is based on warrants issued by judges and magistrates. Arrest is based on crimes committed in the presence of law enforcement officials. Arrest or "probable cause."
3. **Hearing and Bail**
   Preliminary hearing in which prosecutor presents testimony that a crime was committed and that there is probable cause for charging the accused.
4. **Indictment**
   Prosecutor or grand jury, in federal cases, issues formal document naming the accused and specifying the charges.
5. **Arraignment**
   Judge reads indictment to the accused and ensures that the accused understands charges and rights and has counsel. Judge asks defendant to choose a plea: guilty, nolo contendere (no contest), or not guilty.
   If the defendant pleads guilty or no contest, a trial is not necessary and the defendant proceeds to sentencing.
6. **Trial**
   Impartial judge presides, and prosecuting and defense attorneys present witnesses and evidence relevant to the guilt or innocence of the

BOX 19-2

1. ***Powell v. Alabama* (1932)**
   Amendment Six, the right to have a lawyer in capital punishment cases
2. ***Wolf v. Colorado* (1949)**
   Amendment Four, no unreasonable searches and seizures
3. ***Mapp v. Ohio* (1961)**
   Amendment Four, exclusionary rule
4. ***Robinson v. California* (1962)**
   Amendment Eight, no cruel and unusual punishment
5. ***Malloy v. Hogan* (1964)**
   Amendment Five, no compulsory self-incrimination
6. ***Parker v. Gladden* (1966)**
   Amendment VI, right to an impartial jury
7. ***Benton v. Maryland* (1969)**
   Amendment Five, no double jeopardy
8. ***Klopfer v. North Carolina* (1967)**
   Amendment Six, right to a speedy trial

defendant, and make arguments to the jury. Jury deliberates in secret and issues a verdict.

7. **Sentencing**
   If the defendant is found not guilty, the procedure ends. Defendants who plead guilty or no contest and defendants found guilty by a jury are sentenced by fine, imprisonment, or both by the judge.
8. **Appeal**
   Defendants found guilty may appeal to higher courts for reversal of verdict or a new trial based on errors made anywhere in the process.

■ CONCLUSION

Civil liberties are freedoms protected by law and have been established to keep one free from unwarranted government intrusion in one's life. We must, however, reassess civil liberties as politics and society change. Some have argued that the Patriot Act is in direct violation of our civil liberties, and that our nation is moving toward a police state. Others have stated that the act was passed to help fight the war on terrorism, and those who argue that we as a nation are moving toward a police state are simply overreacting.

Nonetheless, the framers of the Constitution felt the Bill of Rights necessary to keep government within its reasonable boundaries. Box 19-2 shows a few civil liberties cases which have dealt with other Amendments of the Bill of Rights.

Suggested Readings

Elshtain, Jean Bethke. *Democracy on Trial*. New York: Basic Books, 1995.

Epstein, Lee. *Constitutional Law for a Changing America: Rights, Liberties and Justice*. 3rd ed. Washington, D.C.: Congressional Quarterly Press, 1997.

Garrow, David. *Liberty and Sexuality: The Right to Privacy and the Making of Roe v. Wade*. New York: MacMillan, 1994.

Hentoff, Nat. *Free Speech for Me—But Not for Thee*. New York: Harper Collins, 1992.

Hickok, Eugene W., ed. *The Bill of Rights: Original Meaning and Current Understanding*. Charlottesville: University of Virginia Press, 1991.

Kobylka, Joseph F. *The Politics of Obscenity*. Westport, Connecticut: Greenwood Press, 1991.

Lewis, Anthony. *Gideon's Trumpet*. New York: Random House, 1964.

CHAPTER 19
STUDY GUIDE

After reading and reviewing this chapter, one should be able to do the following:

1. Explain the Bowtie Professor's views concerning civil liberties.

_____

_____

_____

2. Name and explain the 10 civil liberties amendments to the U.S. Constitution.

_____

_____

_____

3. Identify the key terms in Table 19-1.

_____

_____

_____

4. Identify the landmark Supreme Court cases in Box 19-1.

_____

_____

_____

5. Explain how the Judeo-Christian principles have been embedded in America's political culture.

_____

_____

_____

6. Identify the cases and key terms in Table 19-2.

_____

_____

_____

7. List those four documents that are the backbone of America's civilization.

_____

_____

_____

8. Give examples of how America as a nation has lost a great deal of morality.

_____

_____

_____

9. Explain the basic steps that one goes through when he or she has either committed a crime or is accused of committing a crime.

_____

_____

_____

10. Identify the "Lemon Test."

_____

_____

_____

11. Identify *Barron v. Baltimore* (1833).

_____

_____

_____

TRUE/FALSE MULTIPLE CHOICE SAMPLE TEST

1. Reserved powers are found in the Tenth Amendment to the U.S. Constitution.
   a. True
   b. False

2. The right to bear arms is found in the Second Amendment to the U.S. Constitution.
   a. True
   b. False

3. Originally, the U.S. Bill of Rights was limited to the national government.
   a. True
   b. False

4. There is such a thing known as "selective incorporation."
   a. True
   b. False

5. No quartering of troops is found in the Third Amendment of the U.S. Constitution.
   a. True
   b. False

6. The Bible is a major backbone of America's political culture.
   a. True
   b. False

7. Morality dictates legislation.
   a. True
   b. False

8. The Lemon Test has been a device for the U.S. Supreme Court.
   a. True
   b. False

9. Religion is a system of values and beliefs.
   a. True
   b. False

10. The First Amendment to the U.S. Constitution has three parts.
    a. True
    b. False

11. There are three major levels of pornography.
    a. True
    b. False

12. *Texas v. Johnson* (1989) dealt with the issue of symbolic speech.
    a. True
    b. False

13. Yates was convicted under the Smith Act (1940).
    a. True
    b. False

14. The Abrams case (1919) dealt with the issue of gun control.
    a. True
    b. False

15. Schenck was convicted under the New York Criminal Code of 1902.
    a. True
    b. False

16. Federal Papers #10 and #51 are *not* major documents of America's political culture.
    a. True
    b. False

17. *Miller v. California* (1973) was a case that dealt with the issue of wearing arm bands.
    a. True
    b. False

18. *Powell v. Alabama* (1932) dealt with the Sixth Amendment to the U.S. Constitution.
   a. True
   b. False

19. Which amendment to the U.S. Constitution gives enumerated powers?
   a. Seventh
   b. Sixth
   c. Eighth
   d. Ninth
   e. Fifth

20. Which amendment to the U.S. Constitution gives the right to have a lawyer in criminal cases?
   a. Seventh
   b. Sixth
   c. Eighth
   d. Ninth
   e. Fifth

21. Which amendment to the U.S. Constitution gives the right to bear arms?
   a. Second
   b. Third
   c. Fourth
   d. Fifth
   e. Sixth

22. No cruel and unusual punishment is found in the _____ Amendment to the U.S. Constitution.
   a. Fifth
   b. Sixth
   c. Seventh
   d. Eighth
   e. Ninth

23. No excessive bails and fines are found in the _____ Amendment to the U.S. Constitution.
   a. Fifth
   b. Sixth
   c. Seventh
   d. Eighth
   e. Ninth

24. Reserved powers are found in the _____ Amendment to the U.S. Constitution.

    a. Tenth

    b. Eleventh

    c. Twelfth

    d. Thirteenth

    e. Fourteenth

25. The freedom of speech is found in the _____ Amendment to the U.S. Constitution.

    a. First

    b. Second

    c. Third

    d. Fourth

    e. Fifth

26. Barron v. Baltimore was ruled in _____.

    a. 1896

    b. 1902

    c. 1833

    d. 1936

    e. 1943

27. Employment Division v. Smith was ruled in_____.

    a. 1990

    b. 1954

    c. 1922

    d. 1976

    e. 1918

28. The _____ Test states that a law affecting religious activity should have a secular purpose.

    a. Litmus

    b. Political

    c. Clear and Present Danger

    d. Compelling Interest

    e. Lemon

29. _____ are actions other than speech itself that are protected by the First Amendment because they constitute the clear sending of a message covered by that amendment.
    a. Commercial Speech
    b. Freedom of Expression
    c. Symbolic Speech
    d. No Establishment Clause
    e. Free Exercise Clause

30. The_____ Test allows the Supreme Court to suppress free speech if it might cause animosity or chaos.
    a. Bad Tendency
    b. Lemon
    c. Clear and Present Danger
    d. No Establishment Clause
    e. Preferred Position

Civil Rights: The Government

Chapter 20

In the 1950's and 60's,
the struggle for Civil Rights was a major theme,
as Martin Luther King made his most famous speech,
"I Have a Dream."

Practically every group in America
was fighting for its rights,
as violence broke out in the streets,
for several days and nights.

America, during this era,
was going through a serious transformation,
because so many groups refused to constantly accept
political and social deprivation.

This movement caused our nation
so much grief and pain.
Even today, the struggles
for Civil Rights still remain.

These struggles will continue,
for many, many years,
some have lost their lives,
while others have shed their tears.

—The Bowtie Professor

Freedom
NEXT EXIT ↗

DAILY GAZE
April 4th, 1968 LATE EDITION
LUTHER K
ASSASSIN
CIVIL RIGHTS LEADER M

Name _____ **Date** _____

Explain:

_____

_____

_____

_____

_____

_____

_____

_____

_____

_____

_____

_____

_____

_____

_____

_____

_____

_____

Civil Rights are those rights which guarantee social equality for all citizens whereby the government sometimes will have to step in and protect its citizenry from one another. These Civil Rights Amendments of the U.S. Constitution are as follows:

1. Thirteenth—Abolished slavery
2. Fourteenth—Gave Blacks citizenship, due process clause, equal protection of the law, and the privileges and immunities clause
3. Fifteenth—Gave black males the right to vote
4. Nineteenth—Gave women the right to vote
5. Twenty-fourth—Struck down the poll tax
6. Twenty-sixth—Gave those 18 years old and older the right to vote

Note: Amendments Thirteen, Fourteen, and Fifteen are also referred to as Civil War Amendments because they became a part of the U.S. Constitution right after the Civil War.

By far, *African Americans* more than any other minority group in American history started the struggle for civil rights, mainly due to the fact that they were slaves, and slavery was protected by the U.S. Constitution and the Supreme Court. African Americans were not considered as citizens or entitled to the rights and privileges of citizenship. The Civil War later ended the institution of slavery and black males were allowed to vote. This was during the Radical Reconstruction Era in which Amendments Thirteen, Fourteen, and Fifteen were added to the U.S. Constitution. Politically and socially, however, African Americans still suffered inequality; and the U.S. Supreme Court did not make it any better by establishing the "separate but equal doctrine" in *Plessy v. Ferguson* in 1896. This decision by the Court practically nullified the civil rights acts of 1865 to 1875.

Box 20-1 is a moment of thought on race relations.

Many would say that the modern *Civil Rights Movement* began in 1955 with the boycott of segregated public transportation in Montgomery, Al-abama. Of course a year before this, legal segregation was declared unconstitutional by the Supreme Court in *Brown v. Board of Education of Topeka* (1954).

Below are major civil rights legislation:

I. *Civil Rights Act 1957*
   - Title I   Established the commission of civil rights.
   - Title II   Authorized the president to appoint, with the advice and consent of the Senate, one additional assistant attorney general in the Justice Department.
   - Title III Extended the jurisdiction of the district courts to include the protection for the right to vote. Also gave the president power to employ troops when necessary.
   - Title IV   Provided further means to secure the right to vote.
   - Title V   Provided punishment for those who violated the Civil Rights Act (1957).

BOX 20-1

When race relations are discussed in the U.S., it is very common for intellectuals, scholars, and even the average American citizen to have a tendency to point to the south or the southern states. In other words, it is assumed that racists are only found in the south in such states as Mississippi, Alabama, Georgia, and the like. Therefore, a lot of northerners would point their fingers at southern racists and rednecks and claim that such individuals and groups are a terror to Blacks; for the most part, they were right. However, let it be known that both segregation and racism were strong in the northern states as well. The only difference was Whites in the south were bold and open with it. They told Blacks to their faces what they thought about them, whereas in the north many Whites were very discreet with their racist views and perceptions. The point that I am making here is that racism in American political history is not a southern problem; it is an American problem. Also it must be understood that African Americans, Hispanics, Asians, Jews, Women, and Gays can be both racist and sexist.

This notion that Whites are the only ones who can be racist is a lie; it simply is not true.

A moment of thought

Professor Yecats

II. *Civil Rights Act of 1960*

Title I   Made it a crime for any person to interfere with any federal court order.
Fine: $1,000, or one year in prison, or both.

Title II   Made it a federal crime to cross state lines to avoid prosecution or punishment for giving evidence on how to bomb or burn buildings and vehicles.
Fine: $5,000, or five years in prison, or both.
Also made it a federal crime to transport or possess explosives with the knowledge or intent that they would be used to blow up any vehicle or building.
Fine: $10,000, or ten years in prison, or death penalty if recommended by the jury.

Title III Required voting records and registration papers be reserved for 22 months.
Fine: $1,000, or one year in prison, or both.

Title IV   Empowered the Civil Rights Commission to administer oaths and take sworn statements.

Title V   Provided schools for military children when the schools those children regularly attended closed to avoid integration.

Title VI   Gave the Attorney General power to ask the court to hold adversary proceedings if there was a pattern or practice of depriving Blacks the right to vote.

Title VII If any provision of this act is held invalid, the remainder of this act shall not be affected thereby.

III. *Civil Rights Act of 1964*

Title I Outlawed arbitrary discrimination in voting.

Title II Outlawed racial discrimination in public accommodations.

Title IV Allowed the Justice Department to sue school districts who would not comply with investigation.

Title VI Banned racial discrimination in federally-funded programs.

Title VII Prohibited discrimination in hiring on the basis of gender or race.

Title IX Prohibited discrimination in higher education.

IV. *Civil Rights Act of 1968*

Prohibited discrimination in the sale or rental of housing. The act struck down:

A. Restrictive covenants

B. Redlining

C. Blockbusting

This act has also been extended to cover the handicapped and families with children.

V. *Voting Rights Act of 1965*

Struck down the:

A. Constitutional test

B. Grandfather clause

C. Literary test

This act extended voting rights to Hispanic, Asian, and Native Americans.

VI. *Civil Rights Act of 1991*

Provided employment protection for women and minority group members. The act made it easier for job discrimination victims (including sexual harassment victims) to sue for damages.

Several of the above acts gave African Americans and other deprived groups the opportunity to experience the "American Dream." As Professor Yecats points out, however, much blood was shed by both Blacks and Whites alike, and many died that others may have a better life. Jim Crowism has been very strong not only in the South but in the North as well. By far, the Civil Rights Movement could have been classified as the fourth Reconstruction period for Blacks. *Reconstruction One* was the period right after the Civil War. *Reconstruction Two* was the Harlem Renaissance. *Reconstruction Three* was the New Deal era; and as stated earlier, *Reconstruction Four* is the Civil Rights Movement. Why these four periods? It is very simple. In each one of these periods there was a great metamorphosis in Black America, politically, economically, socially, and religiously. Also during each of these periods, there was a change in race relations.

Table 20-1 shows a few major Civil Rights leaders and organizations, as well as a few key terms.

By far, there were some major Civil Rights cases that changed the face of American society. These major cases are as follows:

TABLE 20-1

1. Major Civil Rights leaders of the 1950's and 1960's:
   - Martin Luther King
   - Malcolm X
   - Roy Wilkins
   - Whitney Young
   - Philip Randolph
2. Major Civil Rights groups of the 1950's and 1960's:
   - National Association for the Advancement of Colored People (1909)
   - The Urban League (1910)
   - Congress of Racial Equality (1942)
   - Student Non-Violent Coordinating Committee (1960)
   - Southern Christian Leadership Conference (1957)
3. A few key terms dealing with the subject of Civil Rights:
   - **Abolitionist Movement**—A social movement in the 1800's whose goal was to abolish slavery throughout the U.S.
   - **Color Blind Standard**—The views that laws should not take into account race at all and that they should neither favor nor discriminate against any individual based on race. The color blind standard was first espoused by Justice John Harlan.
   - **Comparable Worth**—The argument that pay levels for traditionally-male and traditionally-female jobs should be equalized by paying equally all the jobs that are worth about the same to an employer.
   - **Defacto Segregation**—Segregation based on residential patterns.
   - **Dejure Segregation**—Segregation based on the law.
   - **Direct Discrimination**—The now illegal practice of differential pay for men versus women even when those individuals have equal qualifications and perform the same job.
   - **Glass Ceiling**—Describes the failure of women to rise to the highest positions in corporations and professions due to the "invisible" barriers to such advancement.
   - **Jim Crowism**—The second-class citizen status conferred on Blacks by southern segregation laws. Jim Crow derived from a 19th-century song and dance act (usually performed by a white man in a black face) that stereotyped Blacks.
   - **Nonviolent Direction Action**—A strategy utilized by moderate civil rights leaders in which protests break "unjust" laws openly but in a "loving" fashion in order to bring the injustices of such laws to public attention.
   - **Redistribute**—Refers to government policies meant to shift assets from one group to another.
   - **Separate-But-Equal Doctrine**—A ruling of a Supreme Court case in which facilities of all kinds are deemed legal as long as the facilities are equal.

III. *Plessy v. Ferguson (1896)*:
   A. Thirteenth and Fourteenth Amendments
   B. Plessy sat in the wrong section of the train.
   C. Plessy lost the case.

BOX 20-2

On June 1, 1921, Tulsa—which was called "Black Wallstreet" (the most affluent all-black community in America)—was bombed from the air and burned to the ground by mobs of envious citizens. Within 12 hours, a once prosperous black business district in northern Tulsa was gone (via fire). It was a model community and a major African American economic resource. That night's riot (carnage) left over 3,000 African Americans dead, and 600 successful businesses lost (21 churches, 21 restaurants, 30 grocery stores, two movie theaters, one hospital, one bank, one post office, libraries, schools, law offices, half a dozen private airplanes, and one bus line). This was pre Rosewood! The Rosewood destruction occurred in 1923; Tulsa occurred in 1921. The force behind the Tulsa destruction was the Klan and its sympathizers. "Black Wallstreet" or "Little Africa," as it was known in 1921, could be likened to Beverly Hills, California. It was seen as the golden door of the black community during the 1900's and it proved to many that African Americans still had a strong infrastructure. The dollar circulated 36 to 100 times, often taking a full year to totally leave the community. In 1998, a dollar could leave the black community in less than 15 minutes. During this period, black physicians owned medical schools in Tulsa. There were also jewelry stores and only two airports (six Blacks owned their own planes).

The area was made up of over 600 businesses and 36 square blocks with a population of over 15,000 African Americans. When the lower-economic citizenry discovered what the black community had created, many of them became angry and jealous. When the average black student went to school in this area, he wore a suit and tie due to the fact that morals and respect were being taught at home and in the school system. The main goal of this community was to educate every child, and everyone believed in nepotism. The main streets were Greenwood Avenue, and Archer and Pine, which intersected with Greenwood. From the first letters of these streets you get G.A.P., and that's where the R&B music group The Gap Band got its name. (They are from Tulsa.) Don't forget that Oklahoma was set aside to be a Black and Indian state, and there were over 28 black townships there. Don't forget that one third of the people who traveled in the "Trail of Tears" with the Native American people were black people (1830-1842). When Blacks intermarried into the Indian culture, some received their promised 40 acres and a mule and whatever oil was later found on their properties.

Finally, in 1910, black folk owned over 13 million acres of land at the height of racism in this country.

Source: Wallace, Ron. *Black Wallstreet.* Tulsa, Oklahoma: Dularon, 1995.

    D. Ruling: The Supreme Court agreed with Judge Ferguson.
    E. Significance: Established the separate but equal doctrine and gave Jim Crowism more power in the U.S.
II. *Brown v. Board of Education (1954):*
    A. Fourteenth Amendment
    B. Linda Brown wanted to attend a white school.
    C. NAACP and Linda Brown appealed to the Supreme Court.
    D. Supreme Court ruled in favor of Linda Brown.

    E. Significance: Reversed the decision in *Plessy v. Ferguson.* This case struck down the separate but equal doctrine.

III. *Sweatt v. Painter (1950):*
    A. Fourteenth Amendment
    B. Horman Sweatt wanted to attend the University of Texas law school.
    C. Painter felt that Sweatt should not attend the institution because he was black.
    D. Ruling: Supreme Court ruled in favor of Sweatt.
    E. Significance: This case helped to start integration in higher education.

IV. *The Supreme Court upholds Swann v. Charlotte-MacKlenburg County Board of Education (1971):*
    A. The use of racial balance requirements in schools and the assignment of pupils to schools based on race.
    B. "Close scrutiny" by judges of schools that are predominantly of one race.
    C. Gerrymandering of school attendance zones as well as "clustering" or "grouping" of schools to achieve racial balance.
    D. Court-ordered busing of pupils to achieve racial balance.

■ HISPANICS

Hispanics have also fought for their equal rights in America's society, and their civil rights movement included many tactics drawn from African Americans in their quest for justice. Hispanic Americans have some radical groups, but the movement has been dominated by more conventional organizations, which have pressed for Chicano and Latino studies programs and have built up ties with existing powerful mainstream associations, including unions and the Roman Catholic Church. Two of the most powerful Latino groups are the League of United Latin American Citizens (LULAC), founded in 1929, and the Mexican American Legal Defense and Educational Fund (MALDEF), founded in 1968. Below are the accomplishments of these organizations:

1. They were instrumental in forcing school districts with predominantly low-income minority populations to implement bilingual education.
2. They are responsible for bringing issues which affect Latino Americans to policy makers on every level of American government.
3. They have been successful in litigations to the U.S. Supreme Court.
4. They have worked to expand voting rights to Hispanics.
5. They have been successful in getting Latinos elected into public office.

Box 20-3 has a moment of thought for a great Hispanic Civil Rights Activist:

BOX 20-3

Cesar Chavez was an individual who fought for economic equality since the Civil Rights Movement started in the early 1950's. Chavez fought constantly by leading boycotts and standing in picket lines for the rights of farm workers. He worked in the fields since the age of ten, and left school in the eighth grade because his father became injured. Chavez joined the other 300,000 Mexican Americans who annually migrated from Washington state to southern California in search of a better life. Chavez met an organizer for the Community Services Organization, a Mexican American self-help group, while working in a fruit orchard outside of San Jose in 1952. Chavez became a full-time organizer for the group, joining hundreds of other Mexican Americans to create voter registration drives and campaign against racial discrimination. Chavez encouraged migrant workers and their communities to fight for their rights, and he persuaded 1,200 workers in his organization to join the AFL-CIO's strike against the grape and wine producers in Delano, California. Chavez continued to fight to enforce statutes and called for boycotts of table grapes and lettuce. His tactics were in the Ghandian spirit of nonviolence as he led several hunger strikes. Chavez died in 1993 and over 44,000 people attended his funeral. He received the Presidential Medal of Freedom posthumously in 1994. Cesar Chavez was considered by many the Martin Luther King of the Hispanic Civil Rights Movement.
   Just a Moment of Thought

Source: Larry Berman and Bruce Allen Murphy. Approaching Democracy. Upper Saddle River, New Jersey: Prentice Hall, 2003.

■ NATIVE AMERICANS

Native Americans who are the "true" Americans have also constantly fought for their rights. Under the U.S. Constitution, "Indian tribes" are considered distinct governments, a situation that has affected Native Americans' treatment by the Supreme Court in contrast to other groups of ethnic minorities. In 1924, Native Americans were made U.S. citizens and were given the right to vote. It was not until the 1960's, however, that Indians, too, began to mobilize as other minority groups have done and demanded their share of the American apple pie. In 1973, national attention was drawn to the plight of Native Americans when members of a radical American Indian movement took over Wounded Knee, South Dakota, the site of the massacre of 150 Indians by the U.S. Army in 1890. Two years prior to the protest, the treatment of Indians had been high, as reported in the best-selling book, *Bury My Heart at Wounded Knee,* which served to support public opinion against the oppression of Native Americans in the same way *Uncle Tom's Cabin* had against slavery.

The Chronicle of Higher Education reported that American Indian nicknames and mascots are "offensive" and colleges should stop using them, according to the U.S. Commission on Civil Rights. The federal agency approved a statement saying that the use of such symbols by non-tribal colleges and schools creates a racially hostile educational environment. The commission lacks a legislative or enforcement power to support its recommendation, but proponents of the recommendation say it's an important symbolic gesture. The commission has also made similar statements on behalf of African Americans, Asian Americans, and people with disabilities, as one anti-discrimination strategy.

"Schools should not use their influence to perpetuate misrepresentations of any culture or people," the statement reads. "Stereotypes of American Indians teach all students that stereotyping of minority groups is acceptable, a dangerous lesson in a diverse society."

At least 60 universities continue to use American Indian mascots, according to the National Coalition of Racism in Sports and the Media. Elsie M. Meeks, an American Indian member of the panel, proposed a draft of the statement at a meeting of the commission, but several members objected, arguing that the statement wrongly tried to limit freedom of expression. Now, the statement's wording has been changed to affirm the commission's respect for the First Amendment. The final draft does suggest that mascots "may" violate federal anti-discrimination laws, however.

Do sport teams that use American Indian nicknames and mascots discriminate against American Indians? Ben Nighthorse Campbell thinks so. Campbell is the only Native American in the U.S. Congress and he attempted to introduce legislation to block the approval of a $200 million stadium for the Washington Redskins unless the team changed its name. He failed to convince his colleagues, however. Indian activists picket football games and other professional sports events, as well as colleges using Native American nicknames and mascots.

■ WOMEN

In early U.S. political history, women were considered citizens but had no political rights. Progress was slow. In 1920, however, when the Nineteenth Amendment was ratified, women finally gained the right to vote. The modern women's movement began in the 1960's in the wake of the Civil Rights movement. The National Organization for Women was formed in 1966 to bring about complete equality for women in all walks of life. Below is a list of a few outstanding women who fought for the equality of women across America:

1. Susan B. Anthony
2. Elizabeth Cady Stanton
3. Barbara C. Jordan
4. Eleanor Roosevelt
5. Rosa Parks

6. Ellen Malcolm
7. Mary McLeod Bethune

Table 20-2 deals with the issue of affirmative action, and a few related cases. Table 20-2 also deals with the issue of civil rights and the power to bargain with management.

Box 20-4 deals with the issue of Gays and Lesbians associating their struggle for equality with African Americans.

TABLE 20-2

1. Affirmative action programs more likely to be found constitutional:
   - When they are adopted in response to past history of discrimination.
   - When they are narrowly tailored to remedy the effects of previous discrimination.
   - When they do not absolutely bar Whites or men from competing or participating.
   - When they serve an important social or educational objective.
2. A few cases that have dealt with affirmative action are:
   - United Steel Workers of America v. Weber (1979)—The Supreme Court approved a plan by a private employer and a union to reserve 50% of higher-paying, skilled jobs for minorities.
   - United States v. Paradise (1987)—The court upheld a rigid 50% black quota system for promotions in the Alabama Department of Safety, which had excluded Blacks from the ranks of state troopers prior to 1972 and had not promoted any Blacks higher than corporal prior to 1984.
   - Firefighters v. Local Union v. Scotts (1984)—The Supreme Court ruled that a city could not lay off white firefighters in favor of black firefighters with less seniority.
   - City of Richmond v. Crosen (1989)—The Supreme Court ruled that a minority set-aside program in Richmond, Virginia, which mandated that 30% of all city construction contracts must go to "Blacks, Spanish-speaking, Orientals, Indians, and other minority groups," violated the equal protection clause of the Fourteenth Amendment.
3. Historical Civil Rights Acts are:
   - Civil Rights Act (1866)—Guaranteed newly freed persons the right to purchase, lease, and use real property.
   - Civil Rights Act (1871)—Made it a federal crime for any person acting under the authority of state law to deprive another of rights protected by the Constitution.
   - Civil Rights Act (1875)—Outlawed segregation in privately-owned businesses and facilities, but in the civil rights case of 1883, the Supreme Court declared it an unconstitutional expansion of federal power, ruling that the Fourteenth Amendment limits only "state" action.
4. The issue of civil rights and the power to bargain with the employer came through the following Acts:
   - Clayton Act (1914)—Gave employees the power to organize trade unions.
   - Norris LaGuardia Act (1932)—Prevented employers and federal courts from requiring employees to sign a pledge not to join a union. It also prevented federal courts from giving injunctions against strike.
   - Wagner Act (1935)—Gave employees power to bargain with management.

BOX 20-4

Many African Americans become appalled when gays and lesbians attempt to associate their struggle for equality with that of African Americans. Yet there are both similarities and dissimilarities between the gay and lesbian struggles for equal rights and the African American struggle for equality. Each are outlined below.

1. **Similarities**
   - Both African Americans and gays and lesbians have been discriminated against. African Americans because of their race, and gays and lesbians because of their sexual preference.
   - Both African Americans and gays and lesbians have been mocked and made fun of because of who they are.
   - Historically, in the U.S., to be black in America meant that you were an outcast. Gays and lesbians are considered by many to be outcasts.

2. **Dissimilarities**
   - African Americans came out of a legacy of slavery while gays and lesbians have not.
   - African Americans cannot hide their skin color, but gays and lesbians can hide their sexuality.
   - Gays and lesbians have not suffered the magnitude of political oppression, economic exploitation, and social deprivation that African Americans have in the U.S.
   - The African American struggle has been that of Civil Rights whereas the gay and lesbians' struggle falls along the line of civil liberties, particularly Amendment Nine.
   - African Americans were denied the right to vote and go into public accommodations; this was not the case with homosexuals.
   - African Americans were considered three-fifths of a person in the U.S. Constitution; gays and lesbians did not have to experience this.

As one can see, the dissimilarities between the African American and gay and lesbians' struggle for equality far outweigh the similarities.

A Moment of Thought
Professor Yecats

■ CONCLUSION

There has been a growth in civil rights, and those who truly believe in democracy must be concerned that all groups within the U.S. enjoy these rights. African Americans by far have been the forerunners of the Civil Rights movement; and other minorities, including women, have been able to piggyback off their efforts and successes. This is not to say that women, Hispanics, and Native Americans did not have their own successful movements; but African Americans were and still are today the pioneers when it comes to civil rights.

Suggested Readings

Armor, David. *Forced Justice: School Desegregation and the Law.* New York: Oxford University Press, 1995.

Bergmann, Barbara. *In Defense of Affirmative Action.* New York: Basic Books, 1996.

Blasius, Mark. *Gay and Lesbian Politics: Sexuality and the Emergence of a New Ethic.* Philadelphia: Temple University Press, 1994.

Brown, Dee. *Bury My Heart at Wounded Knee.* New York: Rinehart and Winston, 1971.

Delgado, Richard. *The Coming Race War? And Other Apocalyptic Tales of America After Affirmative Action and Welfare.* New York: New York University Press, 1996.

Eastland, Terry. *Ending Affirmative Action: The Case for Color-Blind Justice.* New York: Basic Books, 1996.

Kahlenberg, Richard D. *The Remedy: Class, Race, and Affirmative Action.* New York: Basic Books, 1996.

CHAPTER 20
STUDY GUIDE

After reading and studying this chapter, one should be able to do the following:

1. Explain the following Civil Rights Acts of:
   a. 1957

   _____

   b. 1960

   _____

   c. 1964

   _____

   d. 1968

   _____

   e. 1991

   _____

   f. 1866

   _____

   g. 1871

   _____

   h. 1875

   _____

2. Explain the Voting Right Act of 1965.

   _____

   _____

   _____

3. Explain the similarities and differences between the African-American struggle for equality and the gay and lesbian struggle for equality.

_____

_____

_____

4. Identify the following:

  a. Wagner Act 1935

_____

  b. Norris LaGuardia Act 1932

_____

  c. Clayton Act 1914

_____

  d. Glass ceiling

_____

  e. Comparable worth

_____

  f. Jim Crowism

_____

  g. Redistribute

_____

  h. Nonviolent direction action

_____

   i. Direct discrimination

_____

   j. Dejure segregation

_____

   k. Defacto segregation

_____

5. Explain the "Black Wallstreet" as outlined in Box 20-2.

_____

_____

_____

6. Explain Cesar Chavez and his impact on Civil Rights for Mexican Americans as discussed in Box 20-3.

_____

_____

_____

7. Identify the five major accomplishments of the League of United Latin American Citizens (LULAC) and the Mexican American Legal Defense and Educational Fund (MALDEF).

_____

_____

_____

_____

_____

8. Explain the role of Native Americans and their struggle for rights and liberties.

_____

_____

_____

9. According to your text, identify a few women who have struggled for civil rights.

_____

_____

_____

10. List the four major reasons Affirmative Action programs are more likely to be found constitutional.

_____

_____

_____

11. List the four Reconstruction Periods and identify each period.

_____

_____

_____

_____

12. Identify the following:
   a. Abolitionist movement

_____

   b. Color blind standard

_____

   c. Separate but Equal Doctrine

_____

   d. *Sweatt v. Painter* (1950)

_____

   e. *Plessy v. Ferguson* (1896)

_____

   f. *Brown v. Board of Education* (1954)

_____

   g. *Swann v. Charlotte-Macklenburg County Board of Education*

_____

   h. *Firefighter Local Union v. Scotts* (1984)

_____

   i. *City of Richmond v. Crosen* (1989)

_____

   j. *United States v. Paradise* (1987)

_____

   k. *United Steel Workers of America v. Weber* (1979)

_____

13. Identify a few civil rights leaders and civil rights organizations.

_____

_____

_____

14. Explain the Bowtie Professor's view concerning civil rights.

_____

_____

_____

15. Name and explain the six civil rights amendments to the U.S. Constitution.

_____

_____

_____

16. Identify Box 20-1.

_____

_____

_____

TRUE/FALSE MULTIPLE CHOICE SAMPLE TEST

1. Civil rights and civil liberties are pretty much the same.
- **a.** True
- **b.** False

2. The Fourteenth Amendment to the U.S. Constitution abolished slavery.
- **a.** True
- **b.** False

3. The Fifteenth Amendment to the U.S. Constitution gave women the right to vote.
- **a.** True
- **b.** False

4. The Thirteenth Amendment to the U.S. Constitution gave blacks citizenship.
   a. True
   b. False

5. Native Americans got the right to vote in 1972.
   a. True
   b. False

6. Cesar Chavez died in 2001.
   a. True
   b. False

7. MALDEF was founded in 1929.
   a. True
   b. False

8. LULAC was founded in 1968.
   a. True
   b. False

9. In 1983, national attention was drawn to the plight of Native Americans.
   a. True
   b. False

10. Philip Randolph was a major civil rights leader.
   a. True
   b. False

11. Defacto segregation is based on residential patterns.
   a. True
   b. False

12. Dejure segregation is based on the law.
   a. True
   b. False

13. The "Black Wall Street" was made up of over 600 businesses.
   a. True
   b. False

14. Linda Brown won her case against the State Board of Education.
   a. True
   b. False

15. There are six civil rights amendments to the U.S. Constitution.
   a. True
   b. False

16. Redlining was outlawed by the:
   a. Civil Rights Act (1968)
   b. Voting Rights Act (1965)
   c. Civil Rights Act (1960)
   d. Civil Rights Act (1957)
   e. Civil Rights Act (1964)

17. The Modern Civil Rights Movement ran from:
   a. 1940s to 1950s
   b. 1960s to 1970s
   c. 1970s to 1980s
   d. 1980s to 1990s
   e. 1990s to present

18. The _____ Amendment to the U.S. Constitution gave women the right to vote.
   a. Seventeenth
   b. Eighteenth
   c. Nineteenth
   d. Twenty-Sixth
   e. Fifteenth

19. The _____ Amendment to the U.S. Constitution gave those who were 18 years of age or older the right to vote.
   a. Fourteenth
   b. Twenty-Sixth
   c. Seventeenth
   d. Thirteenth
   e. Nineteenth

20. Which U.S. act struck down the "Literary Test"?
    a. Civil Rights Act (1991)
    b. Civil Rights Act (1964)
    c. Civil Rights Act (1871)
    d. Voting Rights Act (1965)
    e. Civil Rights Act (1871)

21. According to the text, there are _____ reconstruction periods.
    a. 1
    b. 2
    c. 5
    d. 6
    e. 4

22. Which U.S. act established the commission of civil rights?
    a. Civil Rights Act (1866)
    b. Civil Rights Act (1991)
    c. Civil Rights Act (1960)
    d. Civil Rights Act (1964)
    e. Civil Rights Act (1957)

23. In 1910, at the height of racism in America, African Americans owned _____ acres of land.
    a. 13 million
    b. 10 million
    c. 2 million
    d. 600,000
    e. 14,000

24. Another name for the "Black Wall Street" was:
    a. Black Indian
    b. Little Africa
    c. The GAP
    d. Big Egypt
    e. The Soul Train

25. The second-class-citizen status conferred on blacks by America was known as:

   a. Racism

   b. The glass ceiling

   c. Jim Crowism

   d. Redistribution

   e. Classism

26. The Civil Rights Act of _____ made it a crime for any person to interfere with any federal court Order.

   a. 1957

   b. 1960

   c. 1964

   d. 1968

   e. 1991

27. The Civil Rights Act of_____guaranteed newly freed persons the right to purchase, lease, and use real property.

   a. 1866

   b. 1871

   c. 1875

   d. 1914

   e. 1935

28. Cesar Chavez died in_____and over 44,000 people attended his funeral.

   a. 1983

   b. 1993

   c. 1970

   d. 1968

   e. 2006

29. In_____, national attention was drawn to the plight of Native Americans when members of a radical American Indian movement took over Wounded Knee, South Dakota.

   a. 1924

   b. 1933

   c. 1987

   d. 1973

   e. 2001

30. _____ was a member of the National Coalition of Racism in Sports and the Media.

   a. Cesar Chavez

   b. Horman Sweatt

   c. Linda Brown

   d. Michael Swann

   e. Elsie M. Meeks

The Federal and State Bureaucracy: Red Tape

The federal and state bureaucracies
are complex in their chain of command.
Much of what they do,
the average citizen does not understand.

Whether it is unity of command,
or span of control,
the bureaucracies play
a very vital role.

It doesn't matter whether one is
a Republican or Democrat.
He can regularly observe
the bureaucrat.

These workers sometimes go to work early
and get off late,
as our nation moved from Classical Liberalism
to the Social Welfare State.

The President, Congress, and Special Interests
are the basis for bureaucratic power,
as these Career Civil Servants perform
way past the midnight hour.

The bureaucrats want the system
to function well for everyone,
and this is why
their job is truly never done.

—The Bowtie Professor

Name _____ **Date** _____

Explain:

_____

_____

_____

_____

_____

_____

_____

_____

_____

_____

_____

_____

_____

_____

_____

_____

_____

_____

_____

The modern federal bureaucracy is composed of nearly three million civil workers from all walks of life. Bureaucrats not only make but implement public policy. Iron triangles or public networks often can be used to describe how this policy-making occurs. The federal bureaucracy has such an influence on the American citizenry; some have referred to it as the fourth branch of government.

Below are key terms used in bureaucracies and by bureaucrats:

- **Bureaucracy**—Departments, agencies, bureaus, and offices that perform the functions of government.
- **Bureaucracy**—Large private or public organizations that are hierarchical in structure, and that provide each employee with clearly-defined responsibilities, base actions, and decisions on impersonal rules; they also hire and promote employees based on skills and training.
- **Bureaucrats**—Career government employees who gain office by appointment rather than election.
- **Chain of Command**—There should be a firm line of authority running from the top down and responsibility running from the bottom up.
- **Decentralization**—When possible, administrators should delegate decisions and responsibilities to lower levels.
- **Division of Labor**—Work is divided among many specialized workers in an effort to improve productivity.
- **Goals Orientation**—Organizational goals determining structure, authority, and rules.
- **Impersonality**—All persons within the bureaucracy treated on "merit" principles, and all "clients" served by the bureaucracy treated equally according to rules.
- **Implementation**—The development by the federal bureaucracy of procedures and activities to carry out policies legislated by Congress which include regulation as well as adjudication.
- **Line and Staff**—The staff advises the executive but gives no commands, whereas the line has operating duties.
- **Regulation**—The development by the federal bureaucracy of formal rules for implementing legislation.
- **Span of Control**—A hierarchical structure should be established so that no individuals supervise more agencies directly than they can effectively handle.
- **Specification of Authority**—Clear lines of responsibility with positions and units reporting to superiors.
- **Unity of Command**—Every officer should have a superior to whom to report and from whom to take orders.

Article II, Section 2, states that the president is both commander-in-chief of the armed forces and chief executive officer to whom the heads of all administrative departments would report. As the United States has grown, government has gotten larger; and at the federal, state, and local levels, more than

18 million people work for the government, with the "feds" taking the lead in directing public policies. For every thousand citizens, there are approximately 60 state and local government employees and 12 federal government employees. Government employs more people than the largest industrial corporations. There are three factors which caused the federal bureaucracy to expand in size: the Great Depression, the Industrialization Era, and the Great Society Programs. There have been many attempts to make the federal bureaucracy more open, efficient, and responsive to the needs of U.S. citizens. The most important reforms have included sunshine and sunset laws, contracting out, strategies to provide incentives for increased productivity and efficiency, and protection for whistleblowers.

Table 21-1 shows a few basic facts concerning the federal bureaucracy.

Today, most federal civilian bureaucrats hold positions that are graded under a personnel system administered by the **Office of Personnel Management.** The most widespread system of job grading and classification is the General Schedule. This schedule divides civilian jobs into 18 pay grades ranging from lower level positions (GS-1) to top management, administrative, and professional positions (GS-16, 17, and 18). Most of the top level officials of the career bureaucracy have been organized into a **Senior Executive Service.** These positions (ES-1 through ES-6) are at least comparable to those in the top three grades of the **General Schedule.** Men and women in the SES bridge the gap between the bulk of the career bureaucracy and the executive branch's appointive political leadership. It would be wrong to assume that relations between political executives and career bureaucrats are always characterized by tension and discord. On the average, they are usually productive and supportive. Political executives often rely upon the experience and advice of careerists, and career employees count on political executives for a strong program leadership.

When a president leaves office, nearly all of the members of his administration go with him. Yet the day-to-day functions of government continue without noticeable interruption. Most government employees are not associated with the presidential administration. They are the career employees. Approximately two million of them are found in the uniformed military service. Another three-quarters of a million or so employees work for government corporations. The remainder, roughly two and one-quarter million employees, make up the civilian bureaucracy or the civil service.

Below are other terminologies that are used when dealing with the subject of bureaucracy.

- **Adjudication**—Decision-making by the federal bureaucracy as to whether or not an individual or organization has complied with or violated government laws and regulations.
- **Affirmative Action**—The recruitment and promotion of minorities and women to meet specified goals for representation of these groups in the work force.

TABLE 21-1

1. The five bureaucratic units are as follows:
   - **Executive Office**—Created in 1939 to serve as the managerial arm of the presidency. It includes such agencies as the National Security Council, Office of Management and Budget, the Council of Economic Advisors, and the Domestic Council.
   - **Government Corporation**—A bureaucratic unit that offers some service for which the benefiting individual or institution must pay directly.
     Example: *Amtrak, U.S. Postal Service, the Export-Import Bank, and Federal Deposit Insurance Corporation.*
   - **Independent Agency**—A type of bureaucratic unit organizationally located outside of an executive department and generally headed by a single individual.
     Example: *Central Intelligence Agency, Veterans Administration, Peace Corps, and Environmental Protection Agency.*
   - **Independent Regulatory Commission**—A type of bureaucratic unit organizationally located outside of the executive department, headed by a group of individuals called a commission, and charged with regulating a specific industry or economic priority.
     Example: *Federal Elections Commission, Equal Employment Opportunity Commission, and the Interstate Commerce Commission.*
   - **Cabinet**—Political institutions comprised mainly of executive department heads who collectively serve as a source of advice for the president.
     Example: *Secretary of State, Treasury, Defense and Agriculture.*
2. The five big bureaucratic agencies are:
   - Department of Navy
   - Department of Army
   - Department of Air Force
   - Department of Veterans Administration
   - U.S. Postal Service
3. The Bureau is:
   The largest sub-unit of a government department or agency.
4. Being a good bureaucratic politician involves the four elements:
   - Cultivating a good base of support for one's requests among the public at large and among people served by the agency.
   - Developing interest, enthusiasm, and support for one's program among top political figures and congressional leaders.
   - Winning favorable coverage of agency activities in the media and among special interests.
   - Following strategies that exploit opportunities.
5. The elements that are involved when firing a federal employee are:
   - Written notice at least 30 days in advance of a hearing to determine incompetence or misconduct.
   - A statement of cause, indicating specific dates, places, and actions cited as incompetent or improper.
   - The right to a hearing and decision by an impartial official, with the burden of proof falling on the agency that wishes to fire the employee.
   - The right to have an attorney and to present witnesses in the employee's favor at the hearing.
   - The right to appeal any adverse action to the Merit System Protection Board.
   - The right to appeal any adverse action by the board to the U.S. Court of Appeals.
   - The right to remain on the job and be paid until all appeals are exhausted.

- **Appropriations Act**—A congressional bill that provides money for programs authorized by Congress.
- **Authorization**—An act of Congress that establishes a government program and defines the amount of money it may spend.
- **"Bureaucratic Red Tape"**—Came from the ribbon English civil servants once used to tie up and bind legal documents.
- **Capture Theory of Regulation**—Describes how some regulated industries come to benefit from government regulation and how some regulatory commissions come to represent the industries they are supposed to regulate rather than representing the people.
- **Continuing Resolution**—Authorizes government agencies to keep spending money for a specified period at the same level as in the previous fiscal year.
- **Discrepancy Funds**—Budgeted funds not earmarked for specific purposes, but available to be spent in accordance with the best judgment of a bureaucrat.
- **Hatch Act (1939)**—Is a federal statute barring federal employees from active participation in certain kinds of politics and protecting them from being fired on partisan grounds. The Hatch Act permits most federal civil servants to held party positions and involve themselves in party fund-raising and campaigning. The act, however, still bars federal officials from running as candidates in partisan elections.
- **Merit System**—Selection of employees for government agencies on the basis of competence, with no consideration of an individual's political stance or power.
- **Obligational Authority**—Permits a government agency to enter into contracts that will require the government to make payments beyond the fiscal years in question.
- **Outlays**—Actual dollar amounts to be spent by the federal government in a fiscal year.
- **Spoils System**—Selection of employees for government agencies on the basis of party loyalty, electoral support, and political influence.
- **Whistle Blowers**—An employee of the federal government or of a firm supplying the government who reports waste, mismanagement, and fraud at or to a government agency or contractor.

The basis of bureaucratic power is the president, Congress, the media, special interest groups, and the general public. Policy makers possess different strategies to control bureaucracies in order to ensure that policies are implemented as intended. The strategies that are used are as follows:

1. Change the law or make legislation detailed enough to reduce or eliminate the discretionary authority of an agency.
2. Cut or threaten to reduce the budget of an agency to force compliance with policy objectives.
3. Pressure the bureaucracy with legislative hearings and public disclosures of agency neglect or inadequacies.

4. Transfer the administration of a program to another agency through administrative reorganization, a strategy attempted by the legislature in 1991.
5. Abolish an agency or program through sunset legislation.
6. Protect public employees who reveal incompetence, mismanagement, and corruption through whistleblower legislation.

The actual job of the federal bureaucracy, of course, will never disappear. Federal agencies are the primary means by which the laws of Congress are put into practice. The power of federal agencies gives them significant discretion to make policy because bureaucrats are often specialists in their fields and they are more knowledgeable than members of Congress and the president about specific issues relating to the legislation passed by Congress.

Box 21-1 gives a few facts about the Texas state bureaucracy.

BOX 21-1

1. **There are three essential characteristics of the Texas state bureaucracy that cause a great deal of confusion because:**
   - There is no single, uniform organizational pattern.
   - There are numerous exceptions to the traditional bureaucratic characteristics of hierarchy.
   - The number of state agencies depends upon one's method of counting.
2. **Terms**
   - **Bureaucracy**—The agencies of government and their employees responsible for carrying out policies and providing public services approved by elected officials.
   - **Impeachment**—A procedure by which the legislature can remove a governor or certain other public officials from office for misconduct.
   - **Pay As You Go**—A constitutional prohibition against the state government borrowing money for its operating budget.
   - **Plural Executive**—A fragmented system of authority under which most statewide, executive officeholders are elected independently of the governor.
   - **Railroad Commission**—A three-member elected body that regulates intrastate trucking, bus service, and oil and natural gas production in Texas.
   - **Secretary of State**—Administers state election laws, grants charters to corporations, and processes the extradition of prisoners to other states. The Secretary of State is the only constitutional official appointed by the governor.
   - **Senatorial Courtesy**—An unwritten policy that permits a senator to block the confirmation of a gubernatorial appointee who lives in the senator's district.
   - **Staggered Terms**—A requirement that members of state boards and commissions appointed by the Governor serve terms that begin on different dates.
   - **State Board of Education**—An elected panel that oversees the administration of public education in Texas.

BOX 21-1

3. **The five major types of top policy makers in the Texas state bureaucracy are:**
    - Elected executive
    - Appointed executive
    - An elected commission and an elected board
    - Ex Officio boards and commissions
    - Appointed boards and commissions
4. **A few examples of state bureaucracies are:**
    - Texas Department of Human Services
    - Texas Employment Commission
    - Texas Department of Health
    - Texas Parks and Wildlife Department
    - Higher Education
    - Independent School Districts
5. **"Zero-Based Budgeting" is:**
    A method of budgeting that demands justification for the entire budget request of an agency and not just its requested increase in funding.
6. **"Incremental Budgeting" is:**
    A method of budgeting that focuses on requested increases in funding for existing programs by accepting as legitimate their previous year's expenditures.
7. **"Sunset" is:**
    The process under which most state agencies have to be periodically reviewed and recreated by the legislature or go out of business.

■ CONCLUSION

Both the federal and state bureaucracies are comprised of many groups who occupy a variety of both blue and white-collar positions. They are organized under personnel systems including presidential appointees, the general civil service, executive service systems, career systems, and wage labor systems. Much of what federal bureaucrats do is hidden from the public. Nevertheless, they play important roles in the policy-making process that goes beyond merely administering government programs.

Suggested Readings

Curry, Landon. "Politics of Sunset Review in Texas," *Public Administration Review.* 50 (January/February 1990): 58-68.

Gore, Al. *Creating a Government that Works Better and Costs Less.* Washington, D.C.: Government Printing Office, 1993.

Johnson, Ronald N. and Gary D. Libecap. *The Federal Civil Service System and the Problem of Bureaucracy.* Chicago: University of Chicago Press, 1994.

Kettl, Donald F. *Civil Service Reform.* Washington, D.C.: Brookings Institution, 1996.

Prindle, David. *Petroleum Politics and the Texas Railroad Commission.* Austin: University of Texas Press, 1981.

Schick, Allen. *The Federal Budget: Politics, Policy, Process.* Washington, D.C.: Brookings Institution, 1995.

Slack, James D. "Bureaucracy and Bureaucrats in Texas." *In Texas Public Policy.* Ed. Gerry Riposa, pp. 187-91. Dubuque, Iowa: Kendall/Hunt, 1987.

CHAPTER 21
STUDY GUIDE

After reading and studying this chapter, one should be able to do the following:

1. Identify the following:
   a. Whistle blowers

   _____

   b. Continuing resolution

   _____

   c. Discrepancy funds

   _____

   d. Merit system

   _____

   e. Obligational authority

   _____

   f. Spoils system

   _____

   g. Outlays

   _____

   h. Hatch Act (1939)

   _____

   i. Staggered terms

   _____

   j. Plural executive

_____

   k. Sunset

_____

   l. Incremental budgeting

_____

   m. Zero base budgeting

_____

   n. Senatorial courtesy

_____

   o. Impeachment

_____

   p. Pay as you go

_____

2. Give a few examples of Texas state bureaucratic agencies.

_____

_____

_____

3. Explain three essential characteristics of the state bureaucratic system that cause a great deal of confusion.

_____

_____

_____

Name _____ **Date** _____

4. List the five areas for the basis of bureaucratic power.

_____

_____

_____

_____

5. Explain the six major strategies policy makers use in order to control bureaucratic agencies and ensure that policies are implemented as intended.

_____

_____

_____

_____

_____

6. List the five major types of top policy makers in the Texas state bureaucracy.

_____

_____

_____

_____

7. Explain the seven elements that are involved when trying to fire a federal employee.

_____

_____

_____

_____

_____

_____

_____

8. Name and explain the five major bureaucratic units in America.

_____

_____

_____

_____

_____

9. List the five big bureaucratic agencies in America.

_____

_____

_____

_____

_____

10. Identfy the four major elements that make one a good bureaucratic politician.

_____

_____

_____

_____

11. Identify the following:

   a. Affirmative action

_____

   b. Appropriations act

_____

   c. Authorization

_____

   d. Bureaucratic red tape

_____

   e. Capture theory of regulation

_____

   f. General schedule

_____

   g. Adjudication

_____

   h. Office of Personnel Management

_____

   i. Senior executive service

_____

   j. Bureaucracy

_____

   k. Bureaucrats

_____

    l. Chain of command

_____

    m. Decentralization

_____

    n. Unity of command

_____

12. Explain the term "the Bureau."

_____

_____

_____

13. Identify Article II, Section 2 of the U.S. Constitution.

_____

_____

_____

14. Explain the Bowtie Professor's view concerning the federal and state bureaucracy.

_____

_____

_____

15. Identify the following:
    a. Line and staff

_____

    b. Regulation

_____

   c. Span of control

_____

   d. Specification of authority

_____

   e. Implementation

_____

   f. Goal orientation

_____

   g. Impersonality

_____

   h. Division of labor

_____

TRUE/FALSE MULTIPLE CHOICE SAMPLE TEST

1. Goals orientation and impersonality are just about the same.
   a. True
   b. False

2. Article II, Section 2, of the U.S. Constitution spells out bureaucratic power.
   a. True
   b. False

3. The modern federal bureaucracy is composed of nearly 3 million civil service workers.
   a. True
   b. False

4. The Executive Office of American government was created in 1789.
   a. True
   b. False

5. The Peace Corps would be an example of an independent regulatory commission.
   a. True
   b. False

6. In America, "the Bureau" is the largest subunit of a government department or agency.
   a. True
   b. False

7. When a U.S. president leaves office, the day-to-day functions of governmental bureaucracy continues without noticeable interruption.
   a. True
   b. False

8. Some have referred to the federal bureaucracy as the sixth branch of U.S. government.
   a. True
   b. False

9. There are three factors that have caused the federal bureaucracy to expand.
   a. True
   b. False

10. The Great Society Programs really did *not* expand the bureaucracy in size.
    a. True
    b. False

11. Most federal employees are associated with the presidential administration.
    a. True
    b. False

12. Amtrak would be an example of a government corporation.
    a. True
    b. False

Name _____ **Date** _____

13. There is no such thing as "bureaucratic blue tape."
    a. True
    b. False

14. There are approximately 60 state and local government employees for every thousand citizens.
    a. True
    b. False

15. Which of the following caused an expanded federal bureaucracy?
    a. Span of control
    b. Fair Deal
    c. Depression
    d. Decentralization
    e. Adjudication

16. Which of the following is an independent agency?
    a. Amtrak
    b. U.S. Postal Service
    c. National Security Council
    d. Interstate Commerce Commission
    e. Veterans Administration

17. Which of the following is a government corporation?
    a. Amtrak
    b. Peace Corps
    c. Domestic Council
    d. CIA
    e. FBI

18. There are _____ essential characteristics of the Texas state bureaucracy.
    a. 2
    b. 3
    c. 4
    d. 5
    e. 6

19. Which of the following is not a basis for bureaucratic power?
    a. President
    b. Congress
    c. Interest group
    d. Cabinet
    e. The media

20. In America, there are _____ major types of top policy makers in the state bureaucracy.
    a. 2
    b. 3
    c. 4
    d. 5
    e. 6

21. The Hatch Act came into existence in:
    a. 1939
    b. 1949
    c. 1959
    d. 1969
    e. 1979

22. The Export-Import Bank would be an example of a(n):
    a. Independent agency
    b. Government corporation
    c. Executive office
    d. Independent regulatory commission
    e. "Bureau"

23. When firing a federal bureaucratic employee, a written notice should be at least_____ days in advance prior to the hearing.
    a. 30
    b. 45
    c. 60
    d. 75
    e. 90

24. There are _____ elements that are involved when trying to fire a federal employee.
    a. 7
    b. 6
    c. 5
    d. 4
    e. 3

25. Which of the following is considered to be a bureaucratic agency?
    a. Cabinet
    b. Department of Navy
    c. Executive Office
    d. Federal Elections Commission
    e. C.I.A.

26. Which of the following is a Government Corporation?
    a. National Security Council
    b. Environmental Protection Agency
    c. Amtrak
    d. Department of Air Force
    e. All the above are government corporations

27. Which of the following is an Independent Regulatory Commission?
    a. Veterans Administration
    b. Peace Corps
    c. Export-Import Bank
    d. Interstate Commerce Commission
    e. C.I.A.

28. The U.S. Postal Service is a (an) _____.
    a. Independent Agency
    b. Independent Regulatory Commission
    c. Executive Office
    d. Protective Agency
    e. Government Corporation

29. The _____ is the largest sub—unit of a government department or agency.
    a. C.I.A.
    b. Amtrak
    c. Bureau
    d. Equal Employment Opportunity Commission
    e. Council of Economic Advisors

30. A congressional bill that provides money for programs authorized by Congress is known as:
    a. Appropriations Act
    b. Adjudication
    c. Authorization
    d. Impersonality
    e. Outlays

Political Economy: Poli-ology

Chapter 22

Politics and Economies,
they do relate,
within any entity
of the state.

Economics and Politics
shape many views,
whether it by good
or bad political news.

Unfortunately, many Americans
seem not to really care.
When it comes to these subjects,
they are totally unaware.

Politics and Economies
are known as Political Economy,
as the stock market goes up and down,
and plays with your money.

Political Economy operates
every second, minute, and hour;
however, the masses do not understand
such great power.

—The Bowtie Professor

Name _____ **Date** _____

Explain:

_____

_____

_____

_____

_____

_____

_____

_____

_____

_____

_____

_____

_____

_____

_____

_____

_____

_____

_____

_____

The nature and role of the government in the political economy, especially the national government, has changed a great deal since the beginning of this country. Efforts of the national government to regulate the economy began with the antimonopoly legislation. Under Franklin D. Roosevelt, the classical liberalist philosophy was replaced by modern reform liberalism, or the social welfare state. Even today the national government continues to shape monetary policy by regulating the nation's money supply and interest rates, which are controlled by the Federal Reserve Board. The **Federal Reserve Board** consists of banking regulators who establish banking policy and determine the amount of money put into circulation. The Federal Reserve System consists of 12 regional federal reserve banks, a seven-member board of governors and five regional bank presidents. The 12 members of the Federal Open Market Committee are all professional economists.

The five major political and economic policy areas that the U.S. government must deal with each year are:

1. Social welfare
2. The regulation of corporations
3. Foreign and defense policies
4. Promotion of science and technology
5. Protection of legal and constitutional rights

Other policy areas facing America are the taxation of e-commerce, poverty, crime, the environment, and social security. Policies are created in response to public problems or public demand for government action, and some of the major institutions of economic policy are:

1. Office of Management and Budget (President)
2. Council of Economic Advisors (President)
3. Budget Committee—coordination (Senate)
4. Finance Committee—revenues (Senate)
5. Appropriations—expenditures (Senate)
6. Budget Committee—coordination (House)
7. Ways and Means—revenues (House)
8. Appropriations—expenditures

Economics is the way in which goods and services are produced, distributed, and consumed. When government, however, makes decisions that affect the production, distribution, and consumption of goods, the provision of services, the flow of income, and the accumulation of wealth, this is known as **Economic Policy.** The Economic Fiscal Policy only determines how much money is going to be spent that particular year; it is the use of changes in government expenditures and taxes to alter national economic variables, such as the rate of inflation or unemployment. Fiscal economic policy also emphasizes increasing government spending during recessionary periods and increasing taxes during inflationary boom periods. Whereas **Monetary**

Policy means the use of changes in the amount of money in circulation so as to affect interest rates, credit markets, rate of inflation, and employment.

Table 22-1 defines other key terms used when discussing the subject of political economy.

When the federal government spends more than it receives, it runs a deficit. The deficit is met by the U.S. Treasury borrowing money. This adds to the public debt of the federal government. The federal budget deficit, however, virtually disappeared by 1998, and since then the budget had showed a surplus, prior to the war on terrorism. The federal government's actions in the area of domestic economic policy affects the lives of the American citizenry. The policymaking process is initiated when policymakers become aware through the

TABLE 22-1

- **Classical Economic Theory**—A school of economic thought that focuses on economic efficiency and presumes that the forces of demand and supply will automatically adjust to restore stable prices after a brief period of inflation.
- **Counter Cyclical Policies**—Part of Keynesian theory which emphasizes the notion that the government must take action to counter the effects of recession and inflation.
- **Employment Act of 1946**—Pledges the federal government to promote maximum employment production and purchasing "power" though its taxing and spending policies. This act created the Council of Economic Advisors to "develop and recommend to the president national economic policies."
- **Free Market Economy**—An economic system in which individual choices by consumers and firms determine what shall be produced, how much, and for whom. It relies on voluntary exhanges of buying and selling.
- **Government Bonds**—Certificates of indebtedness that pay interest and promise repayment on a future date.
- **Gross National Product**—A nation's total production of goods and services for a single year.
- **Growth**—Any increase in a nation's economic output; this is often measured in terms of real increases in the gross national product.
- **Hyperinflation**—Annual inflation rates of 100 to 1,000 percent or more.
- **Incidence**—The actual bearer of a tax burden.
- **Inflation**—A rise in the general level of prices, not just the prices of some products.
- **Monetarist Economic Theory**—A school of economic thought that argues that economic stability can only be achieved by holding the rate of monetary growth to the rate of the economy's own growth.
- **Political Economy**—The study of relationships between politics and economics and governments and markets.
- **Stagflation**—The simultaneous occurrence of high rates of inflation and unemployment.
- **Supply Side Economic Theory**—A school of economic thought that focuses on economic growth and argues that government taxing and spending are detrimental to such growth.
- **Tax Expenditures**—Revenues lost to the federal government because of exemptions, exlusions, deductions, and special-treatment provisions in tax laws.
- **Unemployment Rate**—The percentage of the civilian labor force who are not working but who are looking for work or waiting to return to or to begin a job.

media, voters, and special interest groups that a problem has arisen and must be addressed by Congress and the president. The process of policymaking is known as the Rational Comprehensive Approach, which consists of:

1. Policy agenda
2. Policy adoption
3. Policy strategy
4. Policy implementation
5. Policy evaluation

Once the rational comprehensive approach is applied by policymakers, public policy will reflect one of the following models:

1. **Systems Model**—Holds that public policy is the product of an interlocking relationship between the political system and its social, cultural, and economic environment.
2. **Bureaucratic Model**—Holds that bureaucrats play a crucial role in developing public policies because of the commitment and expertise they can provide.
3. **Marxist Model**—Holds that public policy is a reflection of the ruling class at the expense of the workers.
4. **Elitist Model**—Holds that public policy is a reflection of the rich at the expense of the poor.
5. **Pluralist Model**—Holds that public policy is a reflection of competing interest groups struggling against one another.
6. **Incrementalist Model**—Holds that public policies that are made in the present are only slightly different from past decisions.

Many have argued that the problem with public policies is that there is a lack of understanding by policymakers and that policies are written in very vague terms that make it very difficult to understand the major purpose of the policy's intent.

Box 22-1 gives an overview on another area of government policy, regulation. Regulations are rules devised by government agencies that shape the actions of individuals and groups in order to achieve some purposes mandated by law.

The politics of taxes has been a major concern among both the government and citizens alike. Some Americans argue for **Progressive Taxation** in which groups with higher incomes pay a larger percentage of their taxes than do lower income groups. Those who call for **Regressive Taxation** believe that lower income groups should pay more in taxes than the wealthy. Nevertheless, a much fairer system would be **Proportional Taxation** in which all income groups pay the same percentage of their incomes in taxes. **Marginal Utility Theory** argues that high income groups can afford to pay a larger percentage of their income into taxes at no more of a sacrifice than required of lower income groups devoting a smaller proportion of their income to

BOX 22-1

1. **The two general categories of regulations are:**
   - **Economic**—Refers to the government's control on the behavior of business in the marketplace, the entry of individual firms into particular lines of business, the prices that firms may charge, and the standards of services they must offer. Public utilities, transportation, and television are examples of regulated industries.
   - **Social**—Government corrections of a wide variety of side effects, usually unintended, brought about by certain economic activities. Concerns for worker health and safety and for hazards to the environment are the stimulus for social regulation. Social regulation also includes the efforts made by the government to ensure equal rights in employment, education, and housing. Whereas economic regulation is usually organized along industry lines, social regulation cuts across these lines.

2. **A few regulatory agencies are:**
   - **Economic**
     - Federal Communications Commission
     - Interstate Commerce Commission
     - Federal Elections Commission
     - Commodity Future Trading Commission
   - **Social**
     - Environmental Protection Agency
     - Consumer Product Safety Commission
     - Occupational Safety and Health Administration

3. **Areas in which federal regulations are designed to protect workers are:**
   - Public contracts
   - Wages and hours
   - Child labor
   - Industrial safety and occupational health

4. **Regulations have improved the quality of our lives in the following areas:**
   - Bars on "quack" medicines
   - Inspections for livestock diseases
   - Recall of defective automobiles
   - Seat belt and air bag regulations
   - Regulations on industrial pollution
   - Regulations on lead poisoning
   - Regulations to encourage clean water
   - Regulations on asbestos
   - Regulations on unsafe toys
   - Regulations on air traffic

5. **Some problems of regulations are:**
   - Regulations distort and disrupt the operation of the market.
   - Regulations can discourage competition.
   - Regulations may discourage technological development.
   - Regulatory agencies are often "captured" by the industries they regulate.

taxation. Yet higher income groups continue to find loopholes which allow them to reduce their taxable income. **Loopholes** are legal methods by which individuals and businesses are allowed to reduce their tax liabilities owed to government.

The United States has enjoyed a relatively long period of economic growth; however, economic growth does not mean economic development. Economic growth mainly will benefit a few in society, whereas economic development benefits large groups of individuals. If for any reason a recession were to occur and jobs were scarce, the current debate over economic and domestic policy would become much sharper and the issues far more contentious than they currently are.

■ CONCLUSION

The interaction between politics and economics has been an old theme in the study of American politics. Economic issues have been near the top of the political agenda throughout America's history. Also, regulation in the U.S. is neither socialism or laissez-faire policy, but a set of government rules and laws issued to alter or control the operations of economic enterprises, yet based on a widely-held commitment to a free market economy.

Suggested Readings

Derthick, Martha and Paul J. Quirk. *The Politics of Deregulation.* Washington, D.C.: Brookings Institution, 1985.

Eisner, Marc A. *Regulatory Politics in Transition.* Baltimore: John Hopkins University Press, 1993.

Gold, Steven D., ed. *The Fiscal Crisis of the States.* Washington, D.C.: Georgetown University Press, 1995.

Keech, William. *Economic Politics: The Costs of Democracy.* Cambridge: Cambridge University Press, 1995.

Krugman, Paul. *The Age of Diminished Expectations.* Cambridge, MA: The MIT Press, 1994.

Rosenbaum, Walter A. *Environmental Politics and Policy.* 2nd ed., Washington, D.C.: CQ Press, 1996.

Wilson, James Q., ed. *The Politics of Regulation.* New York: Basic Books, 1980.

After reading and studying this chapter, one should be able to either explain, define, or identify the following:

1. Explain the Bowtie Professor's views concerning political economy.

_____

_____

2. Explain the structure of the Federal Reserve Board.

_____

_____

3. List the five major political and economic policy areas of the U.S. government.

_____

_____

_____

_____

_____

4. List the eight major institutions of economic policy.

_____

_____

_____

_____

_____

_____

_____

_____

5. Identify the following:

  a. Economics

_____

  b. Economic policy

_____

  c. Political economy

_____

  d. Monetary policy

_____

  e. Marginal utility theory

_____

  f. Loopholes

_____

  g. Progressive taxation

_____

  h. Regressive taxation

_____

  i. Proportional taxation

_____

6. Explain the two major categories of government regulations.

_____

_____

7. Identify a few regulatory agencies.

_____

_____

8. Identify areas in which federal regulations protect the American worker.

_____

_____

_____

9. List areas of our lives in which federal regulations have helped Americans.

_____

_____

_____

10. List the four major problems of U.S. regulations.

_____

_____

_____

_____

11. Identify the key terms in Table 22-1.

_____

_____

_____

TRUE/FALSE MULTIPLE CHOICE SAMPLE TEST

1. Regulations are both social and economical.
   a. True
   b. False

2. Policy evaluation is a major element of the rational comprehensive approach.
   a. True
   b. False

3. There are four major problems of federal regulations.
   a. True
   b. False

4. The interaction between politics and economics has *not* been an old theme in U.S. politics.
   a. True
   b. False

5. There are six major areas of government policy.
   a. True
   b. False

6. Table 22-1 discusses the Federal Reserve Board.
   a. True
   b. False

7. There are eight major economic policy institutions in American government.
   a. True
   b. False

8. Social welfare is not a major policy area for the federal government.
   a. True
   b. False

9. There are professional economists on the Federal Reserve Board.
   a. True
   b. False

10. The study of the relationship between politics and economics is known as political economy.
   a. True
   b. False

11. When the federal government spends more than it receives, it runs a deficit.
   a. True
   b. False

12. Loopholes are legal methods by which individuals and businesses are allowed to reduce the tax liabilities they owe multinational corporations.
   a. True
   b. False

13. There is no such thing as marginal utility expenditures.
   a. True
   b. False

14. Regulations have *not* improved the quality of our lives.
   a. True
   b. False

15. There are two major types of government regulations.
   a. True
   b. False

16. The Federal Reserve Board consists of _____ regional federal reserve banks.
   a. 8
   b. 9
   c. 10
   d. 11
   e. 12

17. The Federal Reserve Board has a _____ member board of governors.
   a. 4
   b. 5
   c. 6
   d. 7
   e. 8

18. The Federal Reserve Board has _____ regional bank presidents.

   a. 2

   b. 3

   c. 5

   d. 9

   e. 10

19. The Classical Liberalist Philosophy was replaced by the _____ administration.

   a. Roosevelt

   b. Johnson

   c. Reagan

   d. Ford

   e. Truman

20. _____ provides key terms when discussing the subject of political economy.

   a. Table 23-1

   b. Table 22-1

   c. Box 22-1

   d. Box 23-1

   e. Figure 7

21. There are _____ major taxation theories.

   a. 2

   b. 3

   c. 4

   d. 5

   e. 6

22. Certificates of indebtedness that pay interest and promise repayment on a future date are known as:

   a. Government bonds

   b. Tax expenditures

   c. Counter cyclical policies

   d. Free markets

   e. Stagflations

23. There are _____ steps or elements of the Rational Comprehensive Approach.
   a. 3
   b. 4
   c. 5
   d. 6
   e. 7

24. An overview of government regulations are found in:
   a. Table 23-1
   b. Box 23-1
   c. Table 22-1
   d. Box 22-1
   e. Figure 8

25. Which of the following is *not* a model of the rational comprehensive approach?
   a. Systems
   b. Pluralist
   c. Incrementalist
   d. Elitist
   e. Policy agenda

26. Some problems with regulations is that:
   a. they banned public contracts.
   b. they allow lead poisoning.
   c. they can dangerously hinder progress
   d. they can discourage competition
   e. they banned "quack" medicines

27. _____ is any increase in a nation's economic output.
   a. Tax Expenditures
   b. Inflation
   c. Stagflation
   d. Growth
   e. Hyperinflation

28. _____ is the actual bearer of a tax burden.
    a. Incidence
    b. Stagflation
    c. Growth
    d. Supply Side Economics
    e. Government Rate

29. _____ Is the way in which goods and services are produced, distributed, and consumed.
    a. Political Science
    b. Economic Policy
    c. Political Economy
    d. Economics
    e. Stagflation

30. _____ is the study of the relationship between politics and economics and governments and markets.
    a. Political Economy
    b. Sociology
    c. Government
    d. Political Science
    e. Hyperinflation

Poli-ology: The Social Welfare State

The Social Welfare Programs
were designed to help the poor,
as they constantly struggled
to endure.

Welfare in America
began with a great start,
but abusers of the system
caused it to fall apart.

It was designed to help those
who were truly in need,
and not individuals
who were full of greed.

Social welfare's major purpose
was to give needy individuals a sense of respect,
and not just sit home
and receive a government check.

Welfare in America
started off with a good intent,
and its objective was not
to just pay one's rent.

—The Bowtie Professor

BENEFITS

social welfare

Name _____ **Date** _____

Explain:

_____

_____

_____

_____

_____

_____

_____

_____

_____

_____

_____

_____

_____

_____

_____

_____

_____

_____

The major purposes of FDR's New Deal and LBJ's Great Society programs were to end poverty, to have ethnic and racial equality, to develop decent housing, and to have a greater sharing of the wealth in America. By far the New Deal and the Great Society programs were the peak of the social welfare state. Out of the two LBJ's Great Society program had a greater impact on America's political culture. Tons and tons of money has been spent to alleviate poverty in the U.S., yet poverty remains a blight on the record of the world's richest country—the United States. The reason for this is due to the fact that too many politicians and intellectuals fail to realize that poverty is a mentality and not just a socioeconomic condition. By some estimates, the U.S. has transferred well over a trillion dollars to eliminate poverty out of its territories. Money alone cannot get people out of their poverty stricken conditions.

According to Professor Yecats, many people are poor because:

1. They come out of environments which foster negative attitudes.
2. They have been made to believe by the agents of political socialization that they are victims of society and, therefore, many of the poor view themselves as helpless.
3. Many of the poor in the U.S. come from families who do not value education, and many of these families, especially African American and Hispanic families, downplay the importance of an education.
4. Some of the poor do not perceive themselves as being poor.
5. Some people do not have any get-up-and-go about themselves.

Below are terminologies that are used when discussing the subject of the **Social Welfare State.**

- **COLA**—Annual cost-of-living adjustment mandated by law in Social Security and other welfare benefits.
- **Dependency Ratio**—In the Social Security system, the number of recipients as a percentage of the number of contributing workers.
- **Entitlement Program**—Any social welfare program for which there are eligibility requirements, whether financial or contributory.
- **Medicaid**—A public assistance program that provides health care to the poor.
- **Medicare**—A social insurance program that provides health care insurance to the elderly and disabled.
- **Poverty Line**—The official standard regarding what level of annual cash income is sufficient to maintain a "decent standard of living." Those with incomes below this level are eligible for public assistance programs.
- **Public Assistance**—Social welfare programs for which only those living in poverty are eligible; these include programs such as food stamps and AFDC.

- **Social Security**—A social insurance program composed of the old age and survivors insurance program, which pays benefits to retired workers who have paid into the program and to the dependents and survivors of insured workers. The disability insurance program is the second distinct program of Social Security in which it provides monthly cash benefits for disabled workers and their dependants.
- **Supplemental Security Income (SSI)**—A public assistance program that provides monthly case payment to the needy elderly (65 or older), blind, and disabled.
- **Temporary Assistance for Needy Families (TANF)**—A public assistance program that provides monies to the states for their use in helping needy children through payments to the parents of such children.
- **Transfer Payments**—Direct payments (either in cash or in goods and/or services) by governments to individuals as part of a social welfare program and not as a result of any service rendered by the individual.
- **Unemployed Compensation**—A social insurance program that temporarily replaces part of the wages of workers who have lost their jobs.

The **Poverty Line,** the official standard regarding what level of annual cash income is sufficient to maintain a "decent standard of living," has been criticized by both liberals and conservatives.

Liberals have criticized the poverty line because:

1. The official definition does not consider what people think they need to live. The poverty line is well below what most Americans think they need to survive.
2. The official definition does not take into account regional differences in the cost of living, climate, or accepted styles of living.

3. The official definition does not count the many "near poor," the 45 million Americans or 18% of the population which could be living below the poverty level.
4. The official definition includes case income from welfare and social security, and without this government assistance, the number of poor would be much higher, perhaps 25% of the total population.

Conservatives have criticized the poverty line because:

1. The official definition of poverty excludes "in kind" (noncash) benefits given to the poor by governments. If these benefits, including food stamps, free medical care, public housing, and school lunches were "costed out" (calculated as cash income), there might be only half as many poor as shown in official statistics.
2. Many persons (poor and unpoor) underreport their real income, which leads to overestimates of the number of poor.
3. Many families and individuals who are officially counted as poor do not think of themselves as "poor people." For example, students who deliberately postpone their income to secure an education.
4. It does not consider the value of family assets. People who own their own mortgage-free homes, furniture, and automobiles—may have incomes below the poverty lines but do not suffer hardship.

Many of the programs that came out of the social welfare system are:

1. AFDC (TANF)
2. Social Security
3. Job Corp
4. Manpower
5. CETA
6. Educational loans
7. BEOG (Pell Grant)
8. Medicare
9. Medicaid
10. Free lunch programs
11. Supplemental rent for the poor
12. Farmers Agricultural Program
13. Work Project Program
14. Youth Administrative Program
15. Vista (a domestic peace corps and legal aid to the poor)
16. Training programs for health professionals

As stated earlier, the two major stages of which brought the Social Welfare State to its peak were Franklin D. Roosevelt's "New Deal Package" and Lyndon B. Johnson's Great Society "War on Poverty" program. The main vehicle that Johnson used to attack poverty was the **Economic Opportunity Act**

(1964), which provided for community action programs. Without a shadow of doubt, the U.S. government has done more than enough for the its citizenry to experience the "American Dream" and not the "American Nightmare." Anyone in the U.S. can make his or her life better if he or she is an adult, and we as American citizens must stop making excuses for not being productive beings in our society.

Box 23-1 discusses a moment of thought.

Table 23-1 highlights a few welfare issues and defines relevant terms.

The Clinton administration turned the welfare system around. The 1996 welfare reform measures abolished AFDC and replaced it with TANF, **Temporary Assistance to Needy Families,** a state administered program in which grants from the national government are given to the states, which use the funds to provide assistance to those who are eligible. One of the great efforts of the welfare reform program is the amount of time that individuals can spend on the system. Most states limit the federal assistance to about two years; however, they may choose to extend the assistance for a longer period of time. The main goal of the welfare reform is to get people into employment.

BOX 23-1

The junior and community colleges across the United States are the last attempt for individuals to experience the "American Dream." These colleges are very economic and many of them offer classes six days a week. These institutions of higher learning offer a variety of courses which will transfer to four-year colleges and universities. They offer remediation courses for those who missed out on the basics at high school, and guess what? If one did not get his or her high school diploma, the two-year colleges offer G.E.D. classes. The point that I am making here is that we as Americans are without excuses for not reaching the goals that we desire out of life. Therefore, stop blaming others for your shortcomings in life. Losers are those who constantly blame others for their mistakes. Are you a loser? Are you a white male, who blames Blacks and Hispanics for not getting the job you so desperately wanted? Are you an African American male, who claims that you cannot get a job, because the white man has his foot on your neck? Are you a woman, who blames men for all the social ills that come your way? Do you walk around with your feelings on your shoulders ready to lash out at anyone who disagrees with your life style? If you are one of the above, you are probably a loser.

In the United States of America, any person of adult age can prosper in some way, form or fashion and, when we say that we can't, foreigners who come to the U.S. make us out a lie.

A Moment of Thought
Professor Yecats

TABLE 23-1

1. a. **Public Assistance**—aid received from the government because of hardship or need.
   b. **Welfare**—aid provided by the government to the poor or needy people.
2. **The major purpose of the family support act of 1988 was to end long-term dependence on "welfare."**
3. **The Family Act (1988) requires state governments to do the following:**
   a. To develop a federal job training program for most adults receiving AFDC payments except in the case of age, illness, or disability.
   b. To provide childcare for job participants.
   c. To furnish transitional childcare and Medicaid 12 months after a person leaves AFDC to take a job.
   d. To strengthen child support enforcement programs.
4. **Some other ideas for welfare reform have been:**
   a. Use tax credit.
   b. Limit the time people can be on welfare.
   c. Target teenage mothers.
   d. Reduce fraud.
   e. Consolidate programs.
   f. Terminate welfare entirely.
5. a. **Food Stamp Program**—A public assistance program that provides low-income households with coupons redeemable for enough food to provide a minimal nutritious diet.
   b. **In-Kind Assistance**—Refers to public assistance programs in which the benefits are the actual goods and services rather than the cash with which to purchase food and services of the recipient's choice.
   c. **Preferred Provider Organizations (PPO)**—groups of hospitals and physicians who have joined together to offer their services to private insurers at a discount.
   d. **Managed Care**—Refers to programs designed to keep health care costs down by the establishment of strict guidelines regarding when and what diagnostic and therapeutic procedures should be administered to patients under various circumstances.
   e. **Health Maintenance**—Health care provider groups that provide a stipulated list of services to patients for a fixed fee that is usually substantially lower than such care would otherwise cost.
   f. **Managed Competition**—An approach to health care cost control in which individuals and/or companies join health insurance purchasing organizations that negotiate with private health insurance companies, HMOs, PPOs, and private physicians and hospitals to obtain the best care possible at a low cost.
   g. **Health Insurance Purchasing Alliances**—Regional cooperatives that obtain the best care and lowest health care cost for individuals and businesses in a managed competition situation.
6. **The three broad approaches to achieving universal coverage of health for all Americans:**
   a. National health insurance paid for by tax revenues
   b. Mandated private health insurance for everyone, with vouchers given to low income families.

Continued

TABLE 23-1	*Continued*

   c. Mandated employer-sponsored health insurance for all workers and their dependants, together with expanded government insurance for non-workers.

7. **Members of *Generation X* will pay many times more into Social Security than they will ever get out of it.**

8. **Groups that lobby for the poor in Washington are:**
   a. Churches, civil rights groups, and liberal organizations
   b. Organized labor
   c. Welfare program administrators and lawyers

9. **Examples of those groups that lobby for the poor in Washington:**
   a. Urban League and NAACP
   b. National Conference of Catholic Bishops and National Council of Churches
   c. Americans for Democratic Action and Common Cause

10. **Groups that are usually homeless in America:**
   a. Youthful runaways
   b. Alcohol and drug abusers
   c. Mentally ill
   d. People recently evicted from rental units
   e. Those who have previously lived with family or friends

Below are a few myths concerning welfare:

- **Hard work is the answer to the welfare power.** This applies to the low-income worker who is not getting paid enough to make a decent living. Instead of blaming his employer, he blames welfare recipients.

- **Most welfare recipients are African Americans.** According to statistics the majority of individuals who are on welfare are Whites. However, Blacks and Hispanics do have higher percentages.

- **All welfare mothers do is have illegitimate children.** On average welfare mothers have about two children.

- **Welfare is the good life: Cadillacs and color televisions.** This is a projection of society's fantasies.

- **Most welfare recipients are cheaters.** According to the research, this is not true.

- **Welfare takes up most of our taxes.** The military budget has been larger. (Wiley, George. *Welfare Mothers Speak Out.*)

According to political scientists and economists, the welfare reform of 1996 had succeeded in reducing the number of people on welfare in the United States by at least 50 percent. In some states it is even higher, such as Idaho, where the number of people on welfare dropped 85 percent.

■ CONCLUSION

Social welfare policy largely determines who gets what from the government. Over half of the federal budget is devoted to "human resources." The government is a major redistribution of income from group to group.

Suggested Readings

Derthick, Martha. *Agency Under Stress: The Social Security Administration in American Government.* Washington, D.C.: Brookings Institution, 1990.

Handler, Joel. *The Poverty of Welfare Reform.* New Haven, CT: Yale University Press, 1995.

Noble, Charles. *Welfare as We Know It: A Political History of the American Welfare State.* New York: Oxford University Press, 1997.

Page, Benjamin I. and James R. Simmons. *What Government Can Do: Dealing with Poverty and Inequality.* Chicago: University of Chicago Press, 2000.

Peters, Guy B. *American Publicity Policy: Promise and Performance.* 5th ed., New York: Chatham House/Seven Bridges Press, 1999.

Pierson, Christopher. "The 'Exceptional' United States: First New Nation or Last Welfare State," *Social Policy and Administration.* 24 (1990), p. 188.

American Enterprise Institute http://www.aei.org

Electronic Policy Network http://www.epn.org

CHAPTER 23
STUDY GUIDE

After reading and studying this chapter, one should be able to do the following:

1. Identify the following:
   a. Public assistance

   _____

   b. Entitlement program

   _____

   c. Medicaid

   _____

   d. Unemployment compensation

   _____

   e. Transfer payments

   _____

   f. Temporary Assistance for Needy Families (TANF)

   _____

   g. Equal Opportunity Act (1964)

   _____

   h. Poverty line

   _____

   i. COLA

   _____

j. Dependency ratio

_____

k. Welfare

_____

l. Social Security

_____

m. Medicare

_____

n. In-kind assistance

_____

2. Explain the Bowtie Professor's view concerning the social welfare state.

_____

_____

_____

3. List the five reasons why people are poor, according to Yecats.

_____

_____

_____

_____

_____

4. Explain the two major stages of the social welfare state.

_____

_____

5. Identify the four major reasons why Conservatives criticize the poverty line.

_____

_____

_____

_____

6. Identify the four major reasons why Liberals criticize the poverty line.

_____

_____

_____

_____

7. List a few programs that came out of the social welfare state.

_____

_____

_____

8. Explain Box 23-1.

_____

_____

_____

9. Explain or identify the major key points in Table 23-1.

_____

_____

_____

10. Name and explain the six myths concerning welfare.

_____

_____

_____

_____

_____

_____

TRUE/FALSE MULTIPLE CHOICE SAMPLE TEST

1. Social welfare policy largely determines who gets what from the government.
- **a.** True
- **b.** False

2. Over half of the federal budget is devoted to "human resources."
- **a.** True
- **b.** False

3. The government is a major redistribution of income from group to group.
- **a.** True
- **b.** False

4. Idaho is a state in which the number of people on welfare dropped around 85 percent.
- **a.** True
- **b.** False

5. The U.S. Family Act (1988) provided child care for job participants.
- **a.** True
- **b.** False

6. One idea for welfare reform was to use tax credits.
  a. True
  b. False

7. Welfare is aid provided by the government to the poor or needy.
  a. True
  b. False

8. Social workers are usually homeless in America.
  a. True
  b. False

9. There are groups who lobby for the poor in Washington.
  a. True
  b. False

10. According to the Bowtie Professor, losers are *not* those who blame others for their mistakes.
  a. True
  b. False

11. One idea for welfare reform is to target grandmothers.
  a. True
  b. False

12. There are five broad approaches to universal health coverage for all Americans.
  a. True
  b. False

13. The mentally ill are a group who are usually a part of the homeless in America.
  a. True
  b. False

14. There are eight myths concerning welfare.
  a. True
  b. False

15. The major purpose of the U.S. Family Act (1988) was to end long-term dependence on "welfare."
  a. True
  b. False

16. Which of the following was *not* an idea for welfare reform?
   a. In kind assistance
   b. Tax credits
   c. Target teenage mothers
   d. Reduce fraud
   e. Terminate welfare entirely

17. There are _____ myths concerning welfare.
   a. 3
   b. 4
   c. 5
   d. 6
   e. 7

18. The U.S. Family Act of _____ required the state governments to require job training for adults receiving welfare.
   a. 1978
   b. 1986
   c. 1988
   d. 1996
   e. 1998

19. Which group is *not* usually homeless in America?
   a. Youthful runaways
   b. The mentally ill
   c. Alcohol and drug abusers
   d. Social workers
   e. People recently evicted from rental units

20. There are _____ reasons why liberals criticize the poverty line.
   a. 8
   b. 7
   c. 5
   d. 6
   e. 4

21. There are _____ reasons why conservatives criticize the poverty line.

   a. 8

   b. 7

   c. 6

   d. 5

   e. 4

22. _____ highlights a few welfare issues and defines relevant terms.

   a. Table 23-1

   b. Box 23-1

   c. Figure 23

   d. Table 23-2

   e. Box 23-2

23. The official definition of the poverty line does not take into account the _____ percent tof Americans living below the poverty level.

   a. 16

   b. 18

   c. 21

   d. 25

   e. 26

24. The official definition of "poverty line" does not take into account the _____ million Americans living below the poverty line.

   a. 25

   b. 36

   c. 45

   d. 51

   e. 57

25. There are _____ major reasons why many people are poor in America, according to Yecats.

   a. 3

   b. 4

   c. 6

   d. 5

   e. 7

Name _____ **Date** _____

26. According to political scientists and economists, the welfare reforms of _____ had succeeded in reducing the number on people on welfare.
    a. 1936
    b. 1947
    c. 1966
    d. 1985
    e. 1996

27. _____ is a social welfare program for which only those living in poverty are eligible.
    a. Social Security
    b. Dependency Ratio
    c. Supplemental Security Income
    d. Public Assistance
    e. Unemployed Compensation

28. A social insurance program that temporarily replaces part of the wages of workers who have lost their jobs, is known as:
    a. Temporary Assistance to Needy Families
    b. Aid to Families with Dependent Children
    c. Unemployed Compensation
    d. Public Assistance
    e. COLA

29. Most states limit federal assistance programs to about_____.
    a. four-years
    b. two-years
    c. three-years
    d. five years
    e. six years

30. Which of the following is not a social welfare program?
    a. Economic Opportunity Act
    b. Pell Grant
    c. Social Security
    d. Transfer Payments
    e. Medicare

American Foreign Policy: International Politics

American foreign policy
is self-interests with a humanitarian cause,
as the nation is controlled
by international laws.

America by far
is definitely a super power,
as her chief leaders dwell
at the United Nations' tower.

It is truly a nation
which has a great deal of wealth,
the god of materialism
has cost many their health.

The U.S. is a country
that is militarily strong,
and she has definitely done
many Third World nations wrong.

In the end,
American foreign policy is politically bold,
and through the New World order,
she will sell her soul.

—The Bowtie Professor

Name _____ **Date** _____

Explain:

_____

_____

_____

_____

_____

_____

_____

_____

_____

_____

_____

_____

_____

_____

_____

_____

_____

_____

_____

_____

_____

_____

A course in American Government would not be complete without considering the importance of **Foreign Policy,** a nation's policies designed to
affect global affairs. Indeed, foreign and domestic policies many times form
an inseparable relationship, one which affects the lifestyle of every American. On a planet where nations are becoming more interdependent, the
United States and its leaders must try to develop a successful foreign policy
designed to preserve world peace and insure American security. The United
States must conduct its foreign policy and interact with other countries,
known as **International Relations,** the political, economic and social interaction of nation states and how they respond toward one another. In short,
the story of international relations is a tale of many different nations trying
to live in harmony with each other.

For the United States, as for virtually every other nation, the core of national interest has been to protect its territorial integrity and the way of life.
American foreign policy has consisted of strategies or planned courses of
action that would ultimately benefit our national interest.

Box 24-1 gives a moment of thought on America's foreign policy.

Below are a few key terms used when discussing the issue of foreign policy:

- **Balance of Power**—An attempt to bring order to international relations
  in the 19th century by creating a system of alliances among nations so
  that the relative strength of each alliance balances that of the others.
- **Cold War**—The political, military, and ideological struggle between the
  U.S. and the Soviet Union following the end of World War II and ending
  with the collapse of the Soviet Union's communist government in 1991.
- **Collective Security**—An attempt to bring order to international relations by all nations joining together to guarantee each other's "territorial integrity" and "independence" against "external aggression." In
  other words, one for all and all for one.

BOX 24-1

Is it the United States' responsibility to try to police the entire world? Should America try and
feed other nations when she has homeless people living on the streets within her own territories? By far, United States foreign policy is self-interest with a disguised humanitarian cause. If
there is no threat to the U.S., Western Europe, and N.A.T.O., then why does America get into all
these senseless wars, have our soldiers killed, while spending billions and billions of dollars to
upgrade other countries, when we have problems still right here at home such as drugs, crime,
unemployment, health care, etc.? Perhaps the U.S. should clean its own house first instead of
trying to save someone else.

Just a Moment of Thought
Professor Yecats

- **Containment**—A policy of preventing the enemy from expanding its boundaries or influence. This describes the U.S. foreign policy versus the U.S.S.R. during the Cold War.
- **Detente**—The relaxation of strained relations between nations; specifically used to refer to the relation of tensions between the U.S. and the Soviet Union.
- **Deterrence**—The U.S. approach to deterring any nuclear attack from the Soviet Union by maintaining a second-strike capability.
- **Domino Theory**—If one country falls to communism, the others will also.
- **First-Strike Capability**—The ability of a nation's forces to completely destroy its enemy's ability to retaliate.
- **Glasnost**—A Russian term meaning "openness"; refers to the removal of many restrictions on individual freedom in the Soviet Union under Mikhail Gorbachev.
- **Hard Target Kill Capability**—The ability to destroy another nation's land-based missiles in a first-strike.
- **Marshall Plan**—A U.S. program to rebuild the nations of Western Europe in the aftermath of World War II in order to render them less susceptible to communist influence or takeover.
- **NATO**—North Atlantic Treaty organization, which consists of 14 western nations providing for joint military cooperation, formed in 1949.
- **Regional Security**—An attempt to bring order to international relations during the Cold War by creating regional alliances between a superpower and nations of a particular region.
- **SALT I**—Consists of a treaty limiting anti-ballistic missiles (ABMs) and an agreement placing a numerical ceiling on offensive missiles. SALT I was the first step forward on the control of nuclear arms and both sides agreed to continue negotiations. SALT stands for Strategic Arms Limitation Talks. SALT I took place in 1972 during the Nixon administration.
- **SALT II**—In 1979, SALT II set an overall limit on strategic nuclear launch vehicles (ICBMs), bombers, and long-range cruise missiles at 2250 for each side. But when the Soviet Union invaded Afghanistan, President Carter withdrew the SALT II treaty from Senate consideration.
- **Second-Strike Capability**—The ability of a nation's forces to survive a surprise attack by the enemy and then to retaliate effectively.
- **Superpowers**—Refers to the U.S. and the U.S.S.R. after World War II, when these two nations dominated international politics.
- **Third World**—Those nations of the world that remain economically underdeveloped.
- **Truman Doctrine**—A U.S. Foreign policy, first articulated by President Truman, that pledged this nation to "support free people who are resisting attempted subjugation by armed minorities or by outside pressures."

- **Unilateralism**—A political strategy in which a nation conducts its political, social, economic, and military functions alone and does not make any alliances.

Most Americans are uninformed about foreign policy, not only about the reasons behind a particular policy but about who the men and women are who decide which policy this country will pursue overseas. A successful foreign policy must have the support of key decision-makers in the executive and legislative branches, the military, the public, and other influential opinion makers. When one observes the list below, he or she will notice others who help to formulate foreign policy:

1. President/Congress
2. Political elites
3. Multinational corporations
4. National Security Council
5. State Department
6. Defense Department
7. Joint Chiefs of Staff
8. Central Intelligence Agency

The formal power of the president to make foreign policy derives from the U.S. Constitution, which makes the president responsible for the preservation of national security and designates the president commander-in-chief of the armed forces. In principle, the State Department is the executive agency

most directly involved with foreign affairs. The Department's primary objectives in foreign policy for the 21st century are as follows:

1. Promoting democratic values.
2. Fostering global growth by promoting market principles.
3. Promoting the secure global environment.
4. Working with allies against new transitional threats.
5. Reshaping and renewing our alliances and other important ties.

Three major themes have guided U.S. foreign policy:

1. Isolationism
2. Global involvement
3. Containment

TABLE 24-1

1. What is the United Nations?
   An international organization comprising most of the countries of the world, to promote security and economic development. The organization was formed in 1945.
2. What is the structure of the United Nations?
   - General Assembly
   - Security Council
   - The Economic and Social Council
   - The Trusteeship Council
   - The Secretariat
   - International Court of Justice
3. List a few United Nations tactics
   - Negotiation
   - Inquiry
   - Mediation
   - Arbitration
   - Adjudication
4. Name four reasons why the U.S. has appeared to have lost power in the international arena.
   - The renewed economic power of Western Europe and Japan.
   - The strain of the U.S. balance of payment.
   - The new power of OPEC in the Middle Eastern countries in the 1970's.
   - Third World nations calling for a new international economic order.
5. List some of the Western institutions or organizations that possess a great deal of control in the Third World.
   - International Monetary Fund
   - International Bank for Reconstruction and Development
   - General Agreement on Tariffs and Trade (G.A.T.T. now is the World Trade Organization.)
6. What is the direction of the United States and other world nations?
   The direction of the U.S. is to move toward a one-world government, usually referred to as the "New World Order." In fact, this is the major objective of the United Nations.

Isolationism was a period during the 1700's and 1800's whereby the United States had little to do with international politics. The **Monroe Doctrine** of 1823 stated that the U.S. would not accept foreign intervention in the Western Hemisphere and would not meddle in European affairs. Global Involvement came to surface when the United States entered World War I on April 6, 1917, and later World War II. The theory of containment came out of the Truman Doctrine. **Containment** was a policy by the U.S. of preventing the enemy from expanding its boundaries or influence. This described the U.S. foreign policy's attitude toward the Soviet Union during the Cold War.

Table 24-1 presents a short question and answer session.

■ CONCLUSION

Foreign policy includes national goals and the techniques used to achieve them. National security policy is designed to protect the independence and the political and economic integrity of the United States. America's foreign policy tends to be self-interest with the disguise of a humanitarian cause.

Suggested Readings

Ambrose, Stephen. *Rise to Globalism.* Rev. ed., New York: Penguin Books, 1997.

Huntington, Samuel P. *The Clash of Civilizations: Civilizations and the Remaking of World Order.* New York: Simon and Schuster, 1997.

La Fiber, Walter. *America, Russia, and the Cold War, 1945-1990.* New York: McGraw-Hill, 1991.

Mann, James. *About Face: A History of America's Curious Relationship with China, Nixon to Clinton.* New York: Knopf, 1999.

Sen, Amartya Kumar. *Development as Freedom.* New York: Knopf, 1999.

Amnesty International http://www.amnesty.org/

Defense Link http://www.defenselink.mil/

CHAPTER 24
STUDY GUIDE

After reading and studying this chapter, one should be able to do the following:

1. Explain the Bowtie Professor's views concerning American foreign policy.

_____

_____

_____

2. Explain the moments of thought in Box 24-1.

_____

_____

_____

3. Identify the major players that help to influence foreign policy.

_____

_____

_____

4. List the three major themes that have guided America's foreign policy.

_____

_____

_____

5. List the five primary objectives of America's foreign policy for the 21st century.

_____

_____

_____

_____

_____

_____

6. Identify the following:
  a. Foreign policy

_____

  b. International politics

_____

  c. Balance of power

_____

  d. Cold War

_____

  e. Collective security

_____

  f. Containment

_____

  g. Detente

_____

  h. Deterrence

_____

  i. Domino theory

_____

    j. First-strike capability

_____

    k. Glasnost

_____

    l. Hard target kill capability

_____

7. Identify the United Nations and its structure and tactics.

_____

_____

_____

8. List the four reasons why the United States has appeared to have lost power in the international arena.

_____

_____

_____

_____

9. List a few Western institutions that possess a great deal of control in the Third World.

_____

_____

_____

10. Identify the following:
    a. Unilateralism

_____

b. Truman Doctrine

_____

c. Third World

_____

d. Superpowers

_____

e. Second-strike capability

_____

f. SALT I

_____

g. SALT II

_____

h. Regional security

_____

i. NATO

_____

j. Marshall Plan

_____

TRUE/FALSE MULTIPLE CHOICE SAMPLE TEST

1. President Carter withdrew the SALT II treaty from the U.S. Senate consideration.
   a. True
   b. False

2. Global involvement is *not* one of the themes that has guided U.S. foreign policy.
   a. True
   b. False

3. Unilateralism is when nations do not make any alliances but take and make actions alone.
   a. True
   b. False

4. Detente is the relaxation of strained relations between nations.
   a. True
   b. False

5. There is no such thing as "domino theory."
   a. True
   b. False

6. Most Americans are informed about foreign policy.
   a. True
   b. False

7. A successful foreign policy must have the support of key decision makers.
   a. True
   b. False

8. There are three major themes that have guided U.S. foreign policy.
   a. True
   b. False

9. The formal power of the U.S. President to make foreign policy derives from the CIA.
   a. True
   b. False

10. The U.S. State Department is *not* the executive agency most directly involved with foreign affairs.
    a. True
    a. False

11. The Bowtie Professor raises the question whether or not it is America's responsibility to try to police the entire world.
    a. True
    b. False

12. Box 24-1 gives a moment of thought on America's foreign policy.
    a. True
    b. False

13. There is no such thing as "card theory."
    a. True
    b. False

14. There is such a thing as "Glasnost."
    a. True
    b. False

15. The Third World includes those nations that remain economically underdeveloped.
    a. True
    b. False

16. Which of the following does *not* help to influence America's foreign policy?
    a. President
    b. Congress
    c. CIA
    d. Joint Chiefs of Staff
    e. Governor

17. If one country falls to Communism, the others will fall as well. This is known as:
    a. Card theory
    b. Glasnost theory
    c. Detente
    d. Domino theory
    e. SALT I

18. Most Americans are uninformed about:
    a. The Third World
    b. Foreign policy
    c. Detente
    d. The Marshall Plan
    e. Unilateralism

19. NATO consists of _____ Western nations.
  a. 14
  b. 21
  c. 33
  d. 42
  e. 56

20. NATO was formed in:
  a. 1925
  b. 1936
  c. 1949
  d. 1961
  e. 1970

21. SALT I took place during the _____ administration.
  a. Truman
  b. Carter
  c. Nixon
  d. Johnson
  e. Reagan

22. The _____ Plan was designed to rebuild the nations of Western Europe.
  a. Marshall
  b. Detente
  c. NATO
  d. Truman
  e. Glasnost

23. There are _____ major tactics that are used by the United Nations.
  a. 4
  b. 5
  c. 6
  d. 7
  e. 8

24. There are _____ elements that make up the structure of the United Nations.
    a. 3
    b. 4
    c. 5
    d. 6
    e. 7

25. The United Nations was formed in:
    a. 1965
    b. 1971
    c. 1982
    d. 1958
    e. 1945

26. Which of the following is not a tactic used by the United Nations?
    a. Détente
    b. Adjudication
    c. Inquiry
    d. Arbitration
    e. Mediation

27. Another term for "one-world government" is:
    a. Unilateralism
    b. New World Order
    c. Containment
    d. Glasnost
    e. Deterrence

28. Which theme has guided U.S. foreign policy?
    a. Detente
    b. Glasnost
    c. Isolationism
    d. Collective Security
    e. Unilateralism

29. _____ is when a nation conducts it political and economic strategy along.
  a. Negotiation
  b. Arbitration
  c. Globalism
  d. Unilateralism
  e. Inquiry

30. SALT II was considered in_____ which set an overall limit on strategic nuclear launch vehicles and bombers, and long-range cruise missiles 2250 for each side.
  a. 1959
  b. 1964
  c. 1970
  d. 1971
  e. 1979

■ RESOURCES

Federal Government

Books

Bartz, Carl F. *The Department of State.* Chelsea, 1988.

Baum, Lawrence. *The Supreme Court.* Congressional Quarterly, 1988.

Bernstein, Richard B., and Jerome Agel. *The Congress.* Sutton, 1989.

Bernstein, Richard B., and Jerome Agel. *The Presidency.* Walker, 1989.

Bernstein, Richard B., and Jerome Agel. *The Supreme Court.* Walker, 1989.

Bowen, Catherine D. *Miracle at Philadelphia: The Story of the Constitutional Convention, May to September 1787.* Little, 1986.

Congressional Quarterly. *How Congress Works.* Congressional Quarterly, 1983.

Hoopes, Roy. *What a United States Senator Does.* Harper, 1975.

Johnson, Joan. *Justice.* Watts, 1985.

Lindop, Edmund. *The Bill of Rights and Landmark Cases.* Watts, 1989.

Ragsdale, Bruce A. *The House of Representatives.* Chelsea, 1989.

Ritchie, Donald A. *The Senate.* Chelsea, 1988.

Schlesinger, Arthur M., Jr. *The Federal Government: How It Works. Know Your Government Series.* Chelsea, 1989.

Van Doren, Carl. *The Great Rehearsal: The Story of the Making and Ratifying of the Constitution of the United States.* Penguin, 1986.

Weiss, Ann. *The Supreme Court.* Enslow, 1987.

Witt, Elder. *The Supreme Court and Individual Rights.* Congressional Quarterly, 1988.

Periodicals

Peterson, Robert W. "The Bill of Rights." *Boys' Life* magazine series, Boy Scouts of America, January-December, 1991.

Video

The Constitution: That Delicate Balance. John D. and Catherine T. MacArthur Foundation Video Classics. Films Incorporated, 1984. This series of thirteen videocassettes is available in larger public libraries.

Politics and Political Science

Books

Archer, Jules. *Winners and Losers: How Elections Work in America.* Harcourt, 1984.

Choosing the President 1992: A Citizen's Guide to the Electoral Process. Lyons & Burford, 1992.

Eannace, Mary Rose. *The Pizza Problem: Democracy in Action.* PS Associates Croton, 1990.

Kronenwetter, Michael. *Are You a Liberal? Are You a Conservative?* Watts, 1984.

McKissack, Patricia C. *The Civil Rights Movement in America from 1865 to the Present.* Childrens, 1987.

Meltzer, Milton. *American Politics: How It Really Works.* Morrow, 1989.

Samuels, Cynthia K. *It's a Free Country! A Young Person's Guide to Politics and Elections.* Macmillan, 1988.

Sullivan, George. *Campaigns and Elections.* Silver Burdett, 1991.

Sullivan, George. Choosing the Candidates. Silver Burdett, 1992.

Weissberg, Robert. *Politics: A Handbook for Students.* Harcourt, 1985.

Periodicals

Common Cause magazine. Six issues per year. 2030 M Street NW, Washington, D.C. 20036.

Congressional Digest magazine. Ten issues per year. Congressional Corp., 3231 P Street N.W., Washington, D.C. 20007.

Reference

Books

Carruth, Gorton. *The Encyclopedia of American Facts & Dates.* Harper and Row, 1987. Arranged by date and subject; covers one thousand years of American history and culture from 986 to 1986.

Furlong, William Rea, and Byron McCandless. *So Proudly We Hail.* Smithsonian Institution, 1981. A history of the U.S. flag with index of flag protocol and laws.

Lesko, Matthew. *Lesko's Info-Power Sourcebook.* Information USA, 1990. This guide to the U.S. government includes names, addresses, and phone numbers of thousands of government information sources and specialists; a keyword index helps the researcher locate information by subject.

Pharos Books. *The World Almanac and Book of Facts.* Pharos Books, annual. An easy-to-use source of statistics and up-to-date facts on political organizations, census figures, taxes, etc.

Periodicals

Congressional Quarterly, Inc. *Current American Government.* Congressional Quarterly Inc., every spring and fall. Covers current issues, such as the nuclear energy lobby and government budget, and many more legislative and judicial topics.

Congressional Quarterly, Inc. *Washington Information Directory.* Congressional Quarterly, Inc., annual. Lists thousands of private and special-interest organizations in Washington as well as congressional committees and government agencies and their key officials, addresses, phone numbers, functions, and jurisdictions.

U.S. Government Publications

U.S. Bureau of the Census. *Statistical Abstract of the United States.* U.S. Department of Commerce, Bureau of the Census, annual. The standard summary of statistics on the social, political, and economic organization of the United States.

U.S. Government Printing Office. *The United States Government Manual.* U.S. Government Printing Office, annual. Lists the programs and purposes of each government department, agency, and commission; includes organizational charts; and gives names, addresses, and telephone numbers of key officials. Covers the executive, legislative, and judicial branches of government. Many other informative government publications are available. For a catalog, write to the Superintendent of Documents, U.S. Government Printing Office, P.O. Box 371954, Pittsburgh, PA 15250-7954; phone 202-512-1800, or fax your request to 202-512-2250.

The Declaration of Independence of the Thirteen Colonies In CONGRESS, July 4, 1776

The Unanimous Declaration of the Thirteen United States of America,

When in the Course of human Events, it becomes necessary for one People to dissolve the Political Bands which have connected them with another, and to assume among the Powers of the Earth, the separate and equal Station to which the Laws of Nature and of Nature's God entitle them, a decent Respect to the Opinions of mankind requires that they should declare the causes which impel them to the Separation.

We hold these Truths to be self-evident, that all Men are created equal, that they are endowed by their Creator with certain unalienable Rights, that among these are Life, Liberty and the Pursuit of Happiness—That to secure these rights, Governments are instituted among Men, deriving their just powers from the consent of the Governed—that whenever any Form of Government becomes destructive of these Ends, it is the Right of the People to alter or to abolish it, and to institute new Government, laying its Foundation on such principles and organizing its Powers in such Form, as to them shall seem most likely to effect their Safety and Happiness. Prudence, indeed, will dictate that Governments long established should not be changed for light and transient Causes; and accordingly all Experience hath shewn, that Mankind are more disposed to suffer, while Evils are sufferable, than to right themselves by abolishing the Forms to which they are accustomed. But when a long Train of Abuses and Usurpations, pursuing invariably the same Object evinces a Design to reduce them under absolute Despotism, it is their Right, it is their Duty, to throw off such Government, and to provide new Guards for their future Security. Such has been the patient Sufferance of these Colonies; and such is now the Necessity which constrains them to alter their former Systems of Government. The History of the present King of Great Britain is a History of repeated Injuries and Usurpations, all having in direct Object the Establishment of an absolute Tyranny over these States. To prove this, let Facts be submitted to a candid world.

He has refused his Assent to Laws, the most wholesome and necessary for the public good.

He has forbidden his Governors to pass Laws of immediate and pressing Importance, unless suspended in their Operation till his Assent should be obtained; and when so suspended, he has utterly neglected to attend to them.

He has refused to pass other Laws for the Accommodation of large Districts of People, unless those People would relinquish the Right of Representation in the Legislature, a Right inestimable to them and formidable to Tyrants only.

He has called together Legislative Bodies at Places unusual, uncomfortable, and distant from the Depository of their Public Records, for the sole Purpose of fatiguing them into Compliance with his Measures.

He has dissolved Representative Houses repeatedly, for opposing with manly Firmness his invasions on the Rights of the People.

He has refused for a long time, after such Dissolutions, to cause others to be elected; whereby the Legislative Powers, incapable of Annihilation, have returned to the People at large for their exercise; the State remaining in the mean time exposed to all the Dangers of Invasion from without, and Convulsions within.

He has endeavoured to prevent the Population of these States; for that Purpose obstructing the Laws for Naturalization of Foreigners; refusing to pass others to encourage their Migrations hither, and raising the Conditions of new Appropriations of Lands.

He has obstructed the Administration of Justice, by refusing his Assent to Laws for establishing Judiciary Powers.

He has made Judges dependent on his Will alone, for the Tenure of their Offices, and the Amount and payment of their Salaries.

He has erected a Multitude of New Offices, and sent hither Swarms of Officers to harass our People, and eat out their Substance.

He has kept among us, in Times of Peace, Standing Armies without the consent of our Legislatures.

He has affected to render the Military independent of, and superior to the Civil Power.

He has combined with others to subject us to a Jurisdiction foreign to our Constitution and unacknowledged by our Laws; giving his Assent to their Acts of pretended Legislation:

For quartering large Bodies of Armed Troops among us:

For protecting them, by a mock Trial, from punishment for any Murders which they should commit on the Inhabitants of these States:

For cutting off our Trade with all Parts of the World:

For imposing Taxes on us without our Consent:

For depriving us, in many Cases, of the Benefits of Trial by Jury:

For transporting us beyond Seas to be tried for pretended offences:

For abolishing the free System of English Laws in a neighbouring Province, establishing therein an arbitrary Government, and enlarging its Boundaries so as to render it at once an Example and fit Instrument for introducing the same absolute Rule into these Colonies:

For taking away our Charters, abolishing our most valuable Laws, and altering fundamentally the Forms of our Governments:

For suspending our own Legislatures, and declaring themselves invested with Power to legislate for us in all Cases whatsoever.

He has abdicated Government here, by declaring us out of his Protection and waging War against us.

He has plundered our seas, ravaged our Coasts, burnt our towns, and destroyed and Lives of our People.

He is at this Time transporting large Armies of foreign Mercenaries to compleat the works of Death, Desolation and Tyranny, already begun with circumstances of Cruelty and Perfidy scarcely paralleled in the most barbarous Ages, and totally unworthy the Head of a civilized Nation.

He has constrained our fellow Citizens taken Captive on the high Seas to bear Arms against their Country, to become the Executioners of their Friends and Brethren, or to fall themselves by their Hands.

He has excited domestic Insurrections amongst us, and has endeavoured to bring on the Inhabitants of our Frontiers, the merciless Indian Savages, whose known Rule of Warfare, is an undistinguished Destruction of all Ages, Sexes and Conditions.

In every stage of these Oppressions we have Petitioned for Redress in the most humble Terms: Our repeated Petitions have been answered only by repeated Injury. A Prince, whose character is thus marked by every act which may define a Tyrant, is unfit to be the Ruler of a free People.

Nor have we been wanting in Attentions to our British Brethren. We have warned them from Time to Time of Attempts by their Legislature to extend an unwarrantable jurisdiction over us. We have reminded them of the Circumstances of our Emigration and Settlement here. We have appealed to their native Justice and Magnanimity, and we have conjured them by the Ties of our common Kindred to disavow these Usurpations, which, would inevitably interrupt our Connections and Correspondence. They too have been deaf to the Voice of Justice and of Consanguinity. We must, therefore, acquiesce in the Necessity, which denounces our Separation, and hold them, as we hold the rest of Mankind, Enemies in War, in Peace, Friends.

We, therefore, the Representatives of the UNITED STATES OF AMERICA, in General Congress, Assembled, appealing to the Supreme Judge of the World for the Rectitude of our Intentions, do, in the Name, and by the Authority of the good People of these Colonies, solemnly Publish and Declare, That these United Colonies are, and of Right out to be, Free and Independent States; that they are absolved from all Allegiance to the British Crown, and that all political Connection between them and the State of Great Britain, is and ought to be totally dissolved; and that as Free and Independent States, they have full Power to levy War, conclude Peace, contract Alliances, establish Commerce, and to do all other Acts and Things which Independent States may of right do. And for the support of this declaration, with a firm Reliance on the Protection of Divine Providence, we mutually pledge to each other our lives, our Fortunes and our sacred Honor.

Federalist No. 10

The Same Subject Continued:
The Union as a Safeguard Against Domestic Faction and Insurrection

From the New York Packet.
Friday, November 23, 1787.

Author: **James Madison**

To the People of the State of New York:

AMONG the numerous advantages promised by a well constructed Union, none deserves to be more accurately developed than its tendency to break and control the violence of fraction. The friend of popular governments never finds himself so much alarmed for their character and fate, as when he contemplates their propensity to this dangerous vice. He will not fail, therefore, to set a due value on any plan which, without violating the principles to which he is attached, provides a proper cure for it. The instability, injustice, and confusion introduced into the public councils, have, in truth, been the mortal diseases under which popular governments have everywhere perished; as they continue to be the favorite and fruitful topics from which the adversaries to liberty derive their most specious declamations. The valuable improvements made by the American constitutions on the popular models, both ancient and modern, cannot certainly be too much admired; but it would be an unwarrantable partiality, to contend that they have as effectually obviated the danger on this side, as was wished and expected. Complaints are everywhere heard from our most considerate and virtuous citizens, equally the friends of public and private faith, and of public and personal liberty, that our governments are too unstable, that the public good is disregarded in the conflicts of rival parties, and that measures are too often decided, not according to the rules of justice and the rights of the minor party, but by the superior force of an interested and overbearing majority. However anxiously we may wish that these complaints had no foundation, the evidence, of known facts will not permit us to deny that they are in some degree true. It will be found, indeed, on a candid review of our situation, that some of the distresses under which we labor have been erroneously charged on the operation of our governments; but it will be found, at the same time, that other causes will not alone account for many of our heaviest misfortunes; and, particularly, for that prevailing and increasing distrust of public engagements, and alarm for private rights, which are echoed from one end of the continent to the other. These must be chiefly, if not wholly, effects of the unsteadiness and injustice with which a factious spirit has tainted our public administrations.

By a fraction, I understand a number of citizens, whether amounting to a majority or a minority of the whole, who are united and actuated by some common impulse of passion, or of interest, adversed to the rights of other citizens, or to the permanent and aggregate interests of the community.

These are two methods of curing the mischiefs of faction: the one, by removing its causes; the other, by controlling its effects.

There are again two methods of removing the causes of faction: the one, by destroying the liberty which is essential to its existence; the other, by giving to every citizen the same opinions, the same passions, and the same interests.

It could never be more truly said than of the first remedy, that it was worse than the disease. Liberty is to faction what air is to fire, an aliment without which it instantly expires. But it could not be less folly to abolish liberty, which is essential to political life, because it nourishes faction, than it would be to wish the annihilation of air, which is essential to animal life, because it imparts to fire its destructive agency.

The second expedient is as impracticable as the first would be unwise. As long as the reason of man continues fallible, and he is at liberty to exercise it, different opinions will be formed. As long as the connection subsists between his reason and his self-love, his opinions and his passions will have a reciprocal influence on each other; and the former will be objects to which the latter will attach themselves. The diversity in the faculties of men, from which the rights of property originate, is not less an insuperable obstacle to a uniformity of interests. The protection of these faculties is the first object of government. From the protection of different and unequal faculties of acquiring property, the possession of different degrees and kinds of property immediately results; and from the influence of these on the sentiments and views of the respective proprietors, ensues a division of the society into different interests and parties.

The latent causes of faction are thus sown in the nature of man; and we see them everywhere brought into different degrees of activity, according to the different circumstances of civil society. A zeal for different opinions concerning religion, concerning government, and many other points, as well of speculation as of practice; an attachment to different leaders ambitiously contending for pre-eminence and power; or to persons of other descriptions whose fortunes have been interesting to the human passions, have, in turn, divided mankind into parties, inflamed them with mutual animosity, and rendered them much more disposed to vex and oppress each other than to co-operate for their common good. So strong is this propensity of mankind to fall into mutual animosities, that where no substantial occasion presents itself, the most frivolous and fanciful distinctions have been sufficient to kindle their unfriendly passions and excite their most violent conflicts. But the most common and durable source of factions has been the various and unequal distribution of property. Those who hold and those who are without property have ever formed distinct interests in society. Those who are creditors, and those who are debtors, fall under a like discrimination. A landed interest, a manufacturing interest, a mercantile interest, a moneyed interest, with many lesser interests, grow up of necessity in civilized nations, and divide them into different classes, actuated by different sentiments and views. The regulation of these various and interfering interests forms the principal task of modern legislation, and involves the spirit of party and faction in the necessary and ordinary operations of the government.

No man is allowed to be a judge in his own cause, because his interest would certainly bias his judgment, and, not improbably, corrupt his integrity. With equal, nay with greater reason, a body of men are unfit to be both judges and parties at the same time; yet what are many of the most important acts of legislation, but so many judicial determinations, not indeed concerning the rights of single persons, but concerning the rights of large bodies of citizens? And what are the different classes of legislators but advocates and parties to the causes which they determine? Is a law proposed concerning private debts? It is a question to which the creditors are parties on one side and the debtors on the other. Justice ought to hold the balance between them. Yet the parties are, and must be, themselves the judges; and the most numerous party, or, in other words, the most powerful faction must be expected to prevail. Shall domestic manufactures be encouraged, and in what degree, by restrictions on foreign manufactures? are questions which would be differently decided by the landed and the manufacturing classes, and probably by neither with a sole regard to justice and the public good. The apportionment of taxes on the various descriptions of property is an act which seems to require the most exact impartiality; yet there is, perhaps, no legislative act in which greater opportunity and temptation are given to a predominant party to trample on the rules of justice. Every shilling with which they overburden the inferior number, is a shilling saved to their own pockets.

It is in vain to say that enlightened statesmen will be able to adjust these clashing interests, and render them all subservient to the public good. Enlightened statesmen will not always be at the helm. Nor, in many cases, can such an adjustment be made at all without taking into view indirect and remote considerations, which will rarely prevail over the immediate interest which one party may find in disregarding the rights of another or the good of the whole.

The inference to which we are brought is, that the CAUSES of faction cannot be removed, and that relief is only to be sought in the means of controlling its EFFECTS.

If a faction consists of less than a majority, relief is supplied by the republican principle, which enables the majority to defeat its sinister views by regular vote. It may clog the administration, it may convulse the society; but it will be unable to execute and mask its violence under the forms of the Constitution. When a majority is included in a faction, the form of popular government, on the other hand, enables it to sacrifice to its ruling passion or interest both the public good and the rights of other citizens. To secure the public good and private rights against the danger of such a faction, and at the same time to preserve the spirit and the form of popular government, is then the great object to which our inquiries are directed. Let me add that it is the great desideratum by which this form of government can be rescued from the opprobrium under which it has so long labored, and be recommended to the esteem and adoption of mankind.

By what means is this object attainable? Evidently by one of two only. Either the existence of the same passion or interest in a majority at the same time must be prevented, or the majority, having such coexistent passion or interest, must be rendered, by their number and local situation, unable to concert and carry into effect schemes of oppression. If the impulse and the opportunity be suffered to coincide, we well know that neither moral nor religious motives can be relied on as an adequate control. They are not found to be such on the injustice and violence of individuals, and lose their efficacy in proportion to the number combined together, that is, in proportion as their efficacy becomes needful.

From this view of the subject it may be concluded that a pure democracy, by which I mean a society consisting of a small number of citizens, who assemble and administer the government in person, can admit of no cure for the mischiefs of faction. A common passion or interest will, in almost every case, be felt by a majority of the whole; a communication and concert result from the form of government itself; and there is nothing to check the inducements to sacrifice the weaker party or an obnoxious individual. Hence it is that such democracies have ever been spectacles of turbulence and contention; have ever been found incompatible with personal security or the rights of property; and have in general been as short in their lives as they have been violent in their deaths. Theoretic politicians, who have patronized this species of government, have erroneously supposed that by reducing mankind to a perfect equality in their political rights, they would, at the same time, be perfectly equalized and assimilated in their possessions, their opinions, and their passions.

A republic, by which I mean a government in which the scheme of representation takes place, opens a different prospect, and promises the cure for which we are seeking. Let us examine the points in which it varies from pure democracy, and we shall comprehend both the nature of the cure and the efficacy which it must derive from the Union.

The two great points of difference between a democracy and a republic are: first, the delegation of the government, in the latter, to a small number of citizens elected by the rest; secondly, the greater number of citizens, and greater sphere of country, over which the latter may be extended.

The effect of the first difference is, on the one hand, to refine and enlarge the public views, by passing them through the medium of a chosen body of citizens, whose wisdom may best discern the true interest of their country, and whose patriotism and love of justice will be least likely to sacrifice it to temporary or partial considerations. Under such a regulation, it may well happen that the public voice, pronounced by the representatives of the people, will be more consonant to the public good than if pronounced by the people themselves, convened for the purpose. On the other hand, the effect may be inverted. Men of factious tempers, of local prejudices, or of sinister designs, may, by intrigue, by corruption, or by other means, first obtain the suffrages, and then betray the interests, of the people. The question resulting is, whether small or extensive republics are more favorable to the election of proper guardians of the public weal; and it is clearly decided in favor of the latter by two obvious considerations:

In the first place, it is to be remarked that, however small the republic may be, the representatives must be raised to a certain number, in order to guard against the cabals of a few; and that, however large it may be, they must be limited to a certain number, in order to guard against the confusion of a multitude. Hence, the number of representatives in the two cases not being in proportion to that of the two constituents, and being proportionally greater in the small republic, it follows that, if the proportion of fit characters be not less in the large than in the small republic, the former will present a greater option, and consequently a greater probability of a fit choice.

In the next place, as each representative will be chosen by a greater number of citizens in the large than in the small republic, it will be more difficult for unworthy candidates to practice with success the vicious arts by which elections are too often carried; and the suffrages of the people being more free, will be more likely to center in men who possess the most attractive merit and the most diffusive and established characters.

It must be confessed that in this, as in most other cases, there is a mean, on both sides of which inconveniences will be found to lie. By enlarging too much the number of electors, you render the representatives too little acquainted with all their local circumstances and lesser interests; as by reducing it too much, you render him unduly attached to these, and too little fit to comprehend and pursue great and national objects. The federal Constitution forms a happy combination in this respect; the great and aggregate interests being referred to the national, the local and particular to the State legislatures.

The other point of difference is, the greater number of citizens and extent of territory which may be brought within the compass of republican than of democratic government; and it is this circumstance principally which renders factious combinations less to be dreaded in the former than in the latter. The smaller the society, the fewer probably will be the distinct parties and interests composing it; the fewer the distinct parties and interests, the more frequently will a majority be found of the same party; and the smaller the number of individuals composing a majority, and the smaller the compass within which they are placed, the more easily will they concert and execute their plans of oppression. Extend the sphere, and you take a greater variety of parties and interests; you make it less probable that a majority of the whole will have a common motive to invade the rights of other citizens; or if such a common motive exists, it will be more difficult for all who feel it to discover their own strength, and to act in unison with each other. Besides other impediments, it may be remarked that, where there is a consciousness of unjust or dishonorable purposes, communication is always checked by distrust in proportion to the number whose concurrence is necessary.

Hence, it clearly appears, that the same advantage which a republic has over a democracy, in controlling the effects of faction, is enjoyed by a large over a small republic,—is enjoyed by the Union over the States composing it. Does the advantage consist in the substitution of representatives whose enlightened views and virtuous sentiments render them superior to local prejudices and schemes of injustice? It will not be denied that the representation of the Union will be most likely to possess these requisite endowments. Does it consist in the greater security afforded by a greater variety of parties, against the event of any one party being able to outnumber and oppress the rest? In an equal degree does the increased variety of parties comprised within the Union, increase this security. Does it, in fine, consist in the greater obstacles opposed to the concert and accomplishment of the secret wishes of an unjust and interested majority? Here, again, the extent of the Union gives it the most palpable advantage.

The influence of factious leaders may kindle a flame within their particular States, but will be unable to spread a general conflagration through the other States. A religious sect may degenerate into a political faction in a part of the Confederacy; but the variety of sects dispersed over the entire face of it must secure the national councils against any danger from that source. A rage for paper money, for an abolition of debts, for an equal division of property, or for any other improper or wicked project, will be less apt to pervade the whole body of the Union than a particular member of it; in the same proportion as such a malady is more likely to taint a particular county or district, than an entire State.

In the extent and proper structure of the Union, therefore, we behold a republican remedy for the diseases most incident to republican government. And according to the degree of pleasure and pride we feel in being republicans, ought to be our zeal in cherishing the spirit and supporting the character of Federalists.

PUBLIUS

Federalist No. 51

The Structure of the Government Must Furnish the Proper Checks and Balances Between the Different Departments

From the New York Packet.
Friday, February 8, 1788.

Author: **Alexander Hamilton** or **James Madison**

To the People of the State of New York:

TO WHAT expedient, then, shall we finally resort, for maintaining in practice the necessary partition of power among the several departments, as laid down in the Constitution? The only answer that can be given is, that as all these exterior provisions are found to be inadequate, the defect must be supplied, by so contriving the interior structure of the government as that its several constituent parts may, by their mutual relations, be the means of keeping each other in their proper places. Without presuming to undertake a full development of this important idea, I will hazard a few general observations, which may perhaps place it in a clearer light, and enable us to form a more correct judgment of the principles and structure of the government planned by the convention. In order to lay a due foundation for that separate and distinct exercise of the different powers of government, which to a certain extent is admitted on all hands to be essential to the preservation of liberty, it is evident that each department should have a will of its own; and consequently should be so constituted that the members of each should have as little agency as possible in the appointment of the members of the others. Were this principle rigorously adhered to, it would require that all the appointments for the supreme executive, legislative, and judiciary magistracies should be drawn from the same fountain of authority, the people, through channels having no communication whatever with one another. Perhaps such a plan of constructing the several departments would be less difficult in practice than it may in contemplation appear. Some difficulties, however, and some additional expense would attend the execution of it. Some deviations, therefore, from the principle must be admitted. In the constitution of the judiciary department in particular, it might be inexpedient to insist rigorously on the principle: first, because peculiar qualifications being essential in the members, the primary consideration ought to be to select that mode of choice which best secures these qualifications; secondly, because the permanent tenure by which the appointments are held in that department, must soon destroy all sense of dependence on the authority conferring them. It is equally evident, that the members of each department should be as little dependent as possible on those of the others, for the emoluments annexed to their offices. Were the executive magistrate, or the judges, not independent of the legislature in this particular, their independence in every other would be merely nominal. But the great security against a gradual concentration of the several powers in the same department, consists in giving to those who administer each department the necessary constitutional means and personal motives to resist encroachments of the others. The provision for defense must in this, as in all other cases, be made commensurate to the danger of attack. Ambition must be made to counteract ambition. The interest of the man must be connected with the constitutional rights of the place. It may be a reflection on human nature, that such devices should be necessary to control the abuses of government. But what is government itself, but the greatest of all reflections on human nature? If men were angels, no government would be necessary. If angels were to govern men, neither external nor internal controls on government would be necessary. In framing a government which is to be administered by men over men, the great difficulty lies in this: you must first enable the government to control the governed; and in the next place oblige it to control itself. A dependence on the people is, no doubt, the primary control on the government; but experience has taught mankind the necessity of auxiliary precautions. This policy of supplying, by opposite and rival interests, the defect of better motives, might be traced through the whole system of human affairs, private as well as public. We see it particularly displayed in all the subordinate distributions of power, where the constant aim is to divide and arrange the several offices in such a manner as that each may be a check on the other that the private interest of every individual may be a sentinel over the public rights. These inventions of prudence cannot be less requisite in the distribution of the supreme powers of the State. But it is not possible to give to each department an equal power of self-defense. In republican government, the legislative authority necessarily predominates. The remedy for this inconveniency is to divide the legislature into different branches; and to render them, by different modes of election and different principles of action, as little connected with each other as the nature of their common functions and their common dependence on the society will admit. It may even be necessary to guard against dangerous encroachments by still further precautions. As the weight of the legislative authority requires that it should be thus divided, the weakness of the executive may require, on the other hand, that it should be fortified. An absolute negative on the legislature appears, at first view, to be the natural defense with which the executive magistrate should be armed. But perhaps it would be neither altogether safe nor alone sufficient. On ordinary occasions it might not be exerted with the requisite firmness, and on extraordinary occasions it might be perfidiously abused. May not this defect of an absolute negative be supplied by some qualified connection between this weaker department and the weaker branch of the stronger department, by which the latter may be led to support the constitutional rights of the former, without being too much detached from the rights of its own department? If the principles on which these observations are founded be just, as I persuade myself they are, and they be applied as a criterion to the several State constitutions, and to the federal Constitution it will be found that if the latter does not perfectly correspond with them, the former are infinitely less able to bear such a test. There are, moreover, two considerations particularly applicable to the federal system of America, which place that system in a very interesting point of view. First. In a single republic, all the power surrendered by the people is submitted to the administration of a single government; and the usurpations are guarded against by a division of the government into distinct and separate departments. In the compound republic of America, the power surrendered by the people is first divided between two distinct governments, and then the portion allotted to each subdivided among distinct and separate departments. Hence a double security arises to the rights of the people. The different governments will control each other, at the same time that each will be controlled by itself. Second. It is of great importance in a republic not only to guard the society against the oppression of its rulers, but to guard one part of the society against the injustice of the other part. Different interests necessarily exist in different classes of citizens. If a majority be united by a common interest, the rights of the minority will be insecure. There are but two methods of providing against this evil: the one by creating a will in the community independent of the majority that is, of the society itself; the other, by comprehending in the society so many separate descriptions of citizens as will render an unjust combination of a majority of the whole very improbable, if not impracticable. The first method prevails in all governments possessing an hereditary or self-appointed authority. This, at best, is but a precarious security; because a power independent of the society may as well espouse the unjust views of the major, as the rightful interests of the minor party, and may possibly be turned against both parties. The second method will be exemplified in the federal republic of the United States. Whilst all authority in it will be derived from and dependent on the society, the society itself will be broken into so many parts, interests, and classes of citizens, that the rights of individuals, or of the minority, will be in little danger from interested combinations of the majority. In a free government the security for civil rights must be the same as that for religious rights. It consists in the one case in the multiplicity of interests, and in the other in the multiplicity of sects. The degree of security in both cases will depend on the number of interests and sects; and this may be presumed to depend on the extent of country and number of people comprehended under the same government. This view of the subject must particularly recommend a proper federal system to all the sincere and considerate friends of republican government, since it shows that in exact proportion as the territory of the Union may be formed into more circumscribed Confederacies, or States oppressive combinations of a majority will be facilitated: the best security, under the republican forms, for the rights of every class of citizens, will be diminished: and consequently the stability and independence of some member of the government, the only other security, must be proportionately increased. Justice is the end of government. It is the end of civil society. It ever has been and ever will be pursued until it be obtained, or until liberty be lost in the pursuit. In a society under the forms of which the stronger faction can readily unite and oppress the weaker, anarchy may as truly be said to reign as in a state of nature, where the weaker individual is not secured against the violence of the stronger; and as, in the latter state, even the stronger individuals are prompted, by the uncertainty of their condition, to submit to a government which may protect the weak as well as themselves; so, in the former state, will the more powerful factions or parties be gradnally induced, by a like motive, to wish for a government which will protect all parties, the weaker as well as the more powerful. It can be little doubted that if the State of Rhode Island was separated from the Confederacy and left to itself, the insecurity of rights under the popular form of government within such narrow limits would be displayed by such reiterated oppressions of factious majorities that some power altogether independent of the people would soon be called for by the voice of the very factions whose misrule had proved the necessity of it. In the extended republic of the United States, and among the great variety of interests, parties, and sects which it embraces, a coalition of a majority of the whole society could seldom take place on any other principles than those of justice and the general good; whilst there being thus less danger to a minor from the will of a major party, there must be less pretext, also, to provide for the security of the former, by introducing into the government a will not dependent on the latter, or, in other words, a will independent of the society itself. It is no less certain than it is important, notwithstanding the contrary opinions which have been entertained, that the larger the society, provided it lie within a practical sphere, the more duly capable it will be of self-government. And happily for the REPUBLICAN CAUSE, the practicable sphere may be carried to a very great extent, by a judicious modification and mixture of the FEDERAL PRINCIPLE.

PUBLIUS

The Constitution of the United States

We the People of the United States, in Order to form a more perfect Union, establish Justice, insure domestic Tranquility, provide for the common defence, promote the general Welfare, and secure the Blessings of Liberty to ourselves and our Posterity, do ordain and establish this Constitution for the United States of America.

Article I.

Section 1

All legislative Powers herein granted shall be vested in a Congress of the United States, which shall consist of a Senate and House of Representatives.

Section 2

The House of Representatives shall be composed of Members chosen every second Year by the People of the several States, and the Electors in each State shall have the Qualifications requisite for Electors of the most numerous Branch of the State Legislature.

No Person shall be a Representative who shall not have attained to the Age of twenty five Years, and been seven Years a Citizen of the United States, and who shall not, when elected, be an Inhabitant of that State in which he shall be chosen.

[Representatives and direct Taxes shall be apportioned among the several States which may be included within this Union, according to their respective Numbers, which shall be determined by adding to the whole Number of free Persons, including those bound to Service for a Term of Years, and excluding Indians not taxed, three fifths of all other Persons.] The actual Enumeration shall be made within three Years after the first Meeting of the Congress of the United States, and within every subsequent Term of ten Years, in such Manner as they shall by Law direct. The Number of Representatives shall not exceed one for every thirty Thousand, but each State shall have at Least one Representative; and until such enumeration shall be made, the State of New Hampshire shall be entitled to chuse three, Massachusetts eight, Rhode Island and Providence Plantations one, Connecticut five, New York six, New Jersey four, Pennsylvania eight, Delaware one, Maryland six, Virginia ten, North Carolina five, South Carolina five and Georgia three.

When vacancies happen in the Representation from any State, the Executive Authority thereof shall issue Writs of Election to fill such Vacancies.

The House of Representatives shall chuse their Speaker and other Officers; and shall have the sole Power of Impeachment.

Section 3

The Senate of the United States shall be composed of two Senators from each State, chosen by the Legislature thereof, for six Years; and each Senator shall have one Vote.

Immediately after they shall be assembled in Consequence of the first Election, they shall be divided as equally as may be into three Classes. The Seats of the Senators of the first Class shall be vacated at the Expiration of the second Year, of the second Class at the Expiration of the fourth Year, and of the third Class at the Expiration of the sixth Year, so that one third may be chosen every second Year; and if Vacancies happen by Resignation, or otherwise, during the Recess of the Legislature of any State, the Executive thereof may make temporary Appointments until the next Meeting of the Legislature, which shall then fill such Vacancies.

No person shall be a Senator who shall not have attained to the Age of thirty Years, and been nine Years a Citizen of the United States, and who shall not, when elected, be an Inhabitant of that State for which he shall be chosen.

The Vice President of the United States shall be President of the Senate, but shall have no Vote, unless they be equally divided.

The Senate shall chuse their other Officers, and also a President pro tempore, in the absence of the Vice President, or when he shall exercise the Office of President of the United States.

The Senate shall have the sole Power to try all Impeachments. When sitting for that Purpose, they shall be on Oath or Affirmation. When the President of the United States is tried, the Chief Justice shall preside: And no Person shall be convicted without the Concurrence of two thirds of the Members present.

Judgment in Cases of Impeachment shall not extend further than to removal from Office, and disqualification to hold and enjoy any Office of honor, Trust or Profit under the United States: but the Party convicted shall nevertheless be liable and subject to Indictment, Trial, Judgment and Punishment, according to Law.

Section 4

The Times, Places and Manner of holding Elections for Senators and Representatives, shall be prescribed in each State by the Legislature thereof; but the Congress may at any time by Law make or alter such Regulations, except as to the Place of Chusing Senators.

The Congress shall assemble at least once in every Year, and such Meeting shall be on the first Monday in December, unless they shall by Law appoint a different Day.

Section 5

Each House shall be the Judge of the Elections, Returns and Qualifications of its own Members, and a Majority of each shall constitute a Quorum to do Business; but a smaller number may adjourn from day to day, and may be authorized to compel the Attendance of absent Members, in such Manner, and under such Penalties as each House may provide.

Each House may determine the Rules of its Proceedings, punish its Members for disorderly Behavior, and, with the Concurrence of two-thirds, expel a Member.

Each House shall keep a Journal of its Proceedings, and from time to time publish the same, excepting such Parts as may in their Judgment require Secrecy; and the Yeas and Nays of the Members of either House on any question shall, at the Desire of one fifth of those Present, be entered on the Journal.

Neither House, during the Session of Congress, shall, without the Consent of the other, adjourn for more than three days, nor to any other Place than that in which the two Houses shall be sitting.

Section 6

The Senators and Representatives shall receive a Compensation for their Services, to be ascertained by Law, and paid out of the Treasury of the United States. They shall in all Cases, except Treason, Felony and Breach of the Peace, be privileged from Arrest during their Attendance at the Session of their respective Houses, and in going to and returning from the same; and for any Speech or Debate in either House, they shall not be questioned in any other Place.

No Senator or Representative shall, during the Time for which he was elected, be appointed to any civil Office under the Authority of the United States which shall have been created, or the Emoluments whereof shall have been increased during such time; and no Person holding any Office under the United States, shall be a Member of either House during his Continuance in Office.

Section 7

All bills for raising Revenue shall originate in the House of Representatives; but the Senate may propose or concur with Amendments as on other Bills.

Every Bill which shall have passed the House of Representatives and the Senate, shall, before it become a Law, be presented to the President of the United States; If he approve he shall sign it, but if not he shall return it, with his Objections to that House in which it shall have originated, who shall enter the Objections at large on their Journal, and proceed to reconsider it. If after such Reconsideration two thirds of that House shall agree to pass the Bill, it shall be sent, together with the Objections, to the other House, by which it shall likewise be reconsidered, and if approved by two thirds of that House, it shall become a Law. But in all such Cases the Votes of both Houses shall be determined by Yeas and Nays, and the Names of the Persons voting for and against the Bill shall be entered on the Journal of each House respectively. If any Bill shall not be returned by the President within ten Days (Sundays excepted) after it shall have been presented to him, the Same shall be a Law, in like Manner as if he had signed it, unless the Congress by their Adjournment prevent its Return, in which Case it shall not be a Law.

Every Order, Resolution, or Vote to which the Concurrence of the Senate and House of Representatives may be necessary (except on a question of Adjournment) shall be presented to the President of the United States; and before the Same shall take Effect, shall be approved by him, or being disapproved by him, shall be repassed by two thirds of the Senate and House of Representatives, according to the Rules and Limitations prescribed in the Case of a Bill.

Section 8

The Congress shall have Power To lay and collect Taxes, Duties, Imposts and Excises, to pay the Debts and provide for the common Defence and general Welfare of the United States; but all Duties, Imposts and Excises shall be uniform throughout the United States;

To borrow money on the credit of the United States;

To regulate Commerce with foreign Nations, and among the several States, and with the Indian Tribes;

To establish an uniform Rule of Naturalization, and uniform Laws on the subject of Bankruptcies throughout the United States;

To coin Money, regulate the Value thereof, and of foreign Coin, and fix the Standard of Weights and Measures;

To provide for the Punishment of counterfeiting the Securities and current Coin of the United States;

To establish Post Offices and Post Roads;

To promote the Progress of Science and useful Arts, by securing for limited Times to Authors and Inventors the exclusive Right to their respective Writings and Discoveries;

To constitute Tribunals inferior to the supreme court;

To define and punish Piracies and Felonies committed on the high Seas, and Offenses against the Law of Nations;

To declare War, grant Letters of Marque and Reprisal, and make Rules concerning Captures on Land and Water;

To raise and support Armies, but no Appropriation of Money to that Use shall be for a longer Term than two Years;

To provide and maintain a Navy;

To make Rules for the Government and Regulation of the land and naval Forces;

To provide for calling forth the Militia to execute the Laws of the Union, suppress Insurrections and repel Invasions;

To provide for organizing, arming, and disciplining the Militia, and for governing such Part of them as may be employed in the Service of the United States, reserving to the States respectively, the Appointment of the Officers, and the Authority of training the Militia according to the discipline prescribed by Congress;

To exercise exclusive Legislation in all Cases whatsoever, over such District (not exceeding ten Miles square) as may, by Cession of particular States, and the acceptance of Congress, become the Seat of the Government of the United States, and to exercise like Authority over all Places purchased by the Consent of the Legislature of the State in which the Same shall be, for the Erection of Forts, Magazines, Arsenals, dock-Yards, and other needful Buildings;—And

To make all Laws which shall be necessary and proper for carrying into Execution the foregoing Powers, and all other Powers vested by this Constitution in the Government of the United States, or in any Department or Officer thereof.

Section 9

The Migration or Importation of such Persons as any of the States now existing shall think proper to admit, shall not be prohibited by the Congress prior to the Year one thousand eight hundred and eight, but a tax or duty may be imposed on such Importation, not exceeding ten dollars for each Person.

The privilege of the Writ of Habeas Corpus shall not be suspended, unless when in Cases of Rebellion or Invasion the public Safety may require it.

No Bill of Attainder or ex post facto Law shall be passed.

No capitation, or other direct, Tax shall be laid, unless in Proportion to the Census or Enumeration herein before directed to be taken.

No Tax or Duty shall be laid on Articles exported from any State.

No Preference shall be given by any Regulation of Commerce or Revenue to the Ports of one State over those of another: nor shall Vessels bound to, or from, one State, be obliged to enter, clear, or pay Duties in another.

No Money shall be drawn from the Treasury, but in Consequence of Appropriations made by Law; and a regular Statement and Account of the Receipts and Expenditures of all public Money shall be published from time to time.

No Title of Nobility shall be granted by the United States: And no Person holding any Office of Profit or Trust under them, shall, without the Consent of the Congress, accept of any present, Emolument, Office, or Title, of any kind whatever, from any King, Prince or foreign State.

Section 10

No State shall enter into any Treaty, Alliance, or Confederation; grant Letters of Marque and Reprisal; coin Money; emit Bills of Credit; make any Thing but gold and silver Coin a

Tender in Payment of Debts; pass any Bill of Attainder, ex post facto Law, or Law impairing the Obligation of Contracts, or grant any Title of Nobility.

No State shall, without the Consent of the Congress, lay any Imposts or Duties on Imports or Exports, except what may be absolutely necessary for executing it's inspection Laws: and the net Produce of all Duties and Imposts, laid by any State on Imports or Exports, shall be for the Use of the Treasury of the United States; and all such Laws shall be subject to the Revision and Controul of the Congress.

No State shall, without the Consent of Congress, lay any duty of Tonnage, keep Troops, or Ships of War in time of Peace, enter into any Agreement or Compact with another State, or with a foreign Power, or engage in War, unless actually invaded, or in such imminent Danger as will not admit of delay.

Article II.

Section 1

The executive Power shall be vested in a President of the United States of America. He shall hold his Office during the Term of four Years, and, together with the Vice-President chosen for the same Term, be elected, as follows:

Each State shall appoint, in such Manner as the Legislature thereof may direct, a Number of Electors, equal to the whole Number of Senators and Representatives to which the State may be entitled in the Congress: but no Senator or Representative, or Person holding an Office of Trust or Profit under the United States, shall be appointed an Elector.

The Electors shall meet in their respective States, and vote by Ballot for two persons, of whom one at least shall not lie an Inhabitant of the same State with themselves. And they shall make a List of all the Persons voted for, and of the Number of Votes for each; which List they shall sign and certify, and transmit sealed to the Seat of the Government of the United States, directed to the President of the Senate. The President of the Senate shall, in the Presence of the Senate and House of Representatives, open all the Certificates, and the Votes shall then be counted. The Person having the greatest Number of Votes shall be the President, if such Number be a Majority of the whole Number of Electors appointed; and if there be more than one who have such Majority, and have an equal Number of Votes, then the House of Representatives shall immediately chuse by Ballot one of them for President; and if no Person have a Majority, then from the five highest on the List the said House shall in like Manner chuse the President. But in chusing the President, the Votes shall be taken by States, the Representation from each State having one Vote; a quorum for this Purpose shall consist of a Member or Members from two-thirds of the States, and a Majority of all the States shall be necessary to a Choice. In every Case, after the Choice of the President, the Person having the greatest Number of Votes of the Electors shall be the Vice President. But if there should remain two or more who have equal Votes, the Senate shall chuse from them by Ballot the Vice-President.

The Congress may determine the Time of chusing the Electors, and the Day on which they shall give their Votes; which Day shall be the same throughout the United States.

No person except a natural born Citizen, or a Citizen of the United States, at the time of the Adoption of this Constitution, shall be eligible to the Office of President; neither shall any Person be eligible to that Office who shall not have attained to the Age of thirty-five Years, and been fourteen Years a Resident within the United States.

In Case of the Removal of the President from Office, or of his Death, Resignation, or Inability to discharge the Powers and Duties of the said Office, the same shall devolve on the Vice President, and the Congress may by Law provide for the Case of Removal, Death, Resignation or Inability, both of the President and Vice President, declaring what Officer shall then act as President, and such Officer shall act accordingly, until the Disability be removed, or a President shall be elected.

The President shall, at stated Times, receive for his Services, a Compensation, which shall neither be increased nor diminished during the Period for which he shall have been elected, and he shall not receive within that Period any other Emolument from the United States, or any of them.

Before he enter on the Execution of his Office, he shall take the following Oath or Affirmation:—"I do solemnly swear (or affirm) that I will faithfully execute the Office of President of the United States, and will to the best of my ability, preserve, protect and defend the Constitution of the United States."

Section 2

The President shall be Commander in Chief of the Army and Navy of the United States, and of the Militia of the several States, when called into the actual Service of the United States; he may require the Opinion, in writing, of the principal Officer in each of the executive Departments, upon any subject relating to the Duties of their respective Offices, and he shall have Power to Grant Reprieves and Pardons for Offenses against the United States, except in Cases of Impeachment.

He shall have Power, by and with the Advice and Consent of the Senate, to make Treaties, provided two thirds of the Senators present concur; and he shall nominate, and by and with the Advice and Consent of the Senate, shall appoint Ambassadors, other public Ministers and Consuls, Judges of the supreme Court, and all other Officers of the United States, whose Appointments are not herein otherwise provided for, and which shall be established by Law: but the Congress may by Law vest the Appointment of such inferior Officers, as they think proper, in the President alone, in the Courts of Law, or in the Heads of Departments.

The President shall have Power to fill up all Vacancies that may happen during the Recess of the Senate, by granting Commissions which shall expire at the End of their next Session.

Section 3

He shall from time to time give to the Congress Information of the State of the Union, and recommend to their Consideration such Measures as he shall judge necessary and expedient; he may, on extraordinary Occasions, convene both Houses, or either of them, and in Case of Disagreement between them, with Respect to the Time of Adjournment, he may adjourn them to such Time as he shall think proper; he shall receive Ambassadors and other public Ministers; he shall take Care that the Laws be faithfully executed, and shall Commission all the Officers of the United States.

Section 4

The President, Vice President and all civil Officers of the United States, shall be removed from Office on Impeachment for, and Conviction of, Treason, Bribery, or other high Crimes and Misdemeanors.

Article III.

Section 1

The judicial Power of the United States, shall be vested in one supreme Court, and in such inferior Courts as the Congress may from time to time ordain and establish. The Judges, both of the supreme and inferior Courts, shall hold their Offices during good Behavior, and shall, at stated Times, receive for their Services a Compensation which shall not be diminished during their Continuance in Office.

Section 2

The judicial Power shall extend to all Cases, in Law and Equity, arising under this Constitution, the Laws of the United States, and Treaties made, or which shall be made, under their Authority; to all Cases affecting Ambassadors, other public Ministers and Consuls; to all Cases of admiralty and maritime Jurisdiction; to Controversies to which the United States shall be a Party; to Controversies between two or more States; between a State and Citizens of another State; between Citizens of different States; between Citizens of the same State claiming Lands under Grants of different States, and between a State, or the Citizens thereof, and foreign States, Citizens or Subjects.

In all Cases affecting Ambassadors, other public Ministers and Consuls, and those in which a State shall be Party, the supreme Court shall have original Jurisdiction. In all the other Cases before mentioned, the supreme Court shall have appellate Jurisdiction, both as to Law and Fact, with such Exceptions, and under such Regulations as the Congress shall make.

The Trial of all Crimes, except in Cases of Impeachment, shall be by Jury; and such Trial shall be held in the State where the said Crimes shall have been committed; but when not committed within any State, the Trial shall be at such Place or Places as the Congress may by Law have directed.

Section 3

Treason against the United States, shall consist only in levying War against them, or in adhering to their Enemies, giving them Aid and Comfort. No Person shall be convicted of

Treason unless on the Testimony of two Witnesses to the same overt Act, or on Confession in open Court.

The Congress shall have power to declare the Punishment of Treason, but no Attainder of Treason shall work Corruption of Blood, or Forfeiture except during the Life of the Person attainted.

Article IV.

Section 1

Full Faith and Credit shall be given in each State to the public Acts, Records, and judicial Proceedings of every other State. And the Congress may by general Laws prescribe the Manner in which such Acts, Records and Proceedings shall be proved, and the Effect thereof.

Section 2

The Citizens of each State shall be entitled to all Privileges and Immunities of Citizens in the several States.

A Person charged in any State with Treason, Felony, or other Crime, who shall flee from Justice, and be found in another State, shall on demand of the executive Authority of the State from which he fled, be delivered up, to be removed to the State having Jurisdiction of the Crime.

No Person held to Service or Labour in one State, under the Laws thereof, escaping into another, shall, in Consequence of any Law or Regulation therein, be discharged from such Service or Labour, But shall be delivered up on Claim of the Party to whom such Service or Labour may be due.

Section 3

New States may be admitted by the Congress into this Union; but no new States shall be formed or erected within the Jurisdiction of any other state; nor any State be formed by the Junction of two or more States, or parts of States, without the Consent of the Legislatures of the States concerned as well as of the Congress.

The Congress shall have Power to dispose of and make all needful Rules and Regulations respecting the Territory or other Property belonging to the United States; and nothing in this Constitution shall be so construed as to Prejudice any Claims of the United States, or of any particular States.

Section 4

The United States shall guarantee to every State in this Union a Republican Form of Government, and shall protect each of them against Invasion; and on Application of the Legislature, or of the Executive (when the Legislature cannot be convened) against domestic Violence.

Article V.

The Congress, whenever two thirds of both Houses shall deem it necessary, shall propose Amendments to this Constitution, or, on the Application of the Legislatures of two thirds of the several States, shall call a Convention for proposing Amendments, which, in either Case, shall be valid to all Intents and Purposes, as part of this Constitution, when ratified by the Legislatures of three fourths of the several States, or by Conventions in three fourths thereof, as the one or the other Mode of Ratification may be proposed by the Congress; Provided that no Amendment which may be made prior to the Year One thousand eight hundred and eight shall in any Manner affect the first and fourth Clauses in the Ninth Section of the first Article; and that no State, without its Consent, shall be deprived of its equal Suffrage in the Senate.

Article VI.

All Debts contracted and Engagements entered into, before the Adoption of this Constitution, shall be as valid against the United States under this Constitution, as under the Confederation.

This Constitution, and the Laws of the United States which shall be made in Pursuance thereof; and all Treaties made, or which shall be made, under the Authority of the United States, shall be the supreme Law of the Land; and the Judges in every State shall be bound thereby, any Thing in the Constitution or Laws of any State to the Contrary notwithstanding.

The Senators and Representatives before mentioned, and the Members of the several State Legislatures, and all executive and judicial Officers, both of the United States and of the several States, shall be bound by Oath or Affirmation, to support this Constitution; but no religious Test shall ever be required as a Qualification to any Office or public Trust under the United States.

Article VII.

The Ratification of the Conventions of nine States, shall be sufficient for the Establishment of this Constitution between the States so ratifying the Same.

Done in Convention by the Unanimous Consent of the States present the Seventeenth Day of September in the Year of our Lord one thousand seven hundred and Eighty seven and of the Independence of the United States of America the Twelfth. In Witness whereof We have hereunto subscribed our Names.

GO WASHINGTON-Presidt. And deputy from Virginia

New Hampshire—John Langdon, Nicholas Gilman

Massachusetts—Nathaniel Gorham, Rufus King

Connecticut—Wm: Saml. Johnson, Roger Sherman

New York—Alexander Hamilton

New Jersey—Wil: Livingston, David Brearley, Wm. Paterson, Jona: Dayton

Pennsylvania—B Franklin, Thomas Mifflin, Robt. Morris, Geo. Clymer, Thos. FitzSimons, Jared Ingersoll, James Wilson, Gouv Morris

Delaware—Geo: Read, Gunning Bedford jun, John Dickinson, Richard Bassett, Jaco: Broom

Maryland—James McHenry, Dan of St Thos. Jenifer, Danl Carroll

Virginia—John Blair, James Madison Jr.

North Carolina—Wm. Blount, Richd. Dobbs Spaight, Hu Williamson

South Carolina—J. Rutledge, Charles Cotesworth Pinckney, Charles Pinckney, Pierce Butler

Georgia—William Few, Abr Baldwin

Attest: William Jackson, Secretary

Amendment I

Congress shall make no law respecting an establishment of religion, or prohibiting the free exercise thereof; or abridging the freedom of speech, or of the press; or the right of the people peaceably to assemble, and to petition the Government for a redness of grievances.

Amendment II

A well regulated Militia, being necessary to the security of a free State, the right of the people to keep and bear Arms, shall not be infringed.

Amendment III

No Soldier shall, in time of peace be quartered in any house, without the consent of the Owner, nor in time of war, but in a manner to be prescribed by law.

Amendment IV

The right of the people to be secure in their persons, houses, papers, and effects, against unreasonable searches and seizures, shall not be violated, and no Warrants shall issue, but upon probable cause, supported by Oath or affirmation, and particularly describing the place to be searched, and the persons or things to be seized.

Amendment V

No person shall be held to answer for a capital, or otherwise infamous crime, unless on a presentment or indictment of a Grand Jury, except in cases arising in the land or naval forces, or in the Militia, when in actual service in time of War or public danger; nor shall any person be subject for the same offense to be twice put in jeopardy of life or limb; nor shall be compelled in any criminal case to be a witness against himself, nor be deprived of life, liberty, or property, without due process of law; nor shall private property be taken for public use, without just compensation.

Amendment VI

In all criminal prosecutions, the accused shall enjoy the right to a speedy and public trial, by an impartial jury of the State and district wherein the crime shall have been committed, which district shall have been previously ascertained by law, and to be informed of the nature and cause of the accusation; to be confronted with the witnesses against him; to have compulsory process for obtaining witnesses in his favor, and to have the Assistance of Counsel for his defence.

Amendment VII

In Suits at common law, where the value in controversy shall exceed twenty dollars, the right of trial by jury shall be preserved, and no fact tried by a jury, shall be otherwise re-examined in any Court of the United States, than according to the rules of the common law.

Amendment VIII

Excessive bail shall not be required, nor excessive fines imposed, nor cruel and unusual punishments inflicted.

Amendment IX

The enumeration in the Constitution, of certain rights, shall not be construed to deny or disparage others retained by the people.

Amendment X

The powers not delegated to the United States by the Constitution, nor prohibited by it to the States, are reserved to the States respectively, or to the people.

Amendment XI

The Judicial power of the United States shall not be construed to extend to any suit in law or equity, commenced or prosecuted against one of the United States by Citizens of another State, or by Citizens or Subjects of any Foreign State.

Amendment XII

The Electors shall meet in their respective states, and vote by ballot for President and Vice-President, one of whom, at least, shall not be an inhabitant of the same state with themselves; they shall name in their ballots the person voted for as President, and in distinct ballots the person voted for as Vice-President, and they shall make distinct lists of all persons voted for as President, and of all persons voted for as Vice-President and of the number of votes for each, which lists they shall sign and certify, and transmit sealed to the seat of the government of the United States, directed to the President of the Senate;—The President of the Senate shall, in the presence of the Senate and House of Representatives, open all the certificates and the votes shall then be counted;—The person having the greatest Number of votes for President, shall be the President, if such number be a majority of the whole number of Electors appointed; and if no person have such majority, then from the persons having the highest numbers not exceeding three on the list of those voted for as President, the House of Representatives shall choose immediately, by ballot, the President. But in choosing the President, the votes shall be taken by states, the representation from each state having one vote; a quorum for this purpose shall consist of a member or members from two-thirds of the states, and a majority of all the states shall be necessary to a choice. And if the House of Representatives shall not choose a President whenever the right of choice shall devolve upon them, before the fourth day of March next following, then the Vice-President shall act as President, as in the case of the death or other constitutional disability of the President.—The person having the greatest number of votes as Vice-President, shall be the Vice-President, if such number be a majority of the whole number of Electors appointed, and if no person have a majority, then from the two highest numbers on the list, the Senate shall choose the Vice-President; a quorum for the purpose shall consist of two-thirds of the whole number of Senators, and a majority of the whole number shall be necessary to a choice. But no person constitutionally ineligible to the office of President shall be eligible to that of Vice-President of the United States.

Amendment XIII

Section 1

Neither slavery nor involuntary servitude, except as a punishment for crime whereof the party shall have been duly convicted, shall exist within the United States, or any place subject to their jurisdiction.

Section 2

Congress shall have power to enforce this article by appropriate legislation.

Amendment XIV

Section 1

All persons born or naturalized in the United States, and subject to the jurisdiction thereof, are citizens of the United States and of the State wherein they reside. No State shall make or enforce any law which shall abridge the privileges or immunities of citizens of the United States; nor shall any State deprive any person of life, liberty, or property, without due process of law; nor deny to any person within its jurisdiction the equal protection of the laws.

Section 2

Representatives shall be apportioned among the several States according to their respective numbers, counting the whole number of persons in each State, excluding Indians not taxed. But when the right to vote at any election for the choice of electors for President and Vice-President of the United States, Representatives in Congress, the Executive and Judicial officers of a State, or the members of the Legislature thereof, is denied to any of the male inhabitants of such State, being twenty-one years of age, and citizens of the United States, or in any way abridged, except for participation in rebellion, or other crime, the basis of representation therein shall be reduced in the proportion which the number of such male citizens shall bear to the whole number of male citizens twenty-one years of age in such State.

Section 3

No person shall be a Senator or Representative in Congress, or elector of President and Vice-President, or hold any office, civil or military, under the United States, or under any State, who, having previously taken an oath, as a member of Congress, or as an officer of the United States, or as a member of any State legislature, or as an executive or judicial officer of any State, to support the Constitution of the United States, shall have engaged in insurrection or rebellion against the same, or given aid or comfort to the enemies thereof. But Congress may be a vote of two-thirds of each House, remove such disability.

Section 4

The validity of the public debt of the United States, authorized by law, including debts incurred for payment of pensions and bounties for services in suppressing insurrection or rebellion, shall not be questioned. But neither the United States nor any State shall assume or pay any debt or obligation incurred in aid of insurrection or rebellion against the United States, or any claim for the loss or emancipation of any slave; but all such debts, obligations and claims shall be held illegal and void.

Section 5

The Congress shall have power to enforce, by appropriate legislation, the provisions of this article.

Amendment XV

Section 1

The right of citizens of the United States to vote shall not be denied or abridged by the United States or by any State on account of race, color, or previous condition of servitude.

Section 2

The Congress shall have power to enforce this article by appropriate legislation.

Amendment XVI

The Congress shall have power to lay and collect taxes on incomes, from whatever source derived, without apportionment among the several States, and without regard to any census or enumeration.

Amendment XVII

The Senate of the United States shall be composed of two Senators from each State, elected by the people thereof, for six years; and each Senator shall have one vote. The electors in each State shall have the qualifications requisite for electors of the most numerous branch of the State legislatures. When vacancies happen in the representation of any State in the Senate, the executive authority of such State shall issue writs of election to fill such vacancies: Provided, That the legislature of any State may empower the executive thereof to make temporary appointments until the people fill the vacancies by election as the legislature may direct.

This amendment shall not be so construed as to affect the election or term of any Senator chosen before it becomes valid as part of the Constitution.

Amendment XVIII

Section 1

After one year from the ratification of this article the manufacture, sale, or transportation of intoxicating liquors within, the importation thereof into, or the exportation thereof from the United States and all territory subject to the jurisdiction thereof for beverage purposes is hereby prohibited.

Section 2

The Congress and the several States shall have concurrent power to enforce this article by appropriate legislation.

Section 3

This article shall be inoperative unless it shall have been ratified as an amendment to the Constitution by the legislatures of the several States, as provided in the Constitution, within seven years from the date of the submission hereof to the States by the Congress.

Amendment XIX

The right of citizens of the United States to vote shall not be defined or abridged by the United States or by any State on account of sex.

Congress shall have power to enforce this article by appropriate legislation.

Amendment XX

Section 1

The terms of the President and Vice President shall end at noon on the 20th day of January, and the terms of Senators and Representatives at noon on the 3d day of January, of the years in which such terms would have ended if this article had not been ratified; and the terms of their successors shall then begin.

Section 2

The Congress shall assemble at least once in every year, and such meeting shall begin at noon on the 3d day of January, unless they shall by law appoint a different day.

Section 3

If, at the time fixed for the beginning of the term of the President, the President elect shall have died, the Vice President elect shall become President. If a President shall not have been chosen before the time fixed for the beginning of his term, or if the President elect shall have failed to qualify, then the Vice President elect shall act as President until a President shall have qualified; and the Congress may by law provide for the case wherein neither a President elect nor a Vice President elect shall have qualified, declaring who shall then act as President, or the manner in which one who is to act shall be selected, and such person shall act accordingly until a President or Vice President shall have qualified.

Section 4

The Congress may by law provide for the case of the death of any of the persons from whom the House of Representatives may choose a President whenever the right of choice shall have devolved upon them, and for the case of the death of any of the persons from whom the Senate may choose a Vice President whenever the right of choice shall have developed upon them.

Section 5

Sections 1 and 2 shall take effect on the 15th day of October following the ratification of this article.

Section 6

This article shall be inoperative unless it shall have been ratified as an amendment to the Constitution by the legislatures of three-fourths of the several States within seven years from the date of its submission.

Amendment XXI

Section 1

The eighteenth article of amendment to the Constitution of the United States is hereby repealed.

Section 2

The transportation or importation into any State, Territory, or possession of the United States for delivery or use therein of intoxicating liquors, in violation of the laws thereof, is hereby prohibited.

Section 3

The article shall be inoperative unless it shall have been ratified as an amendment to the Constitution by conventions in the several States, as provided in the Constitution, within seven years from the date of the submission hereof to the States by the Congress.

Amendment XXII

Section 1

No person shall be elected to the office of the President more than twice, and no person who has held the office of President, or acted as President, for more than two years of a term to which some other person was elected President shall be elected to the office of the President more than once. But this Article shall not apply to any person holding the office of President, when this Article was proposed by the Congress, and shall not prevent any person who may be holding the office of President, or acting as President, during the term within which this Article becomes operative from holding the office of President or acting as president during the remainder of such term.

Section 2

This article shall be inoperative unless it shall have been ratified as an amendment to the Constitution by the legislatures of three-fourths of the several States within seven years from the date of its submission to the States by the Congress.

Amendment XXIII

Section 1

The District constituting the seat of Government of the United States shall appoint in such manner as the Congress may direct: A number of electors of President and Vice President equal to the whole number of Senators and Representatives in Congress to which the District would be entitled if it were a State, but in no event more than the least populous State; they shall be in addition to those appointed by the States, but they shall be considered, for the purposes of the election of President and Vice President, to be electors appointed by a State; and they shall meet in the District and perform such duties as provided by the twelfth article of amendment.

Section 2

The Congress shall have power to enforce this article by appropriate legislation.

Amendment XXIV

Section 1

The right of citizens of the United States to vote in any primary or other election for President or Vice President, for electors for President or Vice President, or for Senator or Representative in Congress, shall not be denied or abridged by the United States or any State by reason of failure to pay any poll tax or other tax.

Section 2

The Congress shall have power to enforce this article by appropriate legislation.

Amendment XXV

Section 1

In case of the removal of the President from office or of his death or resignation, The Vice-President shall become President.

Section 2

Whenever there is a vacancy in the office of the Vice President, the President shall nominate a Vice President who shall take office upon confirmation by a majority vote of both Houses of Congress.

Section 3

Whenever the President transmits to the President pro tempore of the Senate and the Speaker of the House of Representatives his written declaration that he is unable to discharge the powers and duties of his office, and until he transmits to them a written declaration to the contrary, such powers and duties shall be discharged by the Vice President as Acting President.

Section 4

Whenever the Vice President and a majority of either the principal officers of the executive departments or of such other body as Congress may by law provide, transmit to the President pro tempore of the Senate and the Speaker of the House of Representatives their written declaration that the President is unable to discharge the powers and duties of his office, the Vice President shall immediately assume the powers and duties of the office as Acting President.

Thereafter, when the President transmits to the President pro tempore of the Senate and the Speaker of the House of Representatives his written declaration that no inability exists, he shall resume the powers and duties of his office unless the Vice President and a majority of either the principal officers of the executive department or of such other body as Congress may by law provide, transmit within four days to the President pro tempore of the Senate and the Speaker of the House of Representatives their written declaration that the President is unable to discharge the powers and duties of his office. Thereupon Congress shall decide the issue, assembling within forty eight hours for that purpose if not in session. If the Congress, within twenty one days after receipt of the latter written declaration, or, if Congress is not in session, within twenty one days after Congress is required to assemble, determines by two thirds vote of both Houses that the President is unable to discharge the powers and duties of his office, the Vice President shall continue to discharge the same as Acting President; otherwise, the President shall resume the powers and duties of his office.

Amendment XXVI

Section 1

The right of citizens of the United States, who are eighteen years of age or older, to vote shall not be denied or abridged by the United States or by any State on account of age.

Section 2

The Congress shall have power to enforce this article by appropriate legislation.

Amendment XXVII

No law, varying the compensation for the services of the Senators and Representatives, shall take effect, until an election of Representatives hall have intervened.

Models for Reformation

Puritan America

(1620–1776)

The voices of Christian philosophers, authors and poets—men possessed of greater faculties of insight—had much to say about the destiny of our continent long before the United States came into existence. As the colonies began to prosper and grow, a group of English Puritans began to prophesy a new turn in history. While the American colonies were still in their infancy, they predicted growth in power and civilization, heralding a Western empire.

George Herbert (1593–1633), the Anglican poet, seeing the Puritan emigration to America, prompted by conscience and the desire for religious liberty, was inspired to write the famous verses:

"Religion stands on tiptoe in our land,

Ready to pass to the American strand."

Herbert died in 1632, twelve years after the landing of the Pilgrims at Plymouth, and two years after the larger movement of the Massachusetts Company which began the settlement of Boston. These verses were almost suppressed by the English government being unsympathetic to the Puritan cause and refusing the proper license for publication. They at last yielded, however, calling Herbert "a divine poet" and expressing the hope that "the world would not take him for an inspired prophet."[1]

John Milton (1608–1674), author of Paradise Lost and the heroic Sonnets, wrote a treatise on the emigration of English Christians to America:

"What numbers of faithful and free-born Englishmen and good Christians have been constrained to forsake their dear dearest home, their friends and kindred, whom nothing but the wide ocean and the savage deserts of America could hide and shelter from the fury of the bishops! O, if we could but see the shape of our dear mother England, as poets are wont to give a personal form to what they please, how would she appear, think ye, but in a mourning

---

[1]The Church Militant: Herbert's Poetical Works (Little and Brown) p.247, note.

weed, with ashes upon her head, and tears abundantly flowing from her eyes, to behold so many of her children exposed at once and thrust from things of dearest necessity, because their conscience could not assent to things which the bishops thought indifferent? Let the astrologer be dismayed at the portentous blaze of comets and impressions in the air, as fore-telling troubles and changes to states; I shall believe there cannot be a more ill-boding sign to a nation (God turn the omen from us!) than when the inhabitants, to avoid insufferable grievances at home, are enforced by heaps to forsake their native country."[2]

Although such statements are not public prayer proclamations in the strictest sense, the English Puritan writings contain the convenantal model of the blessings and curses of God on nations. It may have been merely a practical understanding that England would suffer by losing its and most intelligent, industrious, prosperous and pious citizens. Yet the prophetic nature of the writings of the Puritans cannot be ignored.

We can view the First Great Awakening of 1740 as the impetus for issuing the Declaration of Independence to King George III in 1776. It would be stretching the truth to say that the Declaration was a type of convenantal lawsuit, yet it is undoubtful that through the waking up of the minds of all classes through the Great Awakening, Puritanism was carried into our form of civil government. The First Great Awakening produced a general discussion of the principles of freedom and human rights, the habit of contending for rights with religious zeal, and the preparation of the mind for all questions pertaining to civil government in the American colonies. Although it is true that there was a strong deistic influence at the time of the signing of the Declaration, there is no question that there were the residual effects of strong Puritan influence. The American Revolution could not have occurred without the 150-year-old Puritan foundation in America.

Thomas Jefferson, a man described by his contemporaries as "a French infidel in respect to religion" was ironically indebted to the Puritans for his model of civil government. The evangelical explosion of the Great Awakening in Puritan New England provided the seeds for the first Baptist churches to be planted in Episcopal Virginia, which held to a Calvinistic theology and a congregational form of church government. Jefferson gained his first clear idea of a republican government from seeing the congregationalism of a Baptist church in his vicinity. It was good politics, too, since he strengthened his party's stance among the people through an alliance with the Baptists and all friends of religious freedom.[3]

The Jeffersonian distinction between Church and State is very different from the idea promoted in our day. The very phrase "separation of Church ad State"is very misleading. It is not a constitutional phrase but it came afterward in the writings of Jefferson. It originated as a Calvinist/Puritan distinction between the spheres of authority of church and civil government. The Church and the State are separate spheres of governmental authority. Separation of Church and State does not mean separation of the civil sphere from God. The issue is not whether the Church should intrude on the State's affairs. The Church should not. Neither should the State intrude on the Church's affairs. But Jesus Christ intercedes in the affairs of both. Civil government is not secular; it still stands under the moral Law of God. This was the understanding of most American legislators until the 20th century.

[2]Reformation in England, Book II: Works, Vol. III, (Pickering) p.45.

[3]Joseph Tracy, The Great Awakening (Tappan and Dennet, Boston, 1842) pp.419.420.

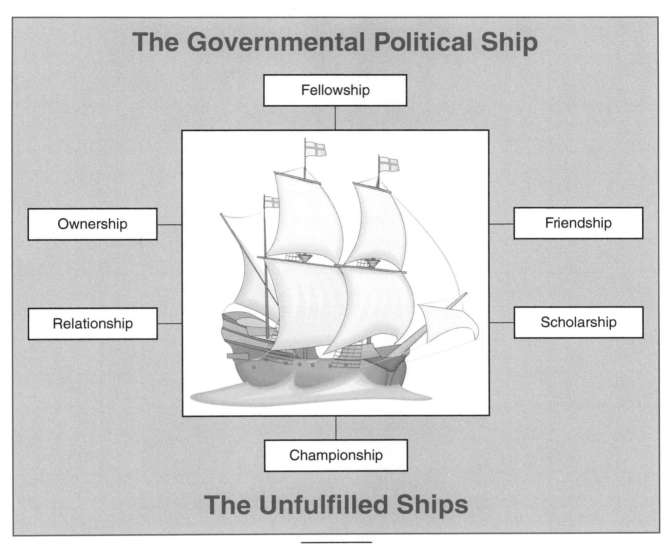

The Governmental Political Ship

Fellowship

Ownership

Friendship

Relationship

Scholarship

Championship

The Unfulfilled Ships

FIGURE A1

Name _____ **Date** _____

Explain:

_____
_____
_____
_____
_____
_____
_____
_____
_____
_____
_____
_____
_____
_____
_____
_____
_____
_____
_____
_____
_____

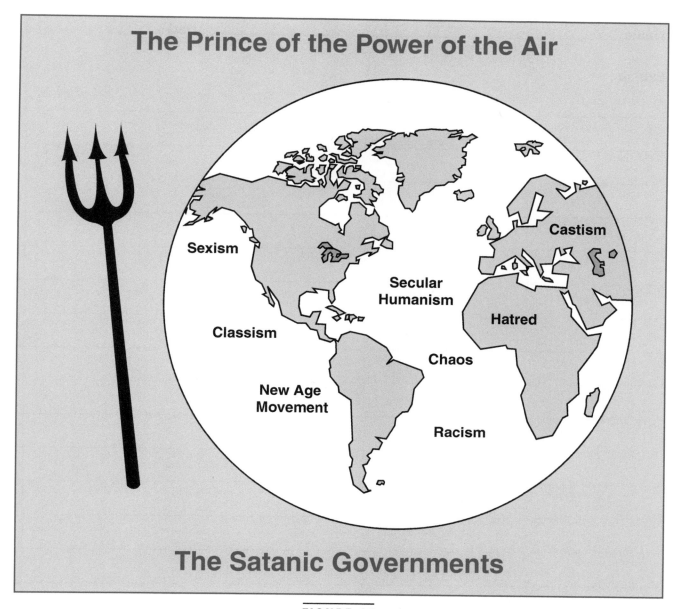

Name _____ **Date** _____

Explain:

_____

_____

_____

_____

_____

_____

_____

_____

_____

_____

_____

_____

_____

_____

_____

_____

_____

_____

_____

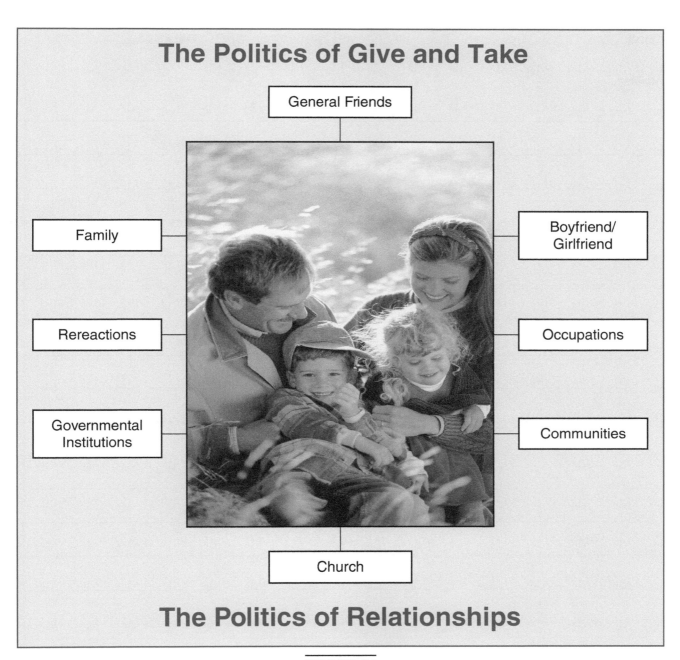

The Politics of Give and Take

General Friends

Family

Boyfriend/
Girlfriend

Rereactions

Occupations

Governmental
Institutions

Communities

Church

The Politics of Relationships

FIGURE A3

Name _____ **Date** _____

Explain:

_____

_____

_____

_____

_____

_____

_____

_____

_____

_____

_____

_____

_____

_____

_____

_____

_____

_____

_____

_____

_____

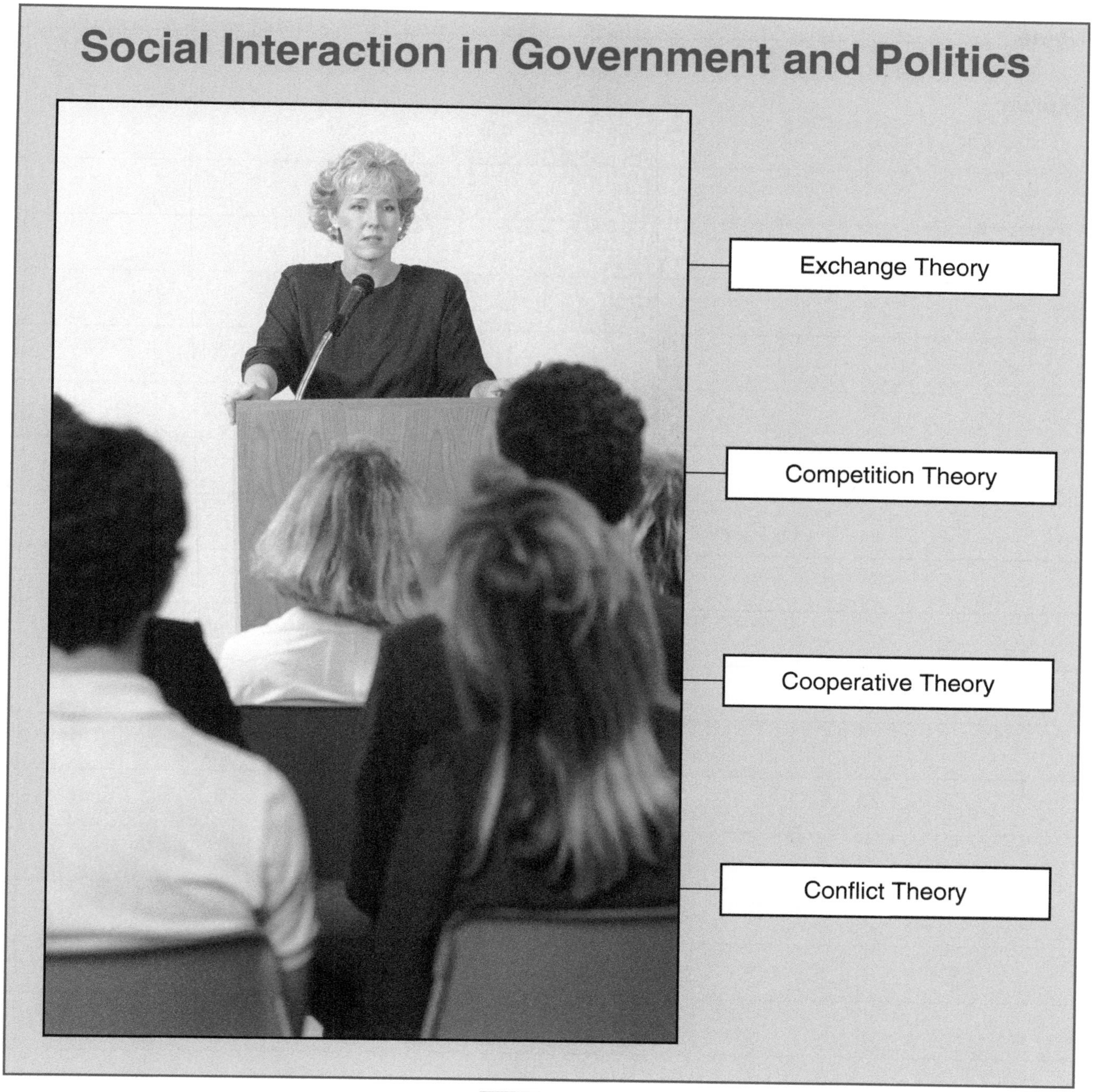

Social Interaction in Government and Politics

Exchange Theory

Competition Theory

Cooperative Theory

Conflict Theory

FIGURE A4

Name _____ **Date** _____

Explain:

_____

_____

_____

_____

_____

_____

_____

_____

_____

_____

_____

_____

_____

_____

_____

_____

_____

_____

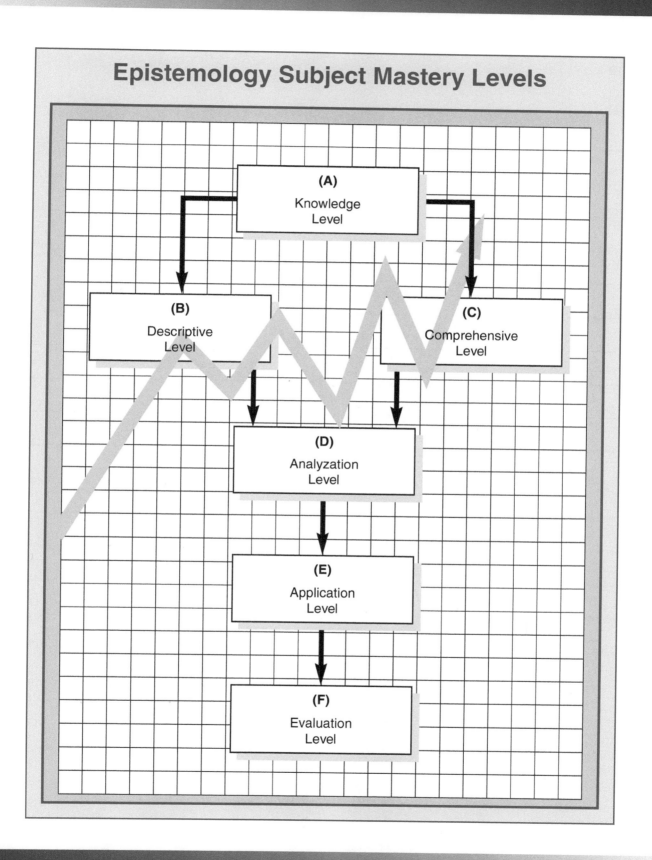

Epistemology Subject Mastery Levels

(A)
Knowledge
Level

(B)
Descriptive
Level

(C)
Comprehensive
Level

(D)
Analyzation
Level

(E)
Application
Level

(F)
Evaluation
Level

Name _____ **Date** _____

Explain:

_____

_____

_____

_____

_____

_____

_____

_____

_____

_____

_____

_____

_____

_____

_____

_____

_____

_____

_____

_____

_____

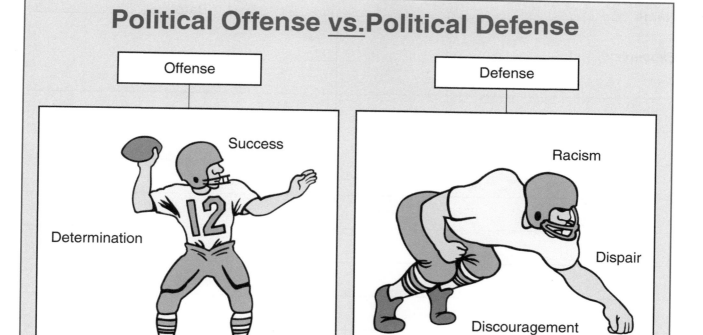

Political Offense vs. Political Defense

Offense

Defense

Success

Determination

12

Accomplishment

Racism

Dispair

Discouragement

Depression

Finances

There will be many obstacles to the "American Dream", Score yourself a touchdown.

FIGURE A6

Name _____ **Date** _____

Explain:

_____

_____

_____

_____

_____

_____

_____

_____

_____

_____

_____

_____

_____

_____

_____

_____

_____

_____

_____

_____

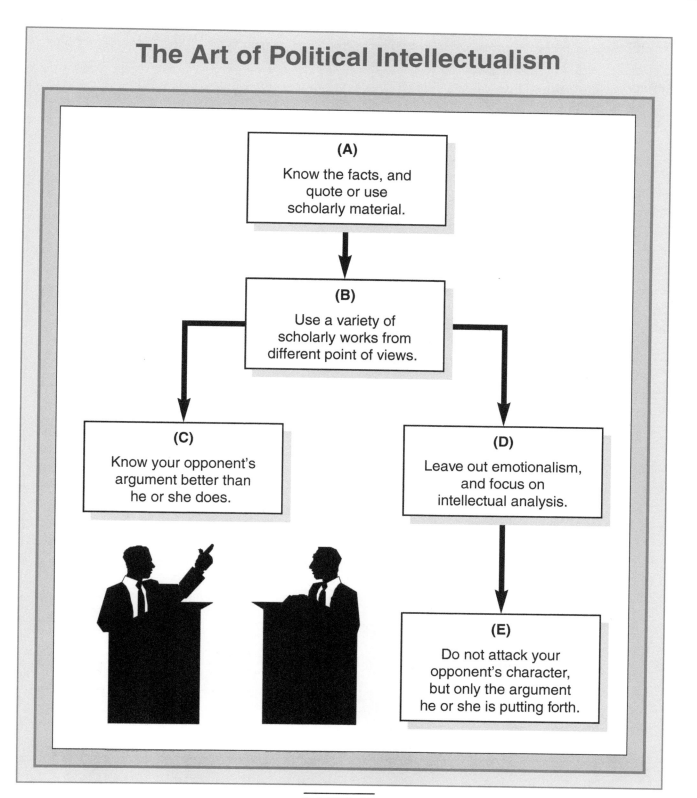

The Art of Political Intellectualism

(A)
Know the facts, and quote or use scholarly material.

(B)
Use a variety of scholarly works from different point of views.

(C)
Know your opponent's argument better than he or she does.

(D)
Leave out emotionalism, and focus on intellectual analysis.

(E)
Do not attack your opponent's character, but only the argument he or she is putting forth.

FIGURE A7

Name _____ **Date** _____

Explain:

_____

_____

_____

_____

_____

_____

_____

_____

_____

_____

_____

_____

_____

_____

_____

_____

_____

_____

_____

Politics: The Destruction of American Civilization

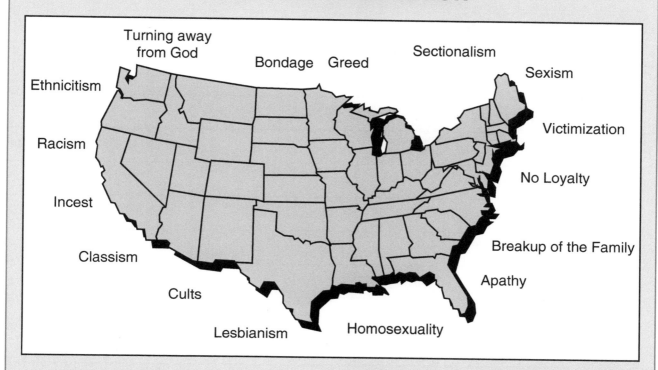

These are the 16 major things which will destroy America.

FIGURE A8

Name _____ **Date** _____

Explain:

_____

_____

_____

_____

_____

_____

_____

_____

_____

_____

_____

_____

_____

_____

_____

_____

_____

_____

_____

_____

_____

_____

The Political Circles of Deception

There is an Enemy Among You

FIGURE A9

Name _____ **Date** _____

Explain:

_____

_____

_____

_____

_____

_____

_____

_____

_____

_____

_____

_____

_____

_____

_____

_____

_____

_____

_____

_____

_____

_____

Money and Power in a Governmental System

1
Money/Power
House
But Not a Home

2
Money/Power
Books
But Cannot Give you
Brains

3
Money/Power
Finery
But Cannot Give you
Beauty

4
Money/Power
Food
But Cannot Give you
an Appetite

5
Money/Power
Bed
But Cannot Give you
Sleep

6
Money/Power
Lust
But Cannot Give you
Love

7
Money/Power
Places
But Cannot Give you
a Sense of Belonging

8
Money/Power
Associates
But Cannot Give you
Friends

9
Money/Power
Crucifix
But Cannot Give you
a Savior

The Examples of what money and power cannot accomplish.

FIGURE A10

Name _____ **Date** _____

Explain:

_____

_____

_____

_____

_____

_____

_____

_____

_____

_____

_____

_____

_____

_____

_____

_____

_____

_____

_____

_____

_____

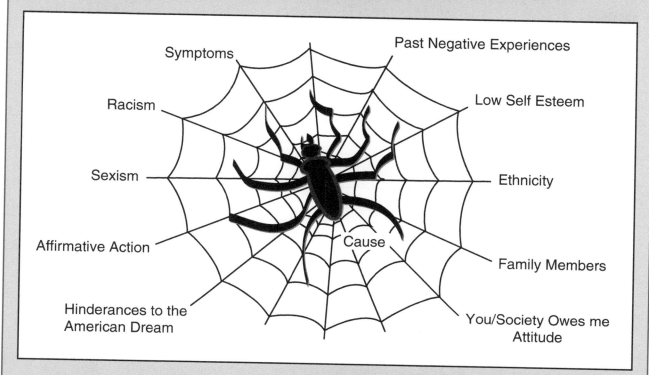

The Deception of Political Victimization

Symptoms

Past Negative Experiences

Racism

Low Self Esteem

Sexism

Ethnicity

Affirmative Action

Cause

Family Members

Hinderances to the American Dream

You/Society Owes me Attitude

The Web of the Spider

FIGURE A11

Name _____ **Date** _____

Explain:

_____

_____

_____

_____

_____

_____

_____

_____

_____

_____

_____

_____

_____

_____

_____

_____

_____

_____

_____

_____

_____

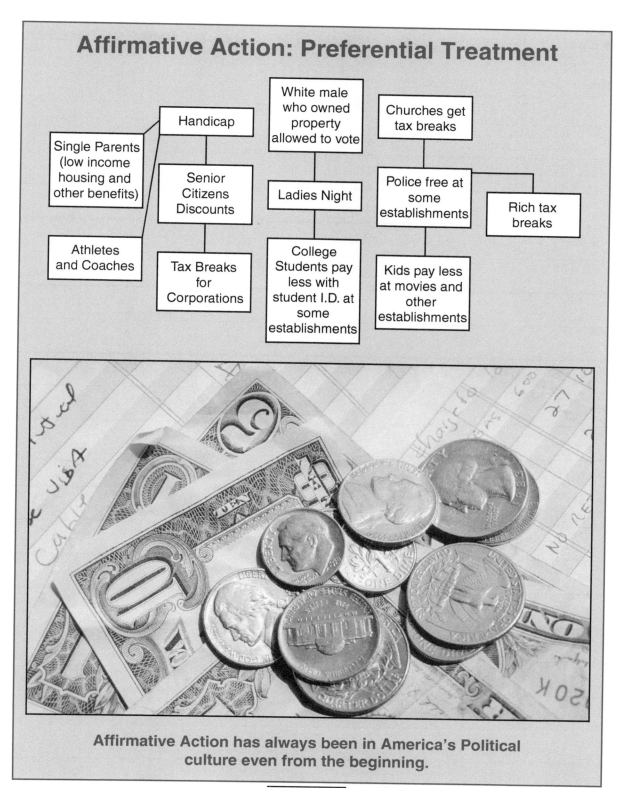

Affirmative Action: Preferential Treatment

Single Parents (low income housing and other benefits)

Handicap

Athletes and Coaches

Senior Citizens Discounts

Tax Breaks for Corporations

White male who owned property allowed to vote

Ladies Night

College Students pay less with student I.D. at some establishments

Churches get tax breaks

Police free at some establishments

Rich tax breaks

Kids pay less at movies and other establishments

Affirmative Action has always been in America's Political culture even from the beginning.

FIGURE A12

Name _____ Date _____

Explain:

_____

_____

_____

_____

_____

_____

_____

_____

_____

_____

_____

_____

_____

_____

_____

_____

_____

_____

_____

_____

_____

_____

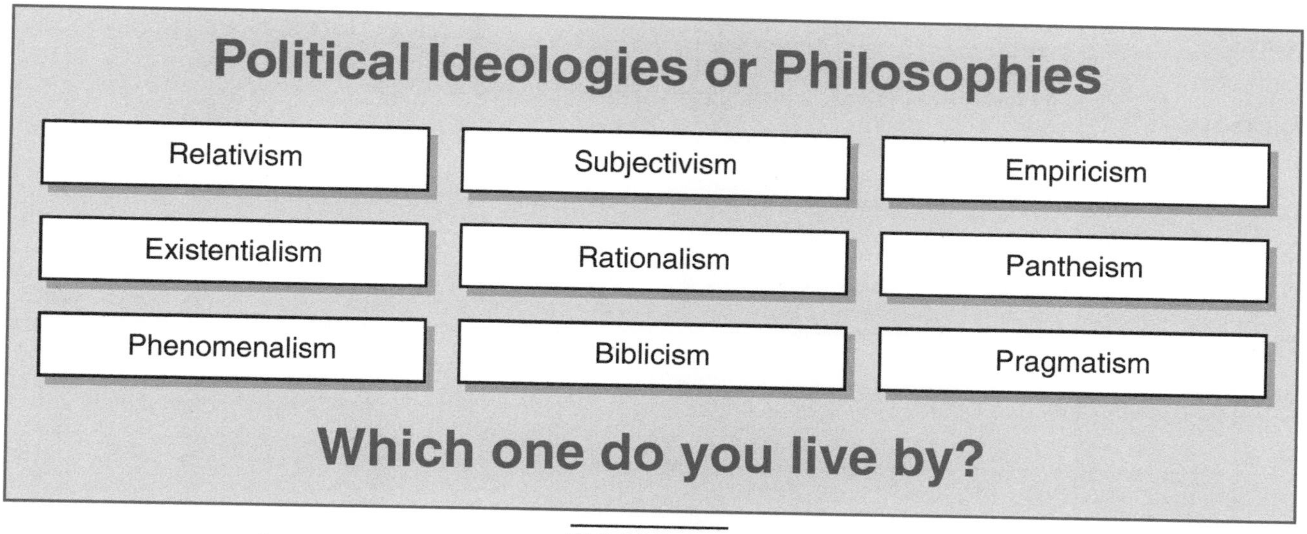

Political Ideologies or Philosophies

Relativism	Subjectivism	Empiricism
Existentialism	Rationalism	Pantheism
Phenomenalism	Biblicism	Pragmatism

Which one do you live by?

FIGURE A13

Name _____ **Date** _____

Explain:

_____

_____

_____

_____

_____

_____

_____

_____

_____

_____

_____

_____

_____

_____

_____

_____

_____

_____

_____

_____

_____

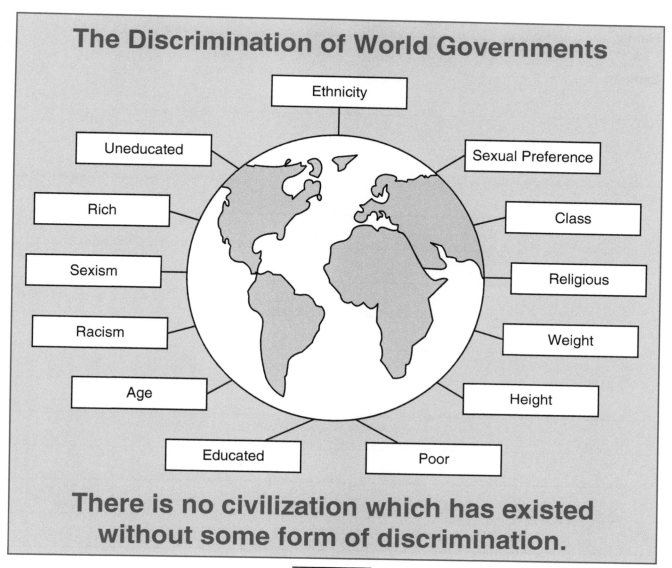

FIGURE A14

Name _____ **Date** _____

Explain:

_____

_____

_____

_____

_____

_____

_____

_____

_____

_____

_____

_____

_____

_____

_____

_____

_____

_____

_____

_____

_____

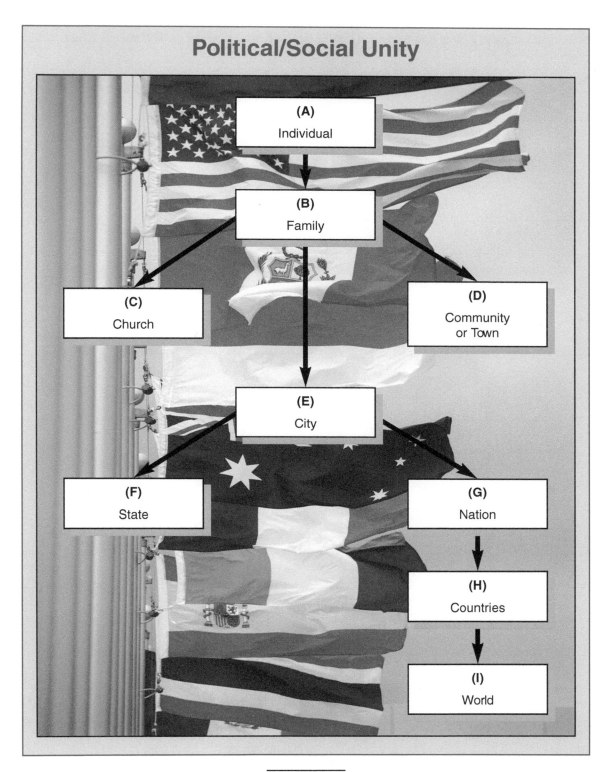

FIGURE A15

Name _____ **Date** _____

Explain:

_____

_____

_____

_____

_____

_____

_____

_____

_____

_____

_____

_____

_____

_____

_____

_____

_____

_____

_____

_____

_____

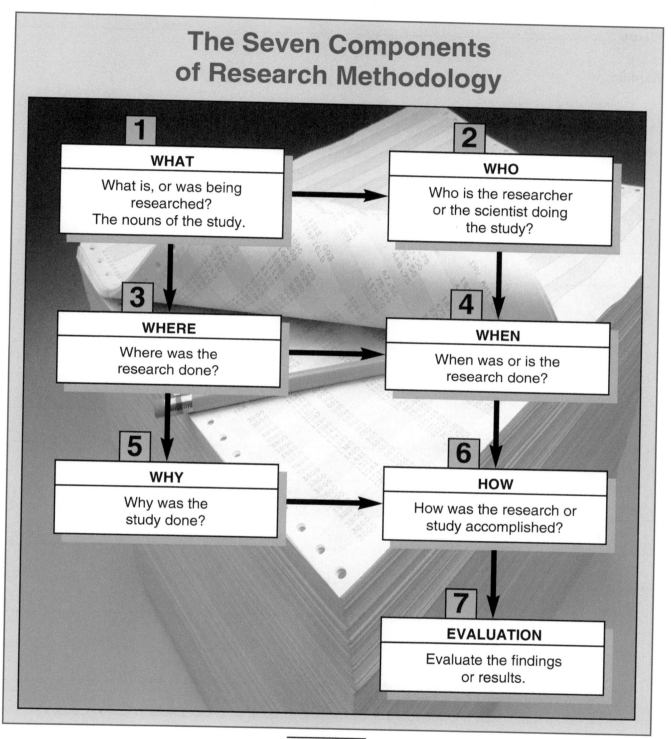

FIGURE A16

Name _____ **Date** _____

Explain:

_____

_____

_____

_____

_____

_____

_____

_____

_____

_____

_____

_____

_____

_____

_____

_____

_____

_____

_____

_____

_____

_____

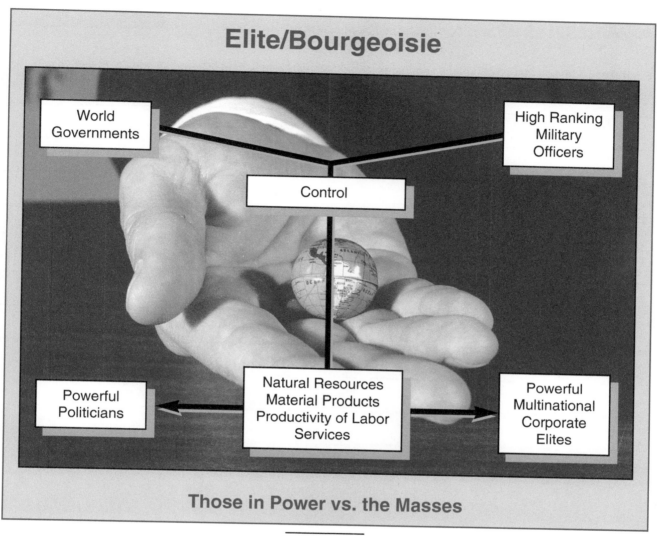

FIGURE A17

Name _____ **Date** _____

Explain:

_____

_____

_____

_____

_____

_____

_____

_____

_____

_____

_____

_____

_____

_____

_____

_____

_____

_____

_____

Cake Theory of Education

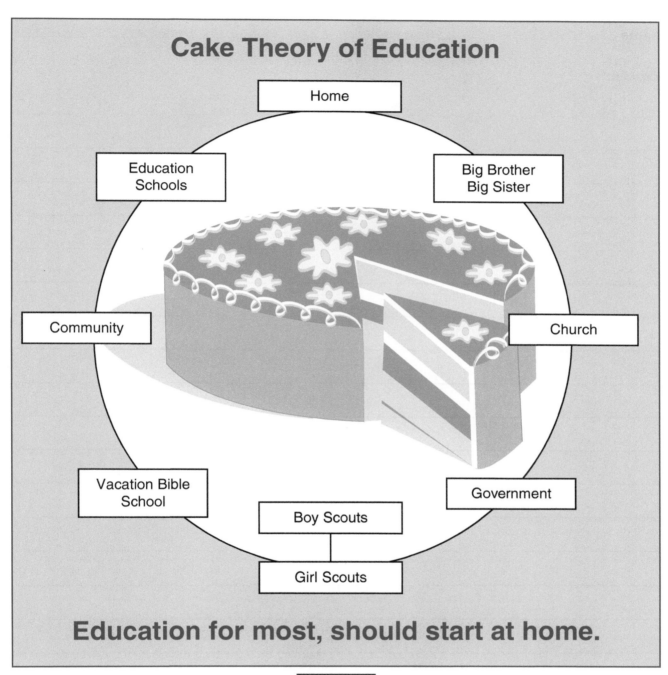

Education for most, should start at home.

FIGURE A18

Name _____ **Date** _____

Explain:

_____

_____

_____

_____

_____

_____

_____

_____

_____

_____

_____

_____

_____

_____

_____

_____

_____

_____

_____

_____

_____